BEST EVER CHICKEN RECIPES

For centuries, the adaptable chicken has provided a ready answer to what's for dinner. The ancient Egyptians roasted chickens in olive oil. American Indians baked them in clay. And wise King Henry IV of France raised and cooked his own chickens, promising every truly loyal subject "a chicken in every pot."

Today's plumper, meatier chickens are even more popular than ever. They are specially bred for roasting, frying or stewing, and are prepared for the market in over 30 ready-to-cook varieties. Whatever your need, or taste, there's a way with chicken:

For families, it's one of the most flavorful, least expensive meats, great for low-budget, high-nutrition meals. Whole roasters can make the most elegant of company meals when stuffed and delicately sauced. Crispy fried chicken is good hot or cold, for party crowds or picnics on the go. In a hurry? Short-fibered, tender broiler-fryers can be poached, broiled, baked or fried in a matter of minutes. On a diet? Chicken is wonderfully low in calories, and responds well to dozens of trim seasonings and sauces. And there's always the leftovers. . . . Odds and ends of cooked chicken are easily transformed into palatable main dishes, soups and

festive appetizers, curries and crêpes.

If you're familiar with any or all of these dinner dilemmas, this magazine is for you. It contains over 400 recipes and cooking suggestions, all carefully developed in our test kitchens. There are economical whole-bird recipes and quick meals-in-a-dish, delectable diet fare and fabulous continental favorites that represent the best of the world's fine cuisines at affordable prices. There are great American grass roots recipes for everything from Southern fried chicken to Cajun gumbos and New England pot pies, plus easy summer salads, sandwiches and barbecues.

Besides this complete guide to chicken cookery, we offer another plus—some winning ways with other popular types of poultry like turkey, capon, duck and Cornish hens. With today's smaller, more tender turkeys your family needn't wait all year for that one 20-pound gobbler. Economical frozen turkeys, turkey parts, and roasts can be the base for everything from a hearty casserole to a delicate pâté.

Try a few of our main dish recipes. Round out the menu with some of the soups, stuffings, gravies and side dishes in our special section, and we think you'll agree—This is chicken at its best —ever!

1

The Whole Bird:
Thrifty recipes that
use every part, page 6

2

Poultry in Parts:
Delicious meals for
drumsticks, breasts,
wings and thighs,
page 12

3

The Bountiful Bird:
Festive roasts for
chicken, turkey,
capon, duck and Cornish
hens, page 18

CONTENTS

4

Appliance Dishes:
Convenient recipes
for the newest
appliances, page 30

5

Easy Summer Meals:
Salads, sandwiches,
picnics and barbecues,
page 38

6

Meals in a Hurry:
Quick ways to broil,
bake and fry, page 50

7

Foreign Classics:
International dishes
with a gourmet flair,
page 60

8

Chicken on a Diet:
Dishes high in flavor,
low on calories, page 72

Special Section: Buying and cutting tips, soups, sauces, gravies, stuffings and go-withs, page 81

Polynesian
Chicken Wings
are stir-fried with
crisp vegetables in a
tangy sweet-sour sauce.
Recipe is on page 14.

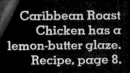

Caribbean Roast
Chicken has a
lemon-butter glaze.
Recipe, page 8.

Buying the whole bird is smart: It's less expensive, and can be cut in any combination of parts to suit your recipe. (Follow our easy cutting guide on page 103.) There's not a speck of waste—you can freeze any unused parts for another recipe.

THE WHOLE BIRD

COUNTRY CAPTAIN

A classic Southern dish with a touch of the Orient.

Makes 8 servings.

2 broiler-fryers (about 2½ pounds each)
¼ cup all-purpose flour
2 teaspoons salt
½ teaspoon pepper
3 tablespoons vegetable oil
1 large onion, chopped (1 cup)
1 large green pepper, halved, seeded, and chopped
1 large clove garlic, crushed
1 tablespoon curry powder
1 can (1 pound) tomatoes
½ cup raisins or currants
  Hot cooked rice

1. Cut chicken into serving-size pieces, following cutting directions on page 103.
2. Combine flour with 1 teaspoon of the salt and ¼ teaspoon of the pepper in a plastic bag. Shake chicken, a few pieces at a time, in flour mixture to coat; tap off excess.
3. Brown chicken, part at a time, in oil in a kettle. Remove chicken; keep warm.
4. Add onion, green pepper, garlic and curry powder to drippings remaining in kettle; sauté until soft. Add tomatoes, breaking with spoon, raisins and reserved chicken, salt and pepper, cover. Simmer 45 minutes, or until chicken is tender. Arrange chicken on a bed of hot cooked rice. Spoon sauce from kettle over top.

CARIBBEAN ROAST CHICKEN

Aromatic bitters and lemon juice add the flavors of the French West Indies to economical whole chicken. Pictured on cover and also on page 6.

Roast at 350° for 1 hour, 30 minutes.
Makes 6 servings.

1 roasting chicken (about 4 pounds)
  Savory Stuffing (recipe, page 87)
¼ cup (½ stick) butter or margarine, melted
2 tablespoons lemon juice
1 teaspoon aromatic bitters
  Lemon Swirl Cups (recipe follows)
  Fresh spinach leaves

1. Stuff chicken neck and body cavities lightly with SAVORY STUFFING. Skewer neck to body; push tail inside bird and secure body cavity closed; tie legs together and draw string up and under wings and knot.
2. Place chicken on rack in shallow roasting pan; brush with a mixture of butter or margarine and lemon juice.

3. Roast in moderate oven (350°) 1 hour, 15 minutes, basting several times with butter-lemon mixture; stir aromatic bitters into remaining butter mixture; brush on chicken to coat evenly with mixture. Roast 15 minutes longer, or until drumstick moves easily at joint; remove string. Arrange on a heated serving platter with LEMON SWIRL CUPS and fresh spinach leaves.

LEMON SWIRL CUPS:

Makes 2 cups.
Hold a lemon vertically and make a one-half-inch lengthwise cut through the center with a sharp paring knife; make the second cut at a 45° angle to the first cut, starting at the base of the first cut. Continue this zig-zag cutting around center of lemon until cuts meet. Pull apart to make two cups.
COOK'S TIP: If lemon does not separate easily after going around the first time, repeat, this time making the same cuts, but pushing knife deeper into fruit.

POULET BRETONNE

A French way of simmering a large chicken to savory tenderness.

Makes 6 servings.

¼ cup (½ stick) butter or margarine
1 stewing chicken (4 to 5 pounds)
2 teaspoons leaf thyme, crumbled
1 can condensed beef broth
3 tablespoons all-purpose flour
1 small can evaporated milk

1. Melt butter or margarine in heavy kettle or Dutch oven; brush part on inside of chicken, then sprinkle chicken with 1 teaspoon of thyme. Brown chicken lightly on all sides in remaining butter or margarine.
2. Turn chicken, breast side up; pour beef broth over; sprinkle with remaining 1 teaspoon thyme; cover tightly.
3. Simmer, basting a few times with pan juices, 1½ hours, or until tender. Remove to heated serving platter; keep hot while making gravy.
4. Pour broth from kettle into 4-cup measure. Let fat rise to top, then skim off. Add water to broth, if needed, to make 2½ cups.
5. Return 3 tablespoons fat to kettle; blend in flour; stir in broth. Cook, stirring constantly, until gravy thickens and bubbles 3 minutes. Blend in evaporated milk; bring just to boiling.
6. Serve chicken with buttered noodles and spoon gravy over all.

JAMBALAYA

This kettle of contrasts from Creole country is filled with chicken, ham and rice.

Makes 12 servings.

2 broiler-fryers (about 3 pounds each)
3 cups diced cooked ham
¼ cup (½ stick) butter or margarine
2 cloves garlic, minced
3 large onions, chopped (3 cups)
3 cans (about 1 pound each) stewed tomatoes
2 teaspoons salt
¼ teaspoon bottled red-pepper seasoning
1 large bay leaf
3 cups sliced celery
1 package (1 pound) frozen deveined shelled raw shrimp
2 cups uncooked rice
¼ cup chopped parsley

1. Cut up chicken, following directions page 103.
2. Brown ham lightly in butter or margarine in a heavy kettle. Stir in garlic and onions; sauté 5 minutes, or until soft. Add chicken.
3. Stir in the tomatoes, salt, red-pepper seasoning and bay leaf.
4. Bring to boiling; lower heat, cover. Simmer 30 minutes. Stir in celery, shrimp and rice, making sure all rice is covered with liquid.
5. Simmer 30 minutes longer, or until chicken and rice are tender; remove bay leaf. Stir in parsley. Serve with hot buttered cornbread and frosty mugs of cold beer.

ORIENTAL CHICKEN

This chicken has a rich honey-and-soy glaze, at once sweet and sour.

Bake at 350° for 1 hour.
Makes 4 servings.

1 broiler-fryer, cut up (about 3 pounds)
½ cup all-purpose flour
1 teaspoon salt
¼ teaspoon pepper
¼ cup (½ stick) butter or margarine
¼ cup honey
¼ cup lemon juice
1 tablespoon soy sauce

1. Cut up chicken, following directions on page 103. Shake in plastic bag with seasoned flour to coat well.
2. Melt 3 tablespoons of the butter or margarine in a 13x9x2-inch baking dish; roll the chicken pieces, one at a time, in melted butter to coat all over. Place, skin-side down, in single layer in baking dish.
3. Bake in moderate oven (350°) for

30 minutes.

4. Melt remaining 1 tablespoon butter or margarine in small saucepan; stir in honey, lemon juice and soy sauce until well mixed. Bring to boiling; remove from heat.

5. Turn chicken; pour honey mixture over. Bake, basting several times with syrup and drippings in pan, 30 minutes longer, or until tender and richly glazed.

POULTRY POINTERS

Here are rules to follow in deciding how much chicken to buy, although you may want to increase these portions for big eaters in the family:

• Chicken for frying: Allow ¾ to 1 pound per serving.
• Chicken for roasting: Allow ¾ to 1 pound per serving.
• Chicken for broiling or barbecuing: Allow ½ chicken or 1 pound per serving.
• Chicken for stewing: Allow ½ to 1 pound per serving.
• Chicken livers: Allow ¼ pound per serving.

CALIFORNIA CHICKEN ROASTS

Lemon marmalade adds a flavor punch to Sunday roast chicken.

Roast at 375° for 1 hour, 15 minutes.
Makes 6 servings.

    2 broiler-fryers (about 2 ½ pounds each)
    ¼ cup (½ stick) butter or margarine
    1 teaspoon salt
    ¼ teaspoon pepper
    ⅔ cup lemon marmalade

1. Remove giblets from body cavities of chickens; save to simmer for soup. Rinse chickens inside and out; pat dry. Tie legs together. Place, breasts-sides up, on a srack in a roasting pan.

2. Melt butter or margarine in a small saucepan; stir in salt and pepper; brush part over chickens.

3. Roast in moderate oven (375°) 45 minutes, brushing once with more butter mixture.

4. While chickens cook, stir lemon marmalade into remaining butter mixture; heat slowly, stirring constantly, until marmalade melts. Brush half of mixture over chickens.

5. Roast 15 minutes; brush with remaining marmalade mixture. Roast 15 minutes longer, or until chickens are tender and richly glazed.

6. Place on a large serving platter; cut away strings. Garnish platter with watercress and lemon slices.

PIMIENTO CHICKEN STEW

A hearty meal topped with peppy pimiento biscuits.

Makes 8 servings.

    1 stewing chicken (4 to 5 pounds)
    ½ cup all-purpose flour
    1 envelope (about 1 ounce) herb salad-dressing mix
    1 large onion, chopped (1 cup)
    1 can (1 pound, 13 ounces) tomatoes
    2 cups water
    2 cups diced celery
    2 cups frozen lima beans
    2 cups frozen whole-kernel corn
    1 can (4 ounces) pimiento
    ¼ cup chopped parsley
       Pimiento Biscuits (recipe follows)

1. Remove all fat from chicken; cut chicken into serving-size pieces, following directions on page 103. Melt fat in large heavy kettle or Dutch oven.

2. Shake chicken with flour and herb salad-dressing mix in plastic bag to coat evenly; brown, a few pieces at at time, in fat in kettle. Remove chicken and reserve.

3. Sauté onion until soft in same kettle; stir in tomatoes and water; add celery, lima beans, corn and chicken; cover kettle.

4. Simmer 1 hour, 30 minutes, or until chicken is tender; let stand 5 to 10 minutes; skim excess fat.

5. Save 1 pimiento for PIMIENTO BISCUITS; dice remaining; stir into stew with parsley; serve with PIMIENTO BISCUITS.

PIMIENTO BISCUITS

Bake at 400° for 10 minutes.
Makes 12 biscuits.

    1 ¾ cups biscuit mix
      ½ cup yellow cornmeal
      2 tablespoons melted butter or margarine
      1 pimiento, chopped
      ⅔ cup water

1. Mix biscuit mix, cornmeal, melted butter or margarine and pimiento with a fork in a medium-size bowl; stir in water just until no dry mix appears; spoon in 12 mounds onto ungreased cooky sheet.

2. Bake in hot oven (400°) 10 minutes, or until golden.

POULTRY POINTERS

• To remove wine and cranberry stains from tablecloths and napkins, soak them in warm water with water softener as soon as possible after the stain occurs. This is safe for all fabrics.

QUICHE AMERICAIN

Turkey can make its final appearance in style when you choose this dish.

Bake at 375° for 40 minutes.
Makes 6 servings.

    1 unbaked 9-inch pie shell
    1 cup shredded Swiss cheese (4 ounces)
    1 cup chopped cooked turkey or chicken
    6 eggs
  1 ½ cups light cream or milk
    1 teaspoon salt
    ¼ teaspoon poultry seasoning

1. Sprinkle pie shell with cheese and turkey.

2. Beat together eggs, cream, salt and poultry seasoning in a medium-size bowl with a wire whip until well blended. Pour over cheese.

3. Bake in moderate oven (375°) 40 minutes or until knife inserted near center comes out clean. Let stand 5 minutes before serving.

PERFECTION CHICKEN

Chicken baked with this spicy sweet-sour glaze can best be described as gorgeous.

Bake at 400° for 1 hour.
Makes 8 servings.

       Curry Glaze (recipe follows)
    2 broiler-fryers, quartered (about 3 pounds each)
    ⅓ cup all-purpose flour
  1 ½ teaspoons salt
    1 teaspoon ground ginger
    ⅓ cup butter or margarine
       Buttered hot rice

1. Make CURRY GLAZE.

2. Shake chicken pieces in mixture of flour, salt and ginger in a plastic bag to coat well.

3. Melt butter or margarine in large shallow roasting pan. Roll chicken in melted butter to coat well, then arrange, skin-side up, in single layer in roasting pan.

4. Bake in hot oven (400°) 20 minutes, or until chicken begins to turn golden. Spoon about half of CURRY GLAZE on top of chicken to make a thick coating; bake 20 minutes. Spoon on remaining glaze; bake 20 minutes longer, or until chicken is tender.

5. Arrange chicken around a mound of buttered hot rice on a heated serving platter. Garnish with lemon cups filled with pepper relish, if you wish. Or, serve chicken along with a tray of assorted curry condiments such as raisins, chutneys, or flaked coconut.

CHICKEN, HUNTER'S STYLE

This is an easy-to-prepare blend of chicken and vegetables.

Makes 4 servings.

    1 broiler-fryer (about 3 pounds)
    1 tablespoon vegetable oil
    1 tablespoon butter or margarine
   ¼ pound mushrooms, trimmed and
          sliced
    2 large tomatoes, peeled, seeded and
          chopped
          OR: 1 can (1 pound) tomatoes
   ¼ cup sliced green onions
    1 small clove garlic, crushed
   ¾ cup water
    2 tablespoons lemon juice
    1 teaspoon leaf chervil or leaf thyme,
          crumbled
    1 teaspoon salt
   ⅛ teaspoon pepper
    1 tablespoon cornstarch

1. Cut chicken into serving-size pieces, following directions on page 103. Brown in oil and butter or margarine in a large skillet.
2. Add mushrooms, tomatoes, green onions, garlic, ½ cup of the water, lemon juice, chervil, salt and pepper; cover. Simmer 45 minutes, or until chicken is tender. Remove chicken to a heated serving platter; keep hot while making gravy.
3. Blend cornstarch with remaining ¼ cup water in a cup; stir into liquid in skillet. Cook, stirring constantly, until mixture thickens and bubbles 1 minute. Pour over chicken.

JUMBO CHICKEN POPOVER

This turns out to be an oversize puffy popover containing browned chicken parts.

Bake at 350° for 1 hour.
Makes 4 servings.

    1 broiler-fryer (about 3 pounds)
   ¼ cup all-purpose flour
    2 teaspoons salt
    1 teaspoon paprika
   ¼ teaspoon pepper
          Fat for frying
   1½ teaspoons baking powder
    4 eggs
   1½ cups milk
    3 tablespoons melted butter or
          margarine
          Creamy Gravy (recipe page 90)

1. Cut chicken into serving-size pieces, following cutting directions on page 103.
2. Shake chicken pieces with the ¼ cup of flour, 1 teaspoon of the salt, paprika and pepper in a plastic bag to coat lightly.
3. Brown, a few at a time, in hot fat in a heavy skillet; drain on paper towels.
4. Sift the 1½ cups flour, baking powder, and remaining 1 teaspoon salt into a medium-size bowl.
5. Beat eggs slightly in second medium-size bowl; blend in milk and melted butter or margarine. Stir into dry ingredients; beat with a rotary beater until smooth.
6. Pour batter into a buttered 8-cup shallow baking dish; arrange chicken in batter.
7. Bake in moderate oven (350°) 1 hour, or until golden. (Keep oven door closed for full hour.) Serve with CREAMY GRAVY.

COACH HOUSE CHICKEN PIE

Hearty and satisfying, this famous recipe from New York's well known Coach House Restaurant is filled with chunks of chicken and just the right balance of vegetables. Pictured on page 11.

Bake at 400° for 45 minutes.
Makes 6 servings.

    1 roasting chicken (4½ to 5 pounds)
   10 cups boiling water
    1 clove garlic, crushed
    4 peppercorns
    1 celery stalk with leaves, coarsely
          chopped
    1 large onion studded with 4 whole
          cloves
    1 tablespoon salt
    3 carrots, pared and cut into 1-inch
          pieces
   12 small white onions, peeled
   ½ pound mushrooms
   ¾ cup (1½ sticks) butter or
          margarine
   ⅔ cup all-purpose flour
   ½ cup cooked peas
    1 tablespoon chopped parsley
          Rich Pie Crust (recipe follows)
    1 egg yolk
    1 tablespoon cream

1. Add the chicken to the kettle of boiling water with the garlic, peppercorns and celery. Press cloves into the onion; add to kettle with salt. Lower heat; cover. Simmer chicken 1 hour and 20 minutes, or until tender.
2. Remove chicken from broth; cool. Remove celery and onion with slotted spoon; discard. Skim fat from broth.
3. Bring broth to boiling; add carrots, onions and mushrooms. Remove mushrooms after 5 minutes' cooking; slice. Continue simmering carrots and onions until tender, about 15 minutes longer. Remove vegetables from broth; strain. Measure 4 cups broth; refrigerate remaining broth for soup.
4. Melt butter or margarine in a heavy skillet; stir in flour. Cook over medium heat, stirring constantly, about 3 minutes, or until bubbly, but not brown. Gradually stir in the 4 cups broth. Cook, stirring constantly, until sauce thickens and bubbles 3 minutes. Remove from heat. Season with salt and pepper to taste.
5. Remove chicken from bones; discard skin and bones. Cut chicken into fairly large pieces. (There should be about 4 cups.)
6. Pour half of sauce into bottom of a 12-cup deep oval casserole. Arrange the chicken, carrots, onions and sliced mushrooms over the sauce. Sprinkle peas and parsley over; pour in remaining sauce. (This much can be done ahead of time. Refrigerate without pastry on top.)
7. Roll out RICH PIE CRUST to about ¼-inch thickness between 2 sheets of wax paper. Measure dish; cut pastry to allow for a 1-inch overhang. Fit pastry over pie; turn edge under. Press pastry against side of dish with fork to seal. Cut steam vents in pastry. Cut leaves and flowers from pastry trims, if you wish. Arrange on top of pastry, moistening them with a little water so they adhere. Combine egg yolk and cream; brush pastry and decorations well with mixture.
8. Bake in hot oven (400°) 45 minutes, or until crust is a deep, golden brown and filling is bubbly. Serve with crisp greens salad and a chilled white wine plus lemon sherbet for desert, if you wish.

RICH PIE CRUST

Makes crust for 12-cup casserole.

   1½ cups sifted all-purpose flour
   ½ cup (1 stick) butter or
          margarine, softened
    1 egg yolk
    1 teaspoon ice water

Place flour in center of a pastry board or large bowl; make a well in center. Cut in the butter or margarine. Add egg yolk and ice water. Work mixture together with fingers until well-blended. Form into ball; wrap in wax paper. Refrigerate at least 1 hour before rolling out.

Chapter 1 continued on page 95.

Chunks of poached chicken baked with vegetables under a flaky crust in Coach House Chicken Pie. Recipe, this page.

POULTRY IN PARTS

White meat or dark, drumsticks, thighs or wings, there are dozens of delicious ways to cook everyone's favorite part of the bird, as this chapter proves.

CHAPTER 3

In this chapter you'll find
recipes for roasting whole chicken,
turkey, duck, goose, capon and Cornish hen.
Complement any of them with the sauces, gravies,
stuffings and side dishes in our special section
beginning on page 81, and turn a simple meal into a
sumptuous feast. Or, try an elegant one-dish specialty.

THE BOUNTIFUL BIRD

CHESTNUT STUFFED TURKEY

The abundant green forests of the young country yielded a great variety of nuts. This stuffing for turkey recalls one of the innovative ways colonists used chestnuts. Pictured on page 18.

Roast at 325° for 3 hours.
Makes 8 servings with leftovers.

- 1 frozen turkey (about 12 pounds)
- 2 large onions, chopped (2 cups)
- 2 cups sliced celery
- ¾ cup (1½ sticks) butter or margarine
  Liver (from giblets), chopped
- ½ cup chopped parsley
- 3 packages (8 ounces each) cornbread stuffing mix
- 1¼ cups boiling water
- ¼ cup sherry cooking wine
- 1 pound fresh chestnuts, cooked and peeled*
  OR: 1 can (15½ ounces) water-packed chestnuts, drained
- ¼ cup (½ cup) butter or margarine, softened
  Giblet Gravy (recipe follows)

1. Thaw turkey.
2. Sauté onions and celery in butter or margarine until soft in large skillet. Add the liver and sauté a few minutes longer. Stir in parsley. Add to stuffing mix in large bowl. Add water and sherry; mix until evenly moist. Coarsely chop the chestnuts and mix into stuffing.
3. Lightly stuff neck and body cavities of turkey with stuffing. Skewer neck skin to back of bird. Turn wing tips under. Secure legs under the band of skin or metal clamp, or tie with kitchen string. Turn any remaining stuffing into a buttered 4-cup casserole.
4. Place stuffed turkey on rack in shallow pan. Rub skin with softened butter or margarine. Make tent of aluminum foil; place over turkey with edges inside pan, not touching bird.
5. Roast in slow oven (325°), basting several times with pan drippings, 3 hours, or until meat thermometer registers 185° and leg joint moves freely. About 1 hour before turkey is done, place extra casserole with stuffing in oven. Bake, covered, until it is heated through (about 1 hour).
6. Remove turkey to heated serving platter. Remove string and skewers. Let stand 20 to 30 minutes before carving. Garnish with dried fruits, nuts and parsley, if you wish. Meanwhile, prepare GIBLET GRAVY.
*Wash fresh chestnuts, dry well. Make a small cross in pointed end with sharp knife. Bake in moderate oven (375°) in a shallow baking pan

15 minutes. Remove shells and skins. Cook, covered, in boiling salted water, 10 minutes or until tender; drain.
GIBLET GRAVY: Makes about 3 cups. Place remaining giblets and neck of turkey in a medium-size saucepan; add a small onion stuck with 2 whole cloves, 3 cups water and 1 teaspoon salt. Bring to boiling; lower heat; cover. Simmer 1½ hours, or until meat is tender. Strain broth. Chop giblets very fine. When turkey has been removed from roasting pan, remove rack. Pour a little of the broth into pan; set pan over a burner and heat while stirring to dissolve browned bits. Strain into a 2-cup measure. Skim fat from drippings. Measure ⅓ cup of the fat into a medium-size saucepan; stir in ⅓ cup all-purpose flour. Heat and stir over medium heat a few minutes to brown flour slightly. Stir in pan drippings and reserved broth. Continue cooking and stirring until gravy thickens and bubbles 3 minutes. Season with salt and pepper. Stir in giblets and 2 tablespoons sherry cooking wine. To be sure that the gravy is always bubbling-hot, when your guests begin to eat, keep gravy simmering in saucepan until ready to serve.

*COLONIAL
THANKSGIVING DINNER
Harvest Pumpkin Soup*
Roast Turkey with Chestnut
Stuffing
Mashed Butternut Squash and Yams*
Baked Stuffed Onions*
Maple-Butter Glazed Carrots*
Orange-Lemon Cranberry Relish*
Assorted Breads
Maple Walnut Tarts
Coffee   Apple Cider
Recipe for Roast Turkey with Chestnut
Stuffing on this page. All other starred
recipes begin on page 93.*

POULTRY POINTERS

• Never stuff a bird *until* just before you are going to roast it because the stuffing could spoil if sitting inside the bird more than 15 minutes at room temperature. *However,* you can prepare the stuffing ahead of time and store in a glass bowl in the refrigerator until ready to put into the bird.
• A good cook's trick for stuffing a turkey is to put a slice of day-old bread or a piece of crust, lightly buttered and rubbed with onion or garlic, at the opening of the body cavity. The slice of bread acts as a lid and keeps stuffing from spilling out.

MOROCCAN COUSCOUS

Couscous is both the name of the semolina grain and the finished dish. Perfect for a party dish.

Makes 16 servings.

- 2 pounds couscous (coarse semolina)
- 6 cups boiling water, well salted
- 1 turkey, cut up (about 8 pounds)
- 6 large onions, (6 cups) chopped
- ½ cup (1 stick) butter or margarine
- ½ cup olive oil or vegetable oil
- 1 tablespoon salt
- 1 teaspoon black pepper
- ½ teaspoon ground turmeric
- ¼ teaspoon cayenne pepper (optional)
- 1 teaspoon saffron threads, crushed
- 1 three-inch piece stick cinnamon
  Water
- 5 large tomatoes, peeled, seeded and chopped (5 cups)
- 6 carrots, pared and cut in 1½-inch pieces
- 1 pound zucchini, cut in 1½-inch lengths
- 3 or 4 white turnips, cut in quarters (optional)
- 1 large or 2 small acorn squash, peeled, seeded and cut in 1½- to 2-inch chunks
- 1 can (1 pound, 13 ounces) chick peas, rinsed
- 1 cup seedless raisins
  Harissa (recipe follows)

1. If you have a couscous pot, prepare semolina by placing it in a large bowl and pouring over it 2 cups of the boiling water. Let stand 20 minutes, fluffing grain occasionally with a fork. Repeat adding water and fluffing twice at 20 minute intervals. Line the top of the couscous pot with a double thickness of clean cheesecloth and set aside. If you do not have a couscous pot, cook semolina, while stew cooks, following instructions on package for boiling, in water or broth from stew.
2. Place turkey and chopped onions, with butter or margarine and oil in the bottom of the couscous pot, or in a large (8-quart) soup pot. Add salt, pepper, turmeric, cayenne, saffron and cinnamon.
3. Cook gently, covered, for 20 minutes, swirling pan and stirring occasionally until meat and onion take on a golden color and look slightly braised. Add enough water to come just to the level of the meat. Cover and simmer for 1½ to 2 hours, or until meat is tender. (This much of the stew can be prepared in advance.) Skim off excess fat.
4. Half an hour before serving, add tomatoes, carrots, zucchini and turnips and simmer until tender. At the

same time, place the couscous grain over the bottom part of the steamer and seal rim of bottom pot to the top by wrapping it in aluminum foil. Cover top and let grain steam as vegetables cook, fluffing grain by tossing it with a fork two or three times. Add squash and chick peas to stew; cook 10 minutes, or until squash is tender. Serve with HARISSA.

HARISSA SAUCE

Makes about 2 cups.
- ⅓ cups crushed, dried Italian hot chili peppers
- 2 cloves garlic, peeled
- 2 teaspoons caraway seeds
- 1 teaspoon fennel seeds (optional)
  Pinch ground cumin (optional)
- ½ teaspoon salt
- 3 tablespoons olive oil, or as needed
- 1½ cups liquid from stew
  Juice of ½ lemon
- 1 tablespoon minced parsley
- 1 tablespoon minced fresh green coriander, if available

Grind chili peppers, garlic, caraway, fennel, cumin and salt, in a mortar and pestle or in a spice mill. Stir in 1 teaspoon olive oil. (This can be done in advance and kept in the refrigerator.) Just before serving, stir 2 teaspoons of this mixture into 1½ cups of broth from stew, adding 2 tablespoons olive oil and lemon juice. Adjust seasonings, adding salt if needed. Stir in chopped parsley and/or coriander. Serve in small sauce bowl, to be spooned over couscous. To serve couscous: Ladle couscous into large individual bowls (old-fashioned soup plates would be perfect), make a well in the center and in it put meat, vegetables and broth. Top with raisins, if you wish.

CHICKEN SAUCE ALLA ROMEO

Leftover chicken goes Italian when combined with wine and Parmesan cheese and tossed with pasta. Great for unexpected company.

Makes 4 servings.
- ¼ cup (½ stick) butter or margarine
- ¼ cup olive oil or vegetable oil
- 1 large onion, finely chopped (1 cup)
- 1 cup water
- 2 cups finely chopped cooked chicken
- ½ teaspoon leaf sage, crumbled
- 1 teaspoon salt
- 1 cup white cooking wine
- 1 package (1 pound) linguini, cooked and drained
Grated Parmesan cheese

1. Heat butter or margarine and oil in a heavy skillet. Add onion and water; boil until onion is soft. (If water boils away before onion is soft, add a little more water.)
2. Stir in chicken, sage, salt and wine. Bring to the boil; reduce heat and simmer 6 to 7 minutes. Serve hot over freshly-cooked pasta with grated Parmesan cheese on the side.

ARUBA CHICKEN SANCOCHO

Caribbean fruit is paired with chicken and pork in this lively dinner-in-a-dish.

Makes 8 servings.
- 1 Spanish onion, sliced
- 2 tablespoons olive oil or vegetable oil
- 1 broiler-fryer, cut up (about 3 pounds)
- 1 pound smoked pork butt, cut into 1-inch cubes
- 2 tablespoons sherry cooking wine
- 2 cups water
- 1 can (8 ounces) tomato sauce
- ¼ cup flaked coconut
- 1½ teaspoons salt
- ½ teaspoon crushed red pepper
- 4 whole cloves
- 1 bay leaf
- ¼ teaspoon leaf thyme
- 2 pounds sweet potatoes
- 2 bananas, peeled and sliced ¾-inch thick
- ¼ cup sliced green onion

1. Sauté onion until golden in oil in a heavy kettle or Dutch oven, about 5 minutes. Remove and reserve.
2. Brown chicken, half at a time, in same kettle, adding more oil if needed. Return all chicken and onion to pan. Add smoked pork and wine.
3. Stir in water, tomato sauce, coconut, and salt. Tie pepper, cloves, bay leaf and thyme in cheesecloth; add to stew. Bring to boiling; lower heat; cover. Simmer 15 minutes.
4. Meanwhile, pare sweet potatoes and cut into ½-inch slices. Add to stew, pushing them down into liquid. Simmer 35 to 40 minutes longer, or until meats and potatoes are tender. Taste and add more salt if needed. (Salt content in pork varies.)
5. Stir bananas and green onions into stew. Cover and simmer 5 to 10 minutes longer. Arrange stew in serving dish. Garnish with additional coconut and green onion, if you wish.

SUGGESTED VARIATION: You can use 2 cups cubed cooked ham or bologna or 2 cups thickly sliced frankfurters for smoked pork.

LONG ISLAND CHRISTMAS DINNER MENU

*King's Soup**
Soda Crackers
*Christmas Goose with Orange Sauce**
Whipped Potatoes
*Whole Cauliflower and Green Beans Platter**
*Supreme Sauce**
*Colonial Turnip Bowl**
*Spicy Cranberry Mold**
Turnip - Carrot - Celery Sticks
*Yuletide Saffron Crown**
*Rum Pumpkin Pie**
*Old-Fashioned Mince Pie**
Sweet Cider   Madeira   Claret
*Festive Holiday Punch**
*Baker Family Christmas Cookies**
*Lillyan Green's Chocolate Cookies**
**Recipes follow.*

Since Colonial days, Christmas has been a time for family and friends to gather at a festive table. This menu is planned to serve 8 for the soup and goose courses, and additional guests, who arrive for dessert and beverages. A variety of cooks can contribute dishes to the dinner, or one cook can prepare it in easy stages. The cookies, pies and saffron bread can be made weeks ahead and frozen, or baked a few days ahead. Refrigerate the Rum Pumpkin Pie and keep all other baked goods wrapped in aluminum foil at room temperature. Wash and trim all the vegetables the day before and store in separate plastic bags until cooking time. The cranberry mold and soup can be made and refrigerated the day before. (All of these foods can be easily transported from one home to another on Christmas Day.) All that really has to be prepared on Christmas Day are the goose and sauces. Allow goose to rest at least 30 minutes before carving.

KING'S SOUP

A recipe for this creamy version of onion soup was published in "The Lady's Companion" in 1753 in the Virginia Colony.

Makes 8 servings.
- 2 large Bermuda onions, thinly sliced
- ½ cup (1 stick) butter or margarine
- 2 teaspoons salt
- ¼ teaspoon ground mace
- ¼ teaspoon white pepper
- 4 cups milk
- 2 cups light cream
- 2 egg yolks
  Chopped parsley

1. Sauté onion slices in butter or margarine until very soft, *but not brown.*

Recipes continued on page 24.

21

THE
STUFFING
MAKES THE
BIRD

1

SUMPTUOUS STUFFINGS

Every cook has a favorite stuffing, and often, so does every member
of the family. Why not surprise the stuffing fans and make two: one for the bird, and
one baked in a casserole alongside, basted with pan juices to keep it moist.
There's a delectable variety to choose from, including those listed below.

Shown on these pages are the ingredients used in making: 1. Orange Pecan Stuffing;
2. Apple and Chestnut Stuffing; 3. Spicy Corn Bread Stuffing; 4. Vegetable and Sausage Stuffing;
5. Fruited Rice Stuffing; 6. Oyster Stuffing. Recipes begin on page 86.

Chinese Wok Chicken is stir-fried in an electric wok along with mixed vegetables in a soy-based sauce. Recipe, page 32.

APPLIANCE DISHES

SKILLET TURKEY SCRAMBLE

Turkey and ham go with rice, tomatoes and seasonings in this timesaver.

Makes 6 servings.

- 1 medium-size onion, chopped (½ cup)
- 1 clove garlic, minced
- 2 tablespoons butter or margarine
- 1 teaspoon salt
- 1 teaspoon chili powder
- ⅛ teaspoon pepper
  Dash cayenne pepper
- 2 cans (1 pound each) stewed tomatoes
- 2 cups diced cooked turkey
- 2 cups diced ham or bologna
- 1 cup uncooked rice
- 3 tablespoons chopped parsley
- 1 bay leaf

1. Sauté onion and garlic in butter or margarine just until soft in an electric frypan set at 360°. Stir in salt, chili powder, pepper and cayenne; cook 2 minutes.
2. Stir in tomatoes, turkey, ham or bologna, rice, parsley, and bay leaf; lower heat to 200°; cover.
3. Simmer, stirring often, 30 minutes, or until rice is tender and liquid is absorbed. Remove bay leaf. Serve with chilled pear halves for dessert.

CHINESE WOK CHICKEN

Stir-fry cooking is the answer to serving a fresh dish, when you're not sure when everyone will arrive. Pictured on page 30.

Makes 4 servings.

- 2 whole chicken breasts (about 12 ounces each)
- ⅓ cup soy sauce
- ⅓ cup sake, dry sherry or chicken broth
- 4 tablespoons peanut oil or vegetable oil
- 1 clove garlic, halved
- 1 small acorn squash, halved, seeded cubed and cooked 5 minutes
- 1 cup cut green beans
- 1 small yellow squash, tipped and sliced
- 1 cup sliced mushrooms
- 1 package (6 ounces) frozen Chinese pea pods, thawed
- 1 package (10 ounces) fresh spinach, washed and trimmed
- 3 cups shredded Chinese cabbage

1. Remove skin from chicken and bone; cut into 1-inch pieces. Combine with soy and sake, sherry or chicken broth in a glass bowl; marinate.
2. Turn electric wok to 375° and add 2 tablespoons of the oil; heat until sizzling; add garlic and cook for 2 minutes; remove and discard garlic.

3. Remove chicken from marinade and drain on paper towels, reserving marinade. Cook chicken quickly in hot oil, stirring constantly; remove and keep warm.
4. Add remaining 2 tablespoons oil and heat; add acorn squash and green beans; toss until glistening with oil; push to one side; add yellow squash and mushrooms; toss in oil, then push to side; add pea pods, spinach and Chinese cabbage and toss until glistening.
5. Return chicken to wok with reserved marinade and toss to blend well; lower temperature to 200° and cover wok.
6. Simmer 5 minutes, or until vegetables are crisply-tender. Serve with boiled rice, if you wish.
HOSTESS TIP: All of the vegetables can be prepared ahead of time and arranged in a decorative pattern on a large flat tray; cover with plastic wrap and chill in refrigerator with marinating chicken. Cook at the table, when all the guests have arrived.

CORNISH HENS IN CASSEROLE

White kidney beans and sweet Italian sausage add a continental touch to tender game hens.

Microwave for 25 minutes.
Makes 4 servings.

- 2 frozen Rock Cornish hens, thawed and split in halves
- 2 tablespoons vegetable oil
- 1 package (2⅜ ounces) seasoned coating for chicken
- ½ pound sweet Italian sausage, diced
- 3 tart apples, peeled, cored and sliced
- 1 green pepper, halved, seeded and diced
- 1 large onion, chopped (1 cup)
- 1 can (1 pound, 4 ounces) white kidney beans (cannellini)
  Few drops bottled red-pepper seasoning
- 1 teaspoon Worcestershire sauce

1. Brush hen halves with oil and roll in coating-mix. Place in a 10-cup shallow microwave-safe casserole; cover with wax paper.
2. Cook in microwave oven 6 minutes, turning halves over after 3 minutes. Remove hens from dish and keep warm.
3. Add sausage, apples, pepper and onion to casserole; cook in oven 3 minutes. Stir in beans and seasonings. Place hens on top of bean mixture; cover with wax paper.
4. Cook in oven 12 to 14 minutes, turning dish twice, or until hens are fork tender.

SALAMI-CHICKEN DUO

These spicy drumsticks taste delicious hot or cold.

Makes 2 servings.

- 2 drumsticks with thighs (about 1 pound)
- 2 slices salami
- 2 tablespoons all-purpose flour
- ½ teaspoon salt
- ¼ teaspoon paprika
- ¼ teaspoon leaf oregano, crumbled
  Dash pepper
- 3 tablespoons vegetable oil

1. Cut through chicken legs at joints to separate drumsticks and thighs, then cut an opening along bone of each drumstick and in meaty part of each thigh with a sharp knife to make a pocket for stuffing.
2. Cut salami into 4 strips; stuff 1 strip into each piece of chicken.
3. Shake pieces in a mixture of flour, salt, paprika, oregano and pepper in a plastic bag to coat evenly.
4. Cook pieces slowly in vegetable oil in an electric fry pan 20 minutes; turn; cover, leaving vent open. Cook 20 minutes longer, or until tender and crisply golden.

PARISIENNE CHICKEN

Stuffed with parsley, simmered in mushroom sauce, the chickens are then sauced and served on noodles.

Makes 8 servings.

- 2 broiler-fryers (about 3 pounds each)
- 1 teaspoon salt
- 2 bunches parsley, washed and trimmed
- 2 tablespoons butter or margarine
- 1 can (3 or 4 ounces) whole mushrooms
  Water
- ¼ teaspoon pepper
- 2 tablespoons all-purpose flour
- ¾ cup light cream
  Hot cooked noodles

1. Sprinkle chicken insides with ½ teaspoon of the salt; place parsley in body cavities, packing in lightly. Skewer neck skin to back; twist wings flat against skewered neck skin; tie the legs to tails with string.
2. Brown chickens in butter or margarine in a deep electric frypan or electric all-purpose cooker at 375°; turn breast side up.
3. Drain liquid from mushrooms into a 1-cup measure; add water to make ¾ cup; pour over chickens. Sprinkle with remaining ½ teaspoon salt and

pepper; cover tightly.

4. Simmer, basting several times with liquid in frypan, 1 hour and 15 minutes, or until tender. Remove from frypan and keep hot while making gravy.

5. Pour liquid from frypan into a 2-cup measure; let stand about a minute, or until fat rises to top, then skim off into a cup. Add water to liquid, if needed, to make 1 cup.

6. Measure 2 tablespoons of the fat and return to frypan; blend in flour; stir in the 1 cup liquid. Cook, stirring constantly, until gravy thickens and bubbles 3 minutes. Stir in mushrooms and cream; heat slowly just to boiling. Darken with a few drips bottled gravy coloring, if you wish.

7. Spoon noodles into a heated large serving bowl. Take out skewers and cut string from chickens; arrange chickens on top of noodles; spoon gravy over all. Garnish with parsley, if you wish. Carve chickens into serving-size pieces.

SOUTHERN TURKEY AND KALE

Second-day turkey, Southern-style, includes chopped kale and a rich, tangy onion-flavored sauce.

Microwave for 24 minutes.
Makes 6 servings.

2 packages (10 ounces each) frozen chopped kale or spinach
1 cup boiling water
1 can (3 or 4 ounces) sliced mushrooms, drained
1 envelope (1½ ounces) onion soup mix
1 container (8 ounces) dairy sour cream
3 cups diced cooked turkey
1 cup heavy cream, softly whipped
2 tablespoons grated Parmesan cheese
2 tablespoons buttered bread crumbs

1. Place kale in an 8-cup shallow microwave-safe casserole, ice-side up; cover with wax paper.

2. Defrost in microwave oven about 8 minutes, breaking up and stirring after 4 minutes. Add water; cook 5 minutes; drain thoroughly.

3. Add mushrooms to casserole. Stir soup mix into sour cream in a small bowl; spread ½ mixture over kale. Top with turkey. Fold whipped cream into remaining soup mixture; spread over turkey.

4. Cook in oven 10 minutes, turning dish several times. Mix cheese and crumbs; sprinkle over casserole. Cook 1 minute longer. Let stand 5 minutes before serving.

POULTRY POINTERS

• The number one rule to remember in preparing poultry is to cook it at the lowest possible temperature for the least amount of time. Poultry is a delicate protein and can become tough when abused by high heat and extra-long cooking periods. Should you see a trace of pink around the bone of a bird that has tested done, don't worry, that's just caused by a chemical reaction and has no effect of the flavor of the bird.

• A wok is a round-bottomed, bowl-shaped Chinese cooking utensil used in stir-fry cooking. Boneless pieces of chicken or turkey can be cooked quickly with a variety of vegetables for a festive easy-on-the-cook meal.

• A pilaf is a rice dish cooked in a savory broth, often with bits of onion, celery, nuts or dried fruits tossed in at the end. It is a perfect accompaniment to barbecued duckling, roast Rock Cornish hens or broiled chicken.

• A gumbo is a Creole stew made with chicken and/or ham and seafood plus tomatoes and okra. Filé powder, made of pulverized dried sassafras leaves, is often used to thicken the gumbo, just before serving.

SLOW COOKER COQ AU VIN

Use a really good red Burgundy to get a great flavor. Flaming the brandy also does something delicious to the dish before it goes into your slow cooker.

Cook on 190° to 200° for 8 hours, or on 290° to 300° for 4 hours.
Makes 4 servings.

2 whole chicken breasts, split (about 12 ounces each)
4 drumsticks or thighs
⅓ cup butter or margarine
¼ cup brandy (optional)
12 small white onions, peeled
2 cloves garlic, crushed
½ pound mushrooms, halved
1 cup red Burgundy or dry red wine
1 cup chicken broth
1 teaspoon salt
¼ teaspoon pepper
1 tablespoon chopped parsley
Dash ground cloves
¼ teaspoon leaf thyme, crumbled
1 bay leaf
2 tablespoons cornstarch
¼ cup cold water

1. Brown chicken pieces in butter or margarine in a large skillet; warm brandy in a small saucepan; pour over chicken and flame; place in slow cooker.

2. Sauté onions, garlic and mush-

rooms in pan drippings; remove to slow cooker with a slotted spoon.

3. Stir in Burgundy wine, chicken broth, salt, pepper, parsley, cloves, thyme and bay leaf and bring to boiling, stirring up all the cooked-on bits in the bottom of the skillet; pour over chicken and vegetables; cover.

4. Cook on low (190° to 200°) 8 hours, or on high (290° to 300°) 4 hours, or until chicken is tender when pierced with a two-tined fork. Remove chicken and vegetables to a heated platter and keep warm while making gravy.

5. Turn heat control to high (290° to 300°). Combine cornstarch and cold water in a cup to make a smooth paste; stir into sauce in slow cooker until well-blended. Cover; simmer 15 minutes longer to thicken sauce. Spoon sauce over chicken and serve with a bottle of the same hearty Burgundy used in the casserole and chunks of crusty French bread for soaking up the sauce.

LIBERIAN CHICKEN

For an authentic touch, serve this African favorite with rice and cottage cheese.

Microwave for 38 minutes.
Makes 4 servings.

1 broiler-fryer, cut up (about 3 pounds)
2 cups boiling water
Juice of 1 lemon
1 teaspoon salt
2 large onions, chopped (2 cups)
¼ cup vegetable oil
3 tablespoons tomato paste
1 to 2 tablespoons chili powder (or to taste)
½ teaspoon ground ginger
¼ teaspoon sugar
¼ teaspoon pepper
¼ cup red wine

1. Place chicken pieces in a 12-cup microwave-safe casserole; add boiling water, lemon juice and salt; cover with wax paper.

2. Cook in microwave oven 10 minutes; remove and reserve. Add onions and oil to casserole; cook in oven 4 minutes.

3. Measure 2 cups of the cooking liquid into casserole. Stir in tomato paste, chili powder, ginger, sugar, pepper and wine. Cook in oven 4 minutes.

4. Add chicken, spooning sauce over so pieces are well coated. Cover; cook in oven 20 minutes, turning pieces over halfway through cooking time. Serve with a well-chilled beer or tart limeade with lots of ice.

SOUTHAMPTON TURKEY

Unexpected company can be treated to this superb dish in minutes. You don't even have to cook the noodles first.

Microwave for 15 minutes.
Makes 4 servings.

1½ cups medium noodles
1 can condensed chicken broth
3 cups cubed cooked turkey
½ cup light cream or evaporated milk
1 pimiento, chopped
½ cup pitted black olives, chopped
1 teaspoon instant minced onion
1 cup shredded sharp Cheddar cheese (4 ounces)

1. Measure uncooked noodles into an 8-cup microwave-safe casserole. Stir in chicken broth, turkey, cream or evaporated milk, pimiento, olives and onion; cover with wax paper.
2. Cook 15 minutes, or until noodles are tender, stirring once or twice during cooking.
3. Add cheese and mix well. Let stand 4 to 5 minutes before serving.

ILE D' ORLÉANS CHICKEN

This suberb dish is named for the Ile d'Orléans near Quebec City, which is noted for its apple orchards. This recipe was developed to cook in an electric slow cooker.

Cook on 190° to 200° for 8 hours, or on 290° to 300° for 4 hours.
Makes 4 servings.

1 broiler-fryer (about 3 pounds)
  Apple brandy or Cognac
1 teaspoon salt
¼ teaspoon freshly ground pepper
2 cups diced white bread (4 slices)
½ cup chopped celery
½ cup chopped apple
¼ cup raisins
3 tablespoons butter or margarine, melted
1 tablespoon chopped parsley
½ teaspoon leaf thyme, crumbled
3 slices thickly-sliced bacon
6 medium-size apples
1 cup light cream

1. Rub chicken inside and out with brandy or Cognac, then with salt and pepper .
2. Combine bread cubes, celery, chopped apple, raisins, butter or margarine, parsley and thyme in a medium-size bowl.
3. Stuff chicken with dressing, packing lightly. Skewer neck skin to back; twist the wing tips flat against skewered neck skin; tie legs to tail with kitchen string.
4. Place bacon in a saucepan; cover with water. Bring to boiling; lower heat and simmer 10 minutes. Dry on paper towels.
5. Fry bacon lightly in an electric slow cooker with a browning unit or a large kettle. Remove bacon and reserve. Brown chicken on all sides in bacon drippings; remove; keep warm.
6. Quarter, core and thickly slice apples; brown lightly in pan drippings. Place chicken on top of apple slices in slow cooker; lay bacon slices over chicken; cover cooker.
7. Cook on low (190° to 200°) 8 hours, or on high (290° to 300°) 4 hours, or until chicken is tender. Pour cream and 2 tablespoons apple brandy or Cognac over the chicken, just before serving. Serve with boiled potatoes sprinkled with chopped parsley and buttered green beans.

BASIC FRIED CHICKEN

Essential to any good cook's repertoire, this chicken can't be hurried—but it is certainly worth waiting for.

Makes 4 servings.

1 broiler-fryer (about 3 pounds)
½ cup all-purpose flour
1 teaspoon salt
⅛ teaspoon pepper
1 cup bacon drippings or part drippings and shortening

1. Cut chicken into 8 serving-size pieces—2 breasts, 2 wings, 2 thighs, 2 drumsticks. (Simmer bony back pieces to make broth for gravy, if you wish.) Wash chicken, but do not dry. This is important so skin will take on a thick flour coating.
2. Mix flour, salt and pepper in a plastic bag. Shake chicken pieces, a few at a time, to coat evenly.
3. Heat bacon drippings ¼-inch deep in a large heavy skillet, or in an electric skillet on 360°. Arrange chicken in a single layer in hot fat.
4. Brown slowly for 15 minutes. When pink juices start to show on top, turn and brown the other side 15 minutes. (Slow cooking, plus turning just once, gives the chicken its crisp coating.)
5. When pieces are browned, pile all back into pan or skillet and cover. Lower range heat to simmer or reset control on electric fry pan to 200°. Let chicken cook 10 minutes longer, or until fork-tender.
SUGGESTED VARIATIONS: For added flavor, mix ½ teaspoon dried leaf thyme, tarragon, basil or poultry seasoning, or 1 teaspoon curry powder into the flour.

MASSACHUSETTS GRILLED CHICKEN

Cranberry sauce in the baste means a colorful and flavorful barbecued bird.

Makes 4 servings.

2 broiler-fryers (about 2½ pounds each)
½ cup (1 stick) butter or margarine, melted
1 can (7 ounces) jellied cranberry sauce
½ cup apple cider
2 tablespoons honey
1 tablespoon orange juice
2 teaspoons cornstarch
½ teaspoon salt

1. Wash chickens; pat dry. Truss and tie. Fasten to an electric rôtisserie spit, following manufacturer's directions.
2. Roast 1 hour, 15 minutes, brushing frequently with melted butter or margarine.
3. Simmer cranberry sauce, cider, honey, orange juice, cornstarch, salt and remaining melted butter in a large saucepan for 15 minutes. Brush over chicken for last 15 minutes.

MANDARIN SUPPER

Cubed chicken, Chinese-style fried rice and soy-seasoned broccoli make this delicious meal-in-a-wok.

Makes 6 servings.

2 whole chicken breasts (about 12 ounces each)
1 tablespoon packaged shrimp spice
1 tablespoon instant minced onion
1 teaspoon salt
2 cups water
1 cup uncooked rice
1 bunch fresh broccoli (about 1½ pounds)
2 large onions, chopped (2 cups)
6 tablespoons peanut oil or vegetable oil
4 tablespoons soy sauce
2 tablespoons wine vinegar or cider vinegar
¼ teaspoon ground ginger
¼ cup coarsely chopped salted peanuts

1. Combine chicken breasts, shrimp spice, instant onion, salt and water in a large saucepan; cover. Simmer 30 minutes, or until chicken is tender. Remove from broth and cool until easy to handle. Strain broth into a 4-cup measure; add water if needed to make 2¼ cups. Pull skin from chicken and take meat from bones; cut into 1-inch cubes.
2. Combine the 2¼ cups chicken broth and rice in a medium-size

saucepan. Cook 25 minutes, or until rice is tender and liquid is absorbed.

3. While rice cooks, trim broccoli; split any large stalks lengthwise, then cut into 2-inch lengths. Cook in boiling salted water in a saucepan 15 minutes; drain; keep warm.

4. Sauté chopped onions in 4 tablespoons of the oil until soft in an electric wok or electric fry pan set at 375°; stir in cooked rice. Sauté, stirring constantly, 5 minutes; add chicken; toss lightly to mix. Arrange cooked broccoli around edge of pan.

5. Combine remaining 2 tablespoons peanut oil or vegetable oil, soy sauce, wine vinegar or cider vinegar and ginger in a cup; drizzle over broccoli. Sprinkle peanuts over rice. Serve right from the wok.

HOLIDAY TURKEY PLATTER INDIENNE

Buy one of the two-pound boneless turkey roasts to cook, slice, and glaze for this easy curry-style dinner.

Roast at 400° for 2 hours,
then bake at 350° for 15 minutes.
Makes 8 servings.

1 packaged frozen boneless turkey roast, (about 2 pounds)
½ cup apricot preserves (from a 12-ounce jar)
¼ cup brandy or apple cider
1 teaspoon curry powder
  Herbed Pilaf (recipe, page 94)
  Golden Spiced Peaches (recipe, page 94)
  Chopped radishes and green onions

1. Roast frozen turkey in its foil package in a large toaster-oven or portable oven, set at 400° following label directions; remove from package; cool. (Meat slices neater if allowed to cool first. Or roast turkey a day ahead and keep chilled until ready to finish dish.).

2. Cut turkey into 24 thin slices; place slices overlapping in a shallow pan.

3. Mix apricot preserves, brandy or cider and curry powder in a small saucepan; heat, stirring constantly, until preserves melt and sauce is hot; brush over turkey slices.

4. Bake in toaster-oven or portable oven, set at 350°, 15 minutes, or until turkey is heated through.

5. Spoon HERBED PILAF onto a large serving platter, mounding it in center; arrange turkey slices, overlapping, in a ring on top.

6. Serve with GOLDEN SPICED PEACHES, and chopped radishes and green onions to sprinkle on top.

NAPOLI CHICKEN

Italian cooking was never so quick.

Microwave for 23 minutes.
Makes 4 servings.

1 broiler-fryer, quartered (about 3 pounds)
1 jar (21 ounces) Italian cooking sauce
¼ cup red cooking wine
1 can (3 or 4 ounces) sliced mushrooms, drained
2 cups diced or shredded mozzarella cheese (8 ounces)
¼ cup grated Parmesan cheese
¼ cup Italian-seasoned dry bread crumbs
2 tablespoons dry parsley flakes

1. Arrange chicken quarters in a 10-cup shallow microwave-safe casserole. Mix sauce, wine and mushrooms in a medium-size bowl. Spoon over chicken.

2. Cook in microwave oven 20 minutes, or until tender, turning casserole midway through cooking.

3. Spread mozzarella cheese over chicken. Combine Parmesan cheese, crumbs and parsley; sprinkle over top of casserole. Cook 3 minutes longer, or until cheese melts.

TURKEY CUTLETS KIEV

If properly prepared, there will be a great spurt of butter from the rolled and fried cutlet when it is pierced with a fork or knife. Although crisply fried shoestring potatoes are the standard accompaniment, some prefer to serve each cutlet on a bed of steamed rice, so the butter can seep into it.

Makes 8 servings.

8 turkey cutlets, thawed if frozen
¾ cup (1½ sticks) butter or margarine
1 teaspoon salt
½ teaspoon pepper
2 eggs
2 tablespoons cold water
¼ cup all-purpose flour
1 cup packaged bread crumbs
  Vegetable oil

1. Pound turkey cutlets between pieces of wax paper until very thin with a mallet or rolling pin.

2. Cut butter into strips 2 to 3 inches long and ½-inch wide. Wrap in wax paper and place in freezer for 10 minutes.

3. Sprinkle turkey cutlets with salt and pepper. Place one piece of chilled butter on each cutlet at the widest edge. Brush edges of cutlets with egg beaten with water in a pie plate and roll meat around butter, tucking sides in as you do so. Roll into a large

sausage shape. (It is absolutely essential that all the butter be enclosed with meat. If edges do not stay closed, fasten with one or two wooden picks.)

4. Gently roll each cutlet in flour on wax paper. Dip into beaten egg and let excess drip off. Roll gently but thoroughly in bread crumbs on wax paper. Arrange all cutlets on plate and chill at least one hour in the refrigerator, or 10 minutes in the freezer. (Cutlets can even be made up 4 or 5 hours in advance and kept in the refrigerator until cooking time.)

5. Pour oil to a depth of 2 inches in an electric deep-fat fryer until it reaches 350° on a fat thermometer or until a cube of bread turns golden in 75 seconds. Fry cutlets, two or three at a time, for 10 minutes.

HONG KONG CHICKEN ALMOND

A simple version of the traditional stir-fried Oriental dish.

Makes 4 servings.

2 whole chicken breasts, (about 12 ounces each)
3 tablespoons vegetable oil
1 cup sliced celery
½ clove garlic, minced
2 envelopes or teaspoons instant chicken broth
1½ cups water
1 tablespoon soy sauce
1 tablespoon chopped crystallized ginger
1 package (6 ounces) frozen Chinese pea pods
2 tablespoons cornstarch
¼ cup toasted slivered almonds
3 cups hot cooked rice

1. Pull skin from chicken breasts; halve breasts and cut meat in one piece from bones, then slice meat into long thin strips.

2. Heat oil in an electric wok or electric frypan set at 375°; add chicken and sauté, stirring constantly, 5 minutes. Stir in celery and garlic; sauté 3 minutes more.

3. Stir in instant broth, water, soy sauce and ginger; bring to boiling; add pea pods; cover wok or frypan. Simmer 5 minutes longer.

4. Smooth cornstarch with a little water to a paste in a cup; stir into chicken mixture. Cook, stirring constantly, until mixture thickens and bubbles 1 minute.

5. Spoon into a heated serving dish; sprinkle with almonds. Serve with hot cooked rice. Pass a bowl of Chinese fried noodles, if you wish.

PARMIGIANA CHICKEN CUTLETS

It's amazing how easily chicken cutlets can be substituted for veal in many classic veal cutlet dishes. Pictured on page 37.

Bake at 350° for 20 minutes.
Makes 4 individual casseroles.

- 8 chicken cutlets (about 1 pound)
- 1 egg
- 2 tablespoons water
- 1 teaspoon salt
- ¼ teaspoon seasoned pepper
- ½ cup Italian-seasoned fine dry bread crumbs
- ¼ cup olive oil or vegetable oil
- 1 jar (21 ounces) Italian cooking sauce
- 4 slices mozzarella cheese (from an 8-ounce package)

1. Place cutlets between pieces of wax paper and pound with a wooden mallet or rolling pin to flatten.
2. Beat egg with water, salt and seasoned pepper in a pie plate; place crumbs on wax paper. Dip cutlets, first into egg mixture, then into crumbs to coat lightly.
3. Brown cutlets, a few at a time, in hot oil in a large skillet. Drain on paper towels.
4. Spoon ¼ cup Italian cooking sauce into each of 4 individual casseroles; place two browned cutlets in each casserole; top with a slice of mozzarella cheese. Cover casseroles with plastic wrap and chill until meal time. Remove plastic wrap.
5. Bake, one or two at a time, in preheated toaster-oven set to moderate (350°) 20 minutes, or until bubbly-hot.
COOK'S TIP: To reheat in microwave oven, replace plastic wrap with wax paper; cook 5 minutes, turn casseroles, cook 5 minutes longer, or until bubbly-hot; let rest 2 minutes before serving.

INDONESIAN RIJSTTAFEL

This is literally a "rice table" for the satays, or kabobs of pungent turkey cubes that are surrounded with deep-fried sweet potato. Pictured on page 37.

Makes 4 servings.

- 3 cups cubed cooked turkey
- ½ cup orange marmalade
- ¼ cup lime juice
- ¼ teaspoon bottled red-pepper seasoning
  Fried Rice (recipe follows)
  Fried Sweet Potato Shreds (recipe, page 94)

1. Thread turkey cubes onto 4 wooden skewers. Combine marmalade, lime juice and bottled red-pepper seasoning in a cup; brush over turkey.
2. Preheat portable electric broiler, following manufacturer's directions. Broil kabobs, turning often and brushing with remaining glaze, 10 minutes, or until golden.
3. Spoon FRIED RICE onto a heated serving platter; arrange kabobs on rice; sprinkle FRIED SWEET POTATO SHREDS around.

FRIED RICE

Makes 4 servings.

- 3 tablespoons vegetable oil
- 1 cup sliced green onions
- 1 cup finely diced cooked ham
- 4 cups cooked rice (1 cup uncooked)
- 2 tablespoons soy sauce
  Dash cayenne pepper

1. Heat oil in an electric frypan set at 375°; sauté green onions in oil until soft; stir in ham and cook 2 minutes.
2. Stir in rice, soy sauce and cayenne pepper until well blended; lower heat control to 200°; cover frypan; cook 15 minutes, or until rice is piping-hot.

MONTEREY CHICKEN AND ARTICHOKES

Artichoke hearts and lemon rind add a California touch to chicken.

Microwave for 13 minutes.
Makes 4 servings.

- 2 whole chicken breasts, boned (about 12 ounces each)
- ¼ cup milk
- 1 package (2⅜ ounces) seasoned coating for chicken
- 2 tablespoons butter or margarine, melted
- 1 package (8 ounces) frozen artichoke hearts
- ½ cup heavy cream
  Salt and pepper
  Grated rind of ½ lemon
- 3 slices bacon, cooked and crumbled

1. Cut chicken breasts in half; dip into milk in a pie plate, then in seasoned coating.
2. Melt butter or margarine in a 6-cup microwave-safe casserole in a microwave oven. Add chicken pieces, skin-side down.
3. Cook, uncovered, 3 minutes. Turn chicken pieces over. Add artichoke hearts, cream, salt and pepper. Cover with wax paper.
4. Cook 5 minutes. Turn dish. Add lemon rind; cover. Cook 5 minutes, or until chicken is tender. Top with crumbled bacon.

LONDONDERRY TURKEY PIE

Pie birds are a traditional touch to meat pies in Great Britain. You can make this recipe without it, but it won't be as much fun. Pictured on page 37.

Bake at 400° for 20 minutes.
Makes 4 servings.

- 1 can condensed cream of onion soup
- ¼ cup light cream or milk
- 1 teaspoon Worcestershire sauce
- 1 can (1 pound) mixed vegetables, drained
- 2 cups diced cooked turkey
- 1 teaspoon leaf savory, crumbled
- 1¼ cups sifted all-purpose flour
- ½ teaspoon salt
- ⅓ cup vegetable shortening
- 3 tablespoons cold water
- 1 egg yolk

1. Combine soup, cream or milk and Worcestershire sauce in a large saucepan; bring to boiling; lower heat; stir in vegetables, turkey and savory; simmer while making pastry.
2. Sift flour and salt into a medium-size bowl; cut in shortening with a pastry blender until mixture is crumbly; stir in water with a fork, just until mixture leaves the side of bowl; pack into ball on wax paper.
3. Turn out dough onto a lightly floured pastry cloth or board; roll out to a ½-inch thick oval or round (match shape of casserole).
4. Invert casserole onto pastry and cut pastry ½-inch wider than dish; make a hole in center of pastry for pie bird base. (Or make several slits in pastry, if not using pie bird.)
5. Place pie bird base in center of casserole; spoon hot turkey mixture into dish; lift pastry from cloth or board to casserole with rolling pin, putting hole over pie bird base; press pastry against side of casserole.
6. Beat egg yolk with a few drops water in a cup; brush over pastry with a soft brush. Cut pastry trims into leaves with paring knife; arrange on pastry; brush with egg mixture.
7. Preheat portable electric oven to hot (400°).
8. Bake pie for 20 minutes, or until crust is golden. Insert pie bird into base before serving.

Chapter 4 continued on page 111.

Top to bottom: Londonderry Turkey Pie, Parmigiana Chicken Cutlets and Indonesian Rijsttafel. Recipes on this page.

EASY-LIVING

Summer is a time for carefree, relaxed living. That means cool salads, picnic finger food like crisp fried chicken, and tangy outdoor barbecues. They're all in this chapter.

Try crisp, refreshing Favorite Chicken Salad. Recipe is on page 41.

SUMMER MEALS

MARIE WALSH'S FRIED CHICKEN

Inspried by the "finger lickin" chicken of that Colonel from Kentucky, this recipe has been the most requested recipe for reprints by Family Circle readers since it was published in 1970. Photo on page 40.

Makes 4 servings.

1 broiler-fryer, cut up (about 2½ pounds)
3 cups water
1 tablespoon salt
2 teaspoons fines herbes
2 teaspoons onion sauté
2 teaspoons seasoned salt
2 envelopes or teaspoons instant chicken broth
¼ teaspoon seasoned pepper
1 cup all-purpose flour
  Fat for frying
  Chicken Broth (recipe follows)
  Chicken Gravy (recipe follows)

1. Cover chicken with a mixture of water and salt in a medium-size bowl. Chill at least 1 hour.
2. Whirl fines herbes, onion sauté, seasoned salt, instant chicken broth, and seasoned pepper in an electric blender or grind in a mortar and pestle until a very fine powder. Combine with flour in a plastic bag.
3. Remove chicken pieces, a few at a time, from water; shake in flour mixture while still wet, until thickly coated with flour.
4. Melt enough shortening or pour in enough vegetable oil to make a 1-inch depth in a large skillet or an electric deepfat fryer; heat to 375° on a deep-fat thermometer or until a cube of bread turns golden in 60 seconds.
5. Fry chicken pieces, turning once, 5 minutes on each side. Lift out with a slotted spoon; drain well on paper towels.
6. When all pieces are fried; drain the fat from skillet. Add 1 cup CHICKEN BROTH to skillet; return chicken pieces; cover skillet.
7. Cook 25 minutes, or until chicken pieces are fork tender. Place on hot serving platter and keep warm in oven while making CHICKEN GRAVY.
CHICKEN BROTH: Makes about 3 cups. Place salted water in which chickens soaked, with chicken giblets in a small saucepan; add 2 onion slices

Marie Walsh's Fried Chicken was inspired by that famous Colonel from Kentucky. Try it—they'll want buckets full. Recipe is on this page.

and a handful of celery leaves. Cover and simmer 30 minutes.
CHICKEN GRAVY: Makes about 2½ cups. Strain and add remaining chicken broth to skillet; bring to boiling, stirring and scraping baked-on juices from bottom and side of pan. Make a smooth paste with ¼ cup all-purpose flour and ½ cup cold water in a small cup. Stir into boiling liquid; continue stirring and boiling for 1 minute. Season to taste with salt and pepper; darken with a little gravy coloring, if you wish. Add chopped giblets and simmer 2 minutes longer.

CHICKEN VERONIQUE

Fresh green grapes and apricots, plus a tangy cucumber dressing, add style to a favorite.

Makes 6 servings.

4 whole chicken breasts (about 12 ounces each)
  Few celery leaves
2 teaspoons salt
6 peppercorns
1 bay leaf
1 envelope instant chicken broth
  OR: 1 chicken bouillon cube
1 cup water
1 cup chopped celery
1 cup seedless green grapes, halved
  Cucumber Dressing (recipe follows)
  Bibb lettuce
6 apricots, washed, halved and pitted

1. Combine the chicken breasts, celery, salt, peppercorns, bay leaf, instant chicken broth or bouillon cube and water in a large skillet; bring to boiling; cover. Simmer 30 minutes, until meat is tender.
2. Cool in broth until easy to handle, then remove and pull off skin; take meat from bones; cube. Place in a large bowl. (Strain broth and chill for making soup another day.)
3. Add celery and grapes to chicken; drizzle with about half of the CUCUMBER DRESSING; toss lightly to mix. Chill at least an hour to season.
4. When ready to serve, line a large bowl with lettuce; pile chicken mixture in center; frame with apricot halves. Serve with remaining dressing.

CUCUMBER DRESSING: Makes about 2 cups. Combine ⅓ cup mayonnaise or salad dressing, 1½ teaspoons salt, 1 teaspoon chopped fresh dill, ¼ teaspoon pepper, ⅓ cup lemon juice and 1 cup buttermilk in a small bowl; beat until well-blended. Stir in 1 small cucumber, pared, diced and drained well. Chill at least an hour.

FAVORITE CHICKEN SALAD

You can vary this recipe by substituting turkey and ham for the chicken, and Swiss or Cheddar for the blue cheese. Pictured on page 38.

Makes 6 servings.

2 whole chicken breasts (about 12 ounces each)
1 cup water
1 small onion, sliced
1 teaspoon herb-seasoned salt
¼ teaspoon lemon-pepper
3 cups broken Boston lettuce
3 cups broken romaine
1 cup sliced celery
6 slices bacon
2 tomatoes, cut into thin wedges
1 ripe avocado
1 tablespoon lemon juice
3 hard-cooked eggs, sliced
4 ounces blue cheese, crumbled
  Herb Vinaigrette Dressing (recipe follows)

1. Cook chicken with water, onion slices, herb-seasoned salt and lemon pepper in a large saucepan 20 minutes; skin and bone; chill; cut meat into thin slices.
2. Combine lettuce, romaine and celery in large bowl; cover; chill.
3. Cook and crumble bacon.
4. Halve avocado; peel and pit. Cut into cubes; sprinkle with lemon juice.
5. Place tomatoes, avocado, chicken, bacon, eggs and cheese over greens.
6. Pour ⅓ of the HERB VINAIGRETTE DRESSING over the salad just before serving; toss gently to coat. Pass remaining dressing. To complete the meal, make one of the chilled soups in our Special Section and a double-crust fruit pie.

HERB VINAIGRETTE DRESSING

Makes 1¼ cups.

¾ cup vegetable oil
½ cup tarragon vinegar
¾ teaspoon salt
¼ teaspoon seasoned pepper
¼ teaspoon leaf basil, crumbled

Shake oil, vinegar, salt, pepper and basil in a screw-top jar. Refrigerate to mellow flavors. Shake again just before pouring over salad.

POULTRY POINTER

Baste poultry with bottled barbecue sauce or a glaze with a sweet ingredient, such as honey, brown sugar or orange marmalade. (Baste only during the last 15 minutes of broiling and last 30 minutes of roasting.)

AVOCADO CHICKEN SALAD

Chilled, seasoned chicken and delicate avocado: A combination everybody loves.

Makes 6 servings.

- 1 stewing chicken (about 4 pounds), cooked
- ¼ cup vegetable oil
- 2 tablespoons fresh lime juice
- ¼ teaspoon ground ginger
- 1 large head iceberg lettuce
- 1 cup sliced celery
- 1 large ripe avocado

1. Cool chicken until easy to handle; remove skin and white and dark meat from bones in chunks as big as possible. (You should have about 4 cups.) Place in medium-size bowl. (Save broth for making soup another day.)
2. Combine oil, lime juice and ginger in a cup; sprinkle over chicken; toss to coat well; cover; chill.
3. At serving time, place a large lettuce leaf on each plate; shred remaining lettuce; toss with celery, and divide evenly onto lettuce leaves. Top with mounds of marinated chicken.
4. Peel avocado, remove seed and cut into thin lengthwise slices; arrange 3 on top of each mound of chicken.

SUMMER CHICKEN DIVAN

A winter casserole turns cool for summer salad days.

Makes 6 servings.

- 3 whole chicken breasts (about 12 ounces each)
- 1 small onion, sliced
- 1 teaspoon salt
  Dash pepper
  Water
- 2 packages (10 ounces each) frozen asparagus spears
- 1 envelope (about 1 ounce) cheese Italian salad dressing mix
  Vegetable oil
  Cider vinegar
- 1 head Boston lettuce, separated into leaves
- 2 cans (3 or 4 ounces each) whole mushrooms, drained
- ½ cup mayonnaise or salad dressing
- 2 hard-cooked egg yolks

1. Combine chicken, onion, salt, pepper and 2 cups water in a large skillet; cover. Simmer 30 minutes, or until chicken is tender. Remove from broth; cool until easy to handle, then pull off skin. Remove meat from each half of breast in one large piece; set aside. (Strain broth and chill for soup another day.)
2. While chicken cooks, cook asparagus, following label directions;

drain; place in a shallow dish.
3. Prepare salad dressing mix with vegetable oil, vinegar and water, following label directions; drizzle ½ cup over asparagus; let stand 30 minutes to season.
4. Line a large shallow serving dish with lettuce; arrange asparagus spears over lettuce, then place chicken breasts, overlapping, in a row on top of asparagus. Pile mushrooms at each end of dish.
5. Blend mayonnaise or salad dressing into remaining dressing in asparagus dish; drizzle over chicken. Press egg yolks through a sieve on top.

SKEWERED CHICKEN LIVERS WITH MUSHROOMS

Tender, crumb-coated chicken livers, paired with fresh mushrooms and a delicate wine sauce, are an epicure's delight.

Makes 4 servings.

- 1 pound chicken livers
- 3 tablespoons butter or margarine, melted
- ¼ cup dry white wine
- ½ cup fine dry bread crumbs
- ¼ teaspoon onion salt
- ¼ teaspoon leaf basil, crumbled
- 4 large mushrooms, quartered
- 8 cherry tomatoes
  White Wine Sauce (recipe follows)

1. Halve chicken livers; combine 2 tablespoons melted butter or margarine and wine in a medium-size bowl; add chicken livers and marinate for ½ hour in the refrigerator.
2. Combine bread crumbs, onion salt and basil on wax paper. Drain excess liquid from chicken livers and roll in bread crumb mixture until completely coated.
3. Thread chicken livers, mushrooms and cherry tomatoes alternately on 4 skewers; brush with remaining butter or margarine and marinade.
4. Grill 15 minutes, turning once, or until liver is slightly brown. Serve with WHITE WINE SAUCE and parslied hot noodles, if you wish.

WHITE WINE SAUCE: Makes about 1¼ cups. Sauté ¼ sliced green onions in 2 tablespoons butter or margarine in a medium-size saucepan 5 minutes, or until tender; stir in 2 tablespoons all-purpose flour, ¼ teaspoon salt and ⅛ teaspoon pepper. Cook, stirring constantly, just until bubbly. Stir in 1 cup dry white wine; continue cooking and stirring until sauce thickens and bubbles 3 minutes. Ladle over livers.

ROSEMARY CHICKEN

Serve this flavorful chicken on the patio for a summer supper.

Bake at 375° for 1 hour.
Makes 4 servings.

- 2 broiler-fryers, cut up (2 pounds each)
- 1 large onion, cut into thick slices
- ⅔ cup catsup
- ⅓ cup vinegar
- ¼ cup (½ stick) butter or margarine
- 1 clove garlic, minced
- 1 teaspoon leaf rosemary, crushed
- 1 teaspoon salt
- ¼ teaspoon dry mustard

1. Place chicken, skin-side down, in a single layer in a shallow baking pan; top with onion slices.
2. Mix catsup, vinegar, butter or margarine, garlic, rosemary, salt and dry mustard in a small saucepan; bring just to boiling; pour over chicken.
3. Bake in moderate oven (375°) 30 minutes. Turn chicken, skin-side up; baste with sauce in pan. Continue baking, basting once or twice, 30 minutes longer, or until tender and richly glazed.

AVOCADO DOUBLE-DECKERS

Fat sandwiches on Italian bread, filled with avocado spread and fruited chicken salad makes a meal from a sandwich.

Makes 8 sandwiches.

- 1 broiler-fryer (about 2½ pounds)
- 1 cup water
- 1½ teaspoons salt
  Few celery leaves
- 1 can (8¼ ounces) crushed pineapple
- ½ cup halved green grapes
- 1 cup mayonnaise or salad dressing
- 1 medium-size firm ripe avocado
- 6 slices crisp bacon, crumbled
  Few drops bottled red-pepper seasoning
- 2 loaves Italian bread

1. Combine chicken with water, 1 teaspoon of salt and celery leaves in a large saucepan; bring to boiling; cover. Simmer 45 minutes.
2. Remove from broth and cool until easy to handle; strain broth and chill for soup or gravy. Pull skin from chicken and take meat from bones; dice. (There should be about 2 cups.) Place in a medium-size bowl.
3. Drain syrup from pineapple into a cup. Add pineapple and grapes to chicken. Blend 2 tablespoons of the syrup with ½ cup mayonnaise or salad dressing and remaining ½ tea-

spoon salt in a small bowl; fold into chicken mixture. Chill.

4. Halve avocado; pit and peel. Mash in a small bowl; stir in crumbled bacon, ¼ cup of the remaining mayonnaise or salad dressing and red-pepper seasoning. (Fix avocado mixture no sooner than an hour ahead so that it keeps its bright color.)

5. Cut each loaf of bread lengthwise into 3 even slices; spread with remaining ¼ cup mayonnaise.

6. Spread avocado mixture on bottom slices and chicken salad on middle slices; stack loaves back in shape; cover with top slices. Cut each loaf crosswise into 4 thick double-decker sandwiches.

GARDEN CHICKEN CASSEROLE

Fresh asparagus, new potatoes and celery combine with chicken quarters in this meal-in-one dish.

Bake at 375° for 1 hour.
Makes 4 servings.

  1 broiler-fryer, quartered (about 3 pounds)
1½ teaspoons salt
  1 teaspoon leaf tarragon, crumbled
  2 tablespoons butter or margarine
  1 pound small new potatoes pared
  2 tablespoons chopped chives
  2 tablespoons chopped parsley
  2 cups sliced celery
  1 pound asparagus (break off ends of stems where they snap easily)
  1 tablespoon lemon juice

1. Sprinkle chicken on both sides with ½ teaspoon of the salt and ½ teaspoon tarragon. Heat butter or margarine in large skillet; add chicken, skin-side down, and brown slowly; turn, and brown other side. Transfer the chicken to a shallow 12-cup casserole.

2. Add potatoes to the butter in skillet; cook slowly over low heat for about 5 minutes and add to casserole. Sprinkle chicken and potatoes with chives, parsley and drippings from skillet. Cover tightly with casserole lid or aluminum foil.

3. Bake in moderate oven (375°) 30 minutes. Remove from oven.

4. Add celery pieces and asparagus. Sprinkle vegetables with remaining 1 teaspoon salt and ½ teaspoon tarragon; spoon juices in casserole over asparagus and celery. Drizzle with lemon juice.

5. Cover tightly and bake 30 minutes longer, or until chicken and vegetables are tender; baste occasionally with the juices in the casserole.

NAPA SONOMA CHICKEN

Nectarines from sunny California make a special summer stuffing for chickens.

Roast at 375° for 1 hour.
Makes 8 servings.

  3 fresh nectarines
  2 cups hot cooked rice
  ½ cup (1 stick) butter or margarine
  ½ cup raisins
  ¾ cup lemon juice
  2 broiler-fryers (about 3 pounds each)
    Salt and pepper
    Parsley

1. Dice nectarines to get about 1½ cups, packed. Mix hot rice with ¼ cup butter or margarine in a large bowl, then add diced nectarines, raisins and ¼ cup of the lemon juice.

2. Stuff mixture into chickens; truss. Sprinkle with salt and pepper and place in large roasting pan. Pour remaining ½ cup lemon juice over. Add remaining ¼ cup butter or margarine to bottom of pan.

3. Roast in moderate oven (375°) 1 hour, or until tender, basting with pan liquids every 15 minutes. Serve with a garnish of parsley.

DUTCH CHICKEN SALAD

Mayonnaise and cream furnish the base for this Netherlands original.

Makes 4 servings.

  1 broiler-fryer, cut up (about 3 pounds)
  2 cups water
1½ teaspoons salt
  1 package (10 ounces) frozen broccoli spears
  3 tablespoons bottled French dressing
  2 medium-size apples
  1 cup chopped celery
  1 small onion, chopped fine (¼ cup)
  ½ cup mayonnaise or salad dressing
  1 tablespoon lemon juice
    Dash pepper
  ½ cup heavy cream
    Iceberg lettuce
  2 tomatoes, cut in wedges
  2 hard-cooked eggs, shelled and sliced

1. Place chicken in a large skillet; add water and 1 teaspoon of the salt. Bring to boiling; cover. Simmer 50 minutes, or until chicken is tender. Remove from broth; cool until easy to handle, then skin chicken and take meat from bones; cut into bite-size pieces. Place in a large bowl; chill.

2. Cook broccoli spears, following label directions; drain. Place in a pie

plate; drizzle with French dressing; let stand a half hour to season.

3. Pare apples; quarter, core and dice. Add to chicken with celery and onion.

4. Blend mayonnaise or salad dressing with lemon juice, remaining ½ teaspoon salt and pepper in a small bowl. Beat cream until stiff in a second small bowl; fold into mayonnaise mixture; fold into chicken mixture.

5. Line a large serving platter with lettuce. Spoon chicken mixture in a mound down center. Arrange broccoli spears on one side, tomato wedges on other side and egg slices at each end of the platter.

BOWLING-NIGHT SALAD

Stash these cooling little salads in the refrigerator for family members to get for themselves.

Makes 4 individual molds.

  1 broiler-fryer, cut up (about 2½ pounds)
  2 cups water
  ½ small onion, sliced
    Few celery leaves
1½ teaspoons salt
  3 peppercorns
  1 envelope unflavored gelatin
  ¼ cup dry white wine or apple juice
  ½ cup mayonnaise or salad dressing
  ¼ cup diced celery
  2 tablespoons chopped toasted slivered almonds
  2 tablespoons chopped stuffed green olives
    Boston lettuce

1. Combine chicken, water, onion, celery leaves, salt and peppercorns in kettle; cover. Simmer 45 minutes, or until chicken is very tender; remove from broth. Strain broth into a 2-cup measure.

2. Soften gelatin in wine or apple juice in a medium-size saucepan; stir in 1½ cups of the broth.

3. Heat gelatin mixture slowly, stirring constantly, until gelatin dissolves; remove from heat; cool.

4. Pull skin from chicken and take meat from bones; dice finely.

5. Blend mayonnaise or salad dressing into gelatin mixture in saucepan; pour into an ice cube tray. Freeze 20 minutes, or until firm about 1 inch in from edges.

6. Spoon into a chilled large bowl; beat until fluffy thick. Fold in diced chicken, celery, almonds and olives. Spoon into 4 individual molds. Chill several hours or until firm.

7. Unmolded onto a lettuce-lined plate and garnish with melon crescents, if you wish.

GRILLED CHICKEN BREASTS SUPREME

This exotic chicken from the Far East is especially good with Tibetan rice and a tangy fruit sauce.

Makes 4 servings.

    4 whole chicken breasts (about 10
      ounces each)
    ½ cup all-purpose flour
    1 teaspoon salt
    ⅛ teaspoon pepper
    ⅛ teaspoon ground nutmeg
    1 egg
    1 tablespoon water
    1 cup finely ground cashew nuts
      (½ pound)
    4 green onions, thinly sliced
    2 tablespoons chopped parsley
    ¼ cup (½ stick) butter or margarine,
      melted
      Tibetan Rice (recipe follows)
      Piquant Fruit Sauce (recipe follows)

1. Wash and dry chicken; cut out any small rib bones and breastbones so breasts will lie flat, butterfly-style Shake in mixture of flour, salt, pepper and nutmeg in plastic bag to coat well.
2. Beat egg with water in pie plate; place ground cashew nuts in second pie plate. Dip chicken in egg mixture, then in nuts.
3. Place each breast, skin-side up, on a 12-inch square of heavy-duty aluminum foil. Sprinkle with green onions and parsley; drizzle melted butter or margarine over.
4. Wrap foil around chicken and seal tightly with a drugstore fold; place on grill above hot coals. Grill, turning often, 1 hour, or until tender.
5. Split foil envelopes open; place each breast on a bed of TIBETAN RICE; serve with PIQUANT FRUIT SAUCE.

PIQUANT FRUIT SAUCE

Makes about 3 cups.

    2 tablespoons brown sugar
    1 teaspoon cornstarch
    1 teaspoon salt
    1 can (1 pound, 4 ounces) pineapple
      chunks
    ½ cup orange juice
    1 tablespoon lemon juice
    ¼ cup water
    1 can (about 11 ounces) mandarin
      orange sections, drained

1. Blend brown sugar, cornstarch and salt in medium-size saucepan; stir in pineapple and syrup, orange and lemon juices and water.
2. Cook, stirring constantly, until sauce thickens slightly and bubbles 1 minute. Stir in mandarin orange sections; heat just to boiling.

TIBETAN RICE

Makes 4 servings.

    ¾ cup uncooked rice
    2 tablespoons vegetable oil
    ½ teaspoon turmeric
    ½ teaspoon curry powder
    ½ teaspoon salt
    ¼ cup seedless raisins
      Water
    1 can condensed chicken broth
      OR: 2 chicken bouillon cubes

1. Stir rice into oil in top of medium-size double boiler; heat over direct heat, stirring constantly, until rice is well coated with the oil.
2. Blend in turmeric, curry powder and salt; stir in raisins. Add enough water to the broth to make 1½ cups (or use bouillon cubes dissolved in 1½ cups boiling water); stir into rice.
3. Cover; cook over simmering water on grill 1 hour, or until rice is fluffed and tender and liquid is absorbed.

POULTRY POINTER

Coatings that Stick:
Chicken coated with seasoned flour before frying has a very thin crust. For a crisp, heavier crust, lightly dust chicken with flour and dip pieces in buttermilk or in a mixture of 1 egg beaten with ⅓ cup milk and 2 tablespoons lemon juice. Then roll in seasoned flour and place on wire racks. Let the chicken stand for 30 minutes for the coating to dry; roll in flour again if the coating is still moist. Proceed as usual for skillet-fried or oven-fried chicken.

SIMPLE SIMON

Chicken is baked in a cheese-cracker coating—delicious hot or cold.

Bake at 375° for 1 hour.
Makes 6 servings.

    1 package (about 5 ounces) cheese
      crackers, finely crushed
    2 teaspoons seasoned salt
    ½ cup vegetable oil
    2 broiler-fryers, cut up (about 3
      pounds each)

1. Place cracker crumbs in a pie plate; stir in seasoned salt. Pour oil into a second pie plate.
2. Dip chicken pieces into oil, then into crushed crumbs to coat well. Place in a single layer in a large shallow baking pan.
3. Bake in moderate over (375°) 1 hour, or until tender and golden-brown. Serve warm or cold.

CHINESE CHICKEN SALAD

Chinese fried noodles and soy dressing give the touch of authenticity to this Oriental-style salad.

Makes 6 servings.

    1 broiler-fryer (about 3 pounds)
    2 cups water
      Handful celery leaves
    1 teaspoon salt
    6 peppercorns
      Soy Dressing (recipe follows)
    1 bunch fresh broccoli (about 2
      pounds)
    6 cups broken salad greens
    1 cup chopped celery
    2 green onions, sliced
    5 large radishes, sliced
    1 can (3 ounces) Chinese fried
      noodles
    1 hard-cooked egg, shelled

1. Simmer chicken with water, celery; salt and peppercorns in kettle 45 minutes, or until tender. Take chicken from broth and let drain until cool enough to handle. (Strain broth and save for soup.)
2. Remove skin from chicken, then pull meat from frame in large pieces. (It comes off easily while still warm.) Cut into bite-size pieces; place in shallow pan; pour ¼ cup SOY DRESSING over. Cover; chill at least an hour to blend flavors.
3. Trim and discard outer leaves from broccoli. Cut off ends to make about 4-inch-long stalks; split large ones lengthwise. Cook, covered, in boiling salted water in a large skillet 10 minutes, or until crisply tender; drain.
4. Place in shallow pan; pour ½ cup SOY DRESSING over. Cover; chill at least an hour.
5. When ready to serve, pile salad greens, celery, green onions and radishes into large shallow salad bowl. Pour remaining ¾ cup SOY DRESSING over; toss lightly to mix.
6. Arrange marinated broccoli with stems toward center in a ring on top; fill ring with marinated chicken. Spoon noodles around broccoli.
7. Press white of egg, then yolk through a sieve onto separate sheets of wax paper. Spoon white on top of chicken; garnish with sieved egg yolk.

SOY DRESSING: Makes 1½ cups. Combine ½ cup soy sauce, ½ cup vegetable oil or peanut oil and ½ cup wine vinegar or cider vinegar with 1 teaspoon salt and ½ teaspoon ground ginger in small jar with tight-fitting cover; shake to mix well. This dressing is also good on a salad of tossed greens and fresh bean sprouts.

44

MRS. McCOLLUM'S FRIED CHICKEN

Mrs. McCollum's recipe comes from Family Circle's Grass Root Cook series: "It's real crispy and brown outside and juicy all the way to the bone. I always make chicken gravy, too, so we can spoon it over hot biscuits."

Makes 4 servings.

    1 broiler-fryer, cut up (about 3
       pounds)
    2 teaspoons salt
    ¼ teaspoon pepper
    ½ cup all-purpose flour
       Lard for frying (or, if you prefer,
       vegetable oil or shortening)
    1 tablespoon water

1. Lay chicken pieces in a shallow baking dish or pan, sprinkle with salt, cover and refrigerate overnight. Next day, pour off all accumulated juices and pat chicken dry on paper towels. Sprinkle chicken well with pepper, then roll in flour to coat, shaking off excess flour.
2. Melt enough lard in a large iron skillet over moderate heat to measure about 1 inch deep. Continue to heat —"when it's frying temperature," says Mrs. McCollum, "you'll begin to see a little steam rising up." Lay in pieces of chicken (it doesn't matter which side first) and adjust heat so chicken doesn't brown too fast. (Heat should be just moderate or moderately low.) Cook chicken 20 minutes on one side, then turn and cook 20 minutes longer. Add water, clap on a skillet lid, and let stand just until the fat stops sputtering. Lay chicken pieces out on paper towels to drain and lay some paper towels on top, too, while you make the gravy. "If the chicken's to be good and crispy, you don't want it to sweat," explains Mrs. McCollum. Serve the fried chicken hot or cold with cold salads, it makes a perfect picnic meal.

CHICKEN GRAVY: Makes about 2 cups. Pour all drippings from skillet, measure out 4 tablespoons and return to skillet. Add ¼ cup all-purpose flour and heat and stir until the flour turns a pretty brown. Add 2 cups water, ½ teaspoon salt and ⅛ teaspoon pepper. Heat and stir slowly until gravy thickens and "you don't get a raw flour taste"—about 5 minutes. Pour into a gravy boat and serve with fresh-baked biscuits. The McCollums don't spoon any gravy over the chicken, but take oven-hot biscuits, split them in half and spoon the gravy over them.

STUFFED SALAD ROLLS

A tasty jumble of chopped chicken, cheese and celery, piled on frankfurter rolls.

Makes 8 rolls.

    2 cups shredded iceberg lettuce
    1 cup diced cooked chicken
    ½ cup diced process American or
       Swiss cheese
    ½ cup chopped celery
    ½ cup mayonnaise or salad dressing
    2 tablespoons pickle relish
    ¼ teaspoon curry powder
    8 frankfurter rolls, split, toasted and
       buttered

1. Combine lettuce with chicken, cheese and celery in medium-size bowl; toss to mix.
2. Blend mayonnaise, pickle relish and curry powder in small bowl; stir into salad mixture to coat well; pile into prepared rolls. Serve with potato chips and lemonade, if you wish.

POULTRY POINTERS

• To baste poultry means to ladle pan drippings, marinade or another liquid over the bird while it roasts to prevent dryness and to add flavor.
• A marinade is a flavorful liquid that contains an acid, such as lemon juice, vinegar or wine in which poultry pieces soak before cooking. It both tenderizes and adds flavor to the birds.
• Many recipes suggest marinating overnight for best results. Marinades are also used to baste the birds while roasting.

OUTDOOR PARTY CHICKEN

Allow plenty of grilling time so that the meat will almost fall off the bones.

Makes 12 servings.

    6 broiler-fryers, split (2½ pounds
       each)
    2 cups vegetable oil
    ½ cup lime or lemon juice
    2 teaspoons salt
    ¼ cup honey

1. Mix oil, lime or lemon juice and salt in small saucepan; brush part over chickens. Place chickens, skin-side up, on grill about 6 inches above coals.
2. Grill, turning and brushing often with more sauce, 1 hour.
3. Stir honey into remaining sauce; brush over chickens. Continue grilling, turning often and brushing with remaining sauce, 15 minutes.

SAN FERNANDO VALLEY SALAD

For a summer party this elegant mélange of tender chicken and fruits is tossed with a creamy curry dressing.

Makes 12 servings.

    2 broiler-fryers (3 pounds each)
    2 cups water
    2 teaspoons salt
    6 peppercorns
       Handful celery leaves
    2 carrots, pared and sliced
       Creamy Boiled Dressing (recipe
       follows)
    3 cups cantaloupe cubes
    2 cups halved green grapes
    2 cups thinly sliced celery
    1 cup toasted slivered almonds
    2 heads Boston or leaf lettuce
       Paprika

1. Simmer broiler-fryers in water with salt, peppercorns, celery and carrots in large saucepan, covered, 45 minutes, or until tender.
2. Remove from broth and let cool just until easy to handle. (Save broth for soup for another meal.) Slip skin from chickens; remove meat from bones in large chunks and cut into cubes. (You should have about 6 cups.)
3. Place chicken in large bowl; toss with just enough CREAMY BOILED DRESSING to coat well; cover; chill.
4. When ready to serve, stir the cantaloupe, grapes, celery and almonds into chicken mixture; toss with enough remaining dressing to coat.
5. Line a salad bowl with lettuce; spoon salad in center; garnish with a sprinkle of paprika.
SUGGESTED VARIATION: Instead of tossing salad with cantaloupe cubes, spoon into cantaloupe halves.

CREAMY BOILED DRESSING

Makes 1½ cups.

    4 tablespoons sugar
    2 tablespoons all-purpose flour
    1 teaspoon salt
    ½ teaspoon curry powder
    2 eggs, beaten
    1 cup water
    ½ cup cider vinegar
    2 tablespoons butter or margarine

1. Combine sugar, flour, salt and curry powder in a medium-size saucepan; stir in egg, water and vinegar.
2. Cook slowly, stirring constantly, 5 minutes, or until thickened. Remove from heat; stir in butter or margarine until melted. This dressing will keep well in a tightly covered jar in the refrigerator.

MUSHROOM-LIVER KABOBS

An interesting variation on the popular kabob.

Makes 4 servings.

    4 slices bacon cut in quarters
   12 small mushroom caps
   12 chicken livers (about 1 pound)
    2 tablespoons melted butter or
       margarine
       Salt and pepper

1. Thread a folded-over piece of bacon, a mushroom cap and a chicken liver on a short skewer; repeat 2 more times, ending with bacon; repeat to fill 4 skewers.
2. Place in shallow baking pan; brush with melted butter or margarine.
3. Place in broiler with top of food 4 inches from unit or tip of flame, and broil 10 minutes, or until livers are cooked through and bacon is crisp, turning once and basting once or twice with drippings. Sprinkle with salt and pepper to taste.
4. Remove food from each skewer onto a hot plate and serve.

CHICKEN LIVER BOUNTIES

Here's a sandwich to please gourmets. Cook the livers gently, then combine with broiled tomatoes and crisp bacon.

Makes 6 sandwiches.

    6 slices bacon
    1 pound chicken livers
    2 tablespoons all-purpose flour
   ¼ teaspoon seasoned salt
    1 can (3 or 4 ounces) chopped
       mushrooms
    3 large tomatoes, each cut in 6 slices
    3 large hamburger buns, split
       Chopped parsley

1. Sauté bacon just until crisp in a large skillet; drain on paper towels, then crumble. Drain off all drippings, then measure 2 tablespoons and return to pan.
2. Halve chicken livers; snip out any veiny parts or skin with scissors. Shake livers with flour and seasoned salt in a plastic bag to coat.
3. Brown slowly in drippings in pan; stir in mushrooms and liquid. Heat, stirring constantly, to boiling; cover. Simmer 3 minutes, or just until livers lose their pink color.
4. While livers cook, place tomato slices and bun halves in a single layer on rack in broiler pan. Broil 3 to 4 minutes, or until tomatoes are heated through and buns are toasted.
5. Place 2 tomato slices on each bun half; spoon hot liver mixture over, dividing evenly. Top each with another tomato slice; sprinkle with crumbled bacon. Garnish with parsley, if you wish.

CHICKEN-CORN SALAD

Filling fare with all white meat chicken, hard-cooked eggs, corn nuggets and tender macaroni.

Makes 6 servings.

    2 whole chicken breasts (about 12
       ounces each)
    2 cups water
    1 slice onion
       Few celery leaves
  1¼ teaspoons salt
    3 tablespoons cider vinegar
    2 teaspoons sugar
   ¼ teaspoon pepper
   ½ cup vegetable oil
    1 package (8 ounces) small
       macaroni shells
    1 can (12 or 16 ounces) whole-
       kernel corn, drained
    1 cup thinly sliced celery
    1 large head Boston lettuce
    3 hard-cooked eggs, shelled and
       coarsely chopped
   ¼ cup mayonnaise or salad dressing
    3 tablespoons chopped parsley

1. Combine chicken breasts with water, onion, celery leaves and ¼ teaspoon of the salt in a medium-size saucepan; cover. Bring to boiling; lower heat; simmer 30 minutes, or until chicken is tender. Remove from broth and cool until easy to handle. (Save broth to add to chicken soup for another day.)
2. Pull skin from chicken and take meat from bones; cut meat into bite-size pieces.
3. Combine vinegar, sugar, remaining 1 teaspoon salt, pepper and vegetable oil in a jar with a tight fitting lid; shake well to mix. Drizzle 3 tablespoons over chicken; chill.
4. Cook macaroni in boiling salted water, following label directions, drain well. Combine with corn, celery and 3 tablespoons of the dressing in a large bowl; toss to mix well; chill.
5. When ready to serve, line shallow salad bowls with lettuce; shred remaining lettuce into pieces and add to bowls. Spoon macaroni mixture on top of lettuce.
6. Add chopped eggs to chicken mixture; toss lightly to mix; spoon over macaroni.
7. Beat remaining dressing into mayonnaise or salad dressing and parsley in a small bowl; pass separately. Serve with tall glasses of iced tea garnished with lemon slices.

HONOLULU JUMBOS

White meat and pineapple in a creamy dressing on raisin bread make delicious stay-moist picnic sandwiches.

Makes 4 sandwiches.

    1 can (8¼ ounces) pineapple slices
   16 thin slices cooked chicken breast
    8 slices cinnamon-raisin bread or
       cracked whole-wheat bread,
       buttered
   ¼ cup mayonnaise or salad dressing
    2 tablespoons chopped pecans

1. Drain syrup from pineapple into a cup; halve slices.
2. Arrange chicken slices and pineapple slices, overlapping, on 4 slices of bread.
3. Blend mayonnaise or salad dressing, 1 tablespoon of the pineapple syrup, and pecans in a cup; spoon a generous tablespoonful over filling for each sandwich. Cover with remaining slices of bread. (Chill remaining syrup to add to a beverage.)
4. Place each sandwich in a plastic bag, or wrap in aluminum foil.

CHICKEN CLUBS

Chicken, bacon and Muenster—a flavory combo—spiked with tomatoes and crisp sliced cucumber.

Bake at 450° for 5 minutes.
Makes 4 sandwiches.

   12 slices bacon
    2 medium-size tomatoes, each cut
       in 4 slices
   ½ small cucumber, sliced
   12 slices whole-wheat bread, toasted
       and buttered
   ¼ cup bottled sandwich spread
    8 slices cooked chicken or turkey
    4 slices Muenster cheese (from an 8-
       ounce package)
    8 pitted ripe olives
    8 small sweet pickles

1. Sauté bacon until crisp in a large skillet; drain on paper towels.
2. Place tomato and cucumber slices and bacon, dividing evenly, on 4 pieces of the toast; add another slice of the toast; spread with bottled sandwich spread.
3. Top with chicken slices, then cheese and remaining toast, buttered side down. Place sandwiches on a cooky sheet.
4. Bake in a very hot oven (450°) 5 minutes, or until cheese melts slightly.
5. Press wooden picks into sandwiches to hold; cut each sandwich diagonally into quarters. Top picks with olives and pickles.

SUMMER SALAD HEROES

Carried to the picnic in an insulated bag, this delightful sandwich is really heroic in flavor and nutrition.

Makes 4 servings.

- ¼ cup milk
- 1 package (3 ounces) cream cheese, softened
- 2½ cups diced cooked chicken
- ¼ cup chopped celery
- ¼ cup chopped pared carrot
- ⅓ cup chopped radishes
- ½ teaspoon onion salt
- Dash pepper
- 4 hero rolls
- Butter or margarine

1. Blend milk into cream cheese and beat until smooth. Add chicken, vegetables, onion salt and pepper; mix.
2. Cut rolls in half and scoop out some of the bread to make a cavity. Spread with butter or margarine.
3. Fill each roll with ¾ cup chicken salad mixture; replace tops and wrap tightly in foil or plastic wrap. Chill before taking to picnic.

TAHITIAN CHICKEN

The exotic flavors of curry and tropical fruits go so well with chicken.

Makes 8 servings.

- 4 whole chicken breasts, split (about 12 ounces each)
- ¾ cup bottled oil-and-vinegar salad dressing
- 2 teaspoons curry powder
- 1 can (15¼ ounces) sliced pineapple
- 2 medium-size bananas or 1 large papaya
- 2 large limes
- 8 preserved kumquats
- ½ cup honey

1. Bone chicken breasts (or buy chicken cutlets already boned) and cut each split chicken breast into 4 pieces.
2. Combine oil-and-vinegar salad dressing and curry powder in a medium-size bowl; add chicken. Marinate 2 hours in the refrigerator.
3. Cut pineapple slices in half. Just before cooking, peel bananas and cut into 2-inch pieces. Halve, seed and pare papaya; cut into 1-inch cubes; cut limes into wedges.
4. Drain chicken; reserve marinade. Thread chicken, pineapple, banana or papaya, kumquats and lime wedges, alternately on 8 long skewers. Stir honey into remaining marinade and brush generously over kabobs.
5. Grill, turning and basting often, 10 minutes, or until chicken is golden.

6. Serve kabobs with kasha or packaged frozen prepared fried rice with almonds, and tall glasses of chilled limeade, if you wish.

CURRIED CHICKEN CORONET

A partylike rich chicken salad mousse delicately spiced with curry and sprinkled with flaked coconut.

Makes 8 servings.

- 2 whole chicken breasts (about 12 ounces each)
- 2 cups water
- 1 medium-size onion, sliced
- Handful celery leaves
- 1½ teaspoons salt
- 3 peppercorns
- 1 envelope unflavored gelatin
- 2 eggs, separated
- ½ cup chopped toasted almonds
- 1 teaspoon curry powder
- ¼ teaspoon pepper
- 1 cup mayonnaise or salad dressing
- 1 cup heavy cream
- 1 can (13¼ ounces) pineapple chunks, drained
- ½ cup flaked coconut

1. Combine chicken breasts, water, onion, celery, 1 teaspoon of the salt and peppercorns in large saucepan; simmer, covered, 45 minutes, or until chicken is tender. Let stand until cool enough to handle, then skin chicken and take meat from bones. Dice chicken fine (you should have about 2 cups diced chicken).
2. Strain stock into a bowl; measure out 1 cup; pour into a medium-size saucepan and cool. (Save any remaining stock for soup for another day.)
3. Soften gelatin in cooled stock in saucepan; heat, stirring constantly, until dissolved.
4. Beat egg yolks slightly in small bowl; slowly stir in dissolved gelatin. Return mixture to saucepan and cook, stirring constantly, 1 minute, or until slightly thickened; remove saucepan from heat.
5. Stir in diced chicken, almonds, curry powder, ½ teaspoon of salt and pepper, blending well. Chill 30 minutes, or until the mixture is syrupy-thick; blend in the mayonnaise.
6. Beat egg whites until stiff in large bowl; fold in chicken mixture until no streaks of white remain.
7. Beat cream until stiff in medium-size bowl; fold into chicken mixture.
8. Pour into a 6-cup ring mold; chill several hours, or until firm.
9. Unmold onto serving plate; fit a shallow bowl into center of mold; fill with pineapple chunks; sprinkle with flaked coconut.

CAPRI CHICKEN BROIL

Grilled chicken breasts brushed with a butter mixture—great indoors or out.

Makes 8 servings.

- ½ cup (1 stick) butter or margarine
- 1 envelope (about 1 ounce) Italian salad dressing mix
- ¼ cup lime juice
- 8 whole chicken breasts (about 12 ounces each)

1. Melt butter or margarine in a small saucepan; stir in salad dressing mix and lime juice. Brush part over both sides of chicken.
2. Place the chicken, skin side down, on grill about 10 inches above hot coals. Grill, turning and brushing pieces often with more butter mixture, 40 minutes, or until chicken is tender and richly glazed.

COOK'S TIP: To cook indoors, place chicken pieces, skin-side up, on rack in broiler pan; brush with butter mixture. Broil, 4 to 6 inches from heat, brushing several times with butter mixture, 15 minutes; turn. Brush again; broil 15 minutes longer.

STROGANOFF ROUNDS

To round out a light supper menu, just add raw relishes and a simple dessert.

Makes 6 servings.

- 1 broiler-fryer, cut up (about 3 pounds)
- 1 medium-size onion, chopped (½ cup)
- ½ cup chopped celery
- 2 tablespoons butter or margarine
- 1 envelope (1 ounce) sour cream sauce mix
- 1 container (8 ounces) dairy sour cream
- 6 split hamburger buns, toasted

1. Simmer chicken, covered, in 2 cups lightly salted boiling water in a large skillet 40 minutes, or until tender. Remove chicken from bones; dice meat. Measure 1 cup of the broth and set aside.
2. Sauté onion and celery in butter or margarine until soft in same pan; stir in chicken.
3. Blend sauce mix with the 1 cup chicken broth in a small bowl; stir into chicken mixture. Bring almost to boiling; cover. Simmer gently 10 minutes longer.
4. Stir about 1 cup of the hot sauce mixture into sour cream in a small bowl; stir back into pan. Heat very slowly just until hot. Spoon over toasted buns to serve open-face style.

BARBECUE CHICKEN DRUMSTICKS

The vegetables can be parboiled early in the day. Then wait for the sun to start setting before beginning the barbecue. Pictured on page 49.

Makes 4 servings

- 8 drumsticks (about 2 pounds)
- ½ cup bottled barbecue sauce
- ¼ cup cider vinegar
- 8 small new potatoes
- 1 small acorn squash
- 1 bunch leeks
  Golden Rice (recipe follows)

1. Place drumsticks in a shallow glass baking dish; pour over a mixture of barbecue sauce and cider vinegar; cover with plastic wrap; chill at least 3 hours to marinate.
2. Pare a thin strip around each potato; halve, seed and slice acorn squash; cook vegetables in separate medium-size saucepans in salted boiling water 10 minutes, or just until crisply-tender; drain and chill.
3. Cut leeks into 2-inch pieces. (Save top leaves for soup kettle.) Soak in salted warm water to remove sand; drain on paper towels.
4. Drain drumsticks; reserve marinade. Thread onto 4 long skewers with potatoes, acorn squash and leeks; brush skewers with reserved marinade.
5. Barbecue, 4 inches from coals, turning often and basting with remaining marinade, 20 minutes, or until drumsticks are tender and vegetables golden. Serve on a platter with GOLDEN RICE.

GOLDEN RICE

Makes 4 servings.

- 1 cup uncooked long-grain rice
- 2 tablespoons vegetable oil
- 2½ cups boiling water
- 2 envelopes or teaspoons instant chicken broth
  Few drops yellow food coloring

1. Sauté rice in oil in a large skillet, just until grains turn golden; combine boiling water, instant chicken broth and yellow food coloring in a 4-cup measure; pour over rice in skillet; cover skillet.
2. Place to the back of the barbecue; cook, shaking pan several times, but *not* uncovering, 30 minutes, or until liquid is absorbed and rice is tender.
COOK'S TIP: To complete cooking indoors, cover skillet and lower heat to simmer; cook 30 minutes. Serve in a heated casserole.

POULTRY POINTERS

Tips for Cooking Poultry Kabobs Outdoors
- Start the barbecue 40 minutes before you are ready to cook; by that time the coals will be grayed and burning at an even heat.
- When cooking kabobs over charcoal, place skewers on barbecue rack, about 4 inches from coals.
- Turn the skewers frequently for even cooking, whether cooking just poultry, or with vegetables.
- When brushing with marinade, remove skewer from barbecue grill to prevent marinade from dripping onto coals and causing unnecessary flaming and smoking.
- Total cooking time will be from 10 to 20 minutes, varying with the number of kabobs as well as the type of poultry and vegetables used.

SESAME SEED GLAZED KABOBS

Toasted sesame seeds and honey add a touch of the Orient to barbecued chicken thighs. Pictured on page 49.

Makes 4 servings.

- 2 tablespoons sesame seeds
- ½ cup honey
- ¼ cup lemon juice
- 1 teaspoon salt
  Few drops bottled red-pepper seasoning
- 8 small white onions, peeled
- 2 small yellow squash
- 1 large green pepper
- 1 large red pepper
- 8 chicken thighs (about 1½ pounds)
- ¼ cup bottled oil and vinegar salad dressing
  Golden Rice (recipe, this page)

1. Sprinkle sesame seeds in an even layer in the bottom of a small saucepan. Toast over low heat, stirring constantly, until golden; stir in honey, lemon juice, salt and red-pepper seasoning.
2. Cut a cross at the root-end of each onion; tip yellow squash and cut into 1-inch slices; cook together in salted boiling water in a medium-size saucepan 10 minutes; drain.
3. Halve and seed peppers; cut into 2-inch pieces.
4. Thread chicken thighs onto 4 long skewers with yellow squash, onions, and green and red pepper pieces; brush well with bottled salad dressing.
5. Barbecue, 4 inches from coals, turning often, 10 minutes; begin to brush with sesame seed glaze, turning and basting 10 minutes longer. Serve with GOLDEN RICE.

MOLDED CHICKEN INDIENNE

All white meat blends with curry and chutney for this inviting supper mold.

Makes 6 servings.

- 2 whole chicken breasts (about 12 ounces each)
- 3½ cups water
- 2 teaspoons salt
- 1 teaspoon curry powder
  Few celery leaves
- 2 envelopes unflavored gelatin
- 1 tablespoon sugar
- 2 tablespoons lemon juice
- ⅓ cup chutney, finely chopped
- 1 cup chopped celery

1. Combine chicken breasts with water, salt, curry powder and celery leaves in a large saucepan; cover; simmer 20 minutes, or until tender.
2. Remove chicken from broth; cool until easy to handle. Strain broth into a 4-cup measure; add water, if needed, to make 3½ cups. Pull skin from chicken and slip meat from bones; chill meat; dice.
3. Soften gelatin with sugar in 1 cup of the broth in a medium-size saucepan; heat, stirring constantly, just until gelatin dissolves; remove from heat. Stir in remaining 2½ cups chicken broth.
4. Measure ½ cup of the gelatin mixture into a small bowl. Stir lemon juice into remaining gelatin in saucepan. Chill about 50 minutes, or until as thick as unbeaten egg white.
5. Stir chutney into gelatin in small bowl; pour into a 6-cup mold; chill about 30 minutes, or until sticky-firm.
6. Fold chicken and celery into thickened gelatin in saucepan; spoon over sticky-firm chutney layer in mold. Chill overnight until firm.
7. To unmold, run a sharp-tip thin-blade knife around top of mold, then dip very quickly in and out of a pan of hot water. Cover mold with serving plate; turn upside down; gently lift off mold. Garnish with leaves of Belgian endive, halved seedless grapes and flaked coconut, if you wish. Serve with hot dinner rolls, if desired.

Chapter 5 continued on page 115.

Left: Barbecue Chicken Drumsticks are grilled with new potatoes and acorn squash. Right: Juicy Sesame Seed Glazed Kabobs with yellow squash and red and green peppers. Recipes are on this page.

GREAT MEALS IN NO TIME AT ALL

Chicken is a natural for quick cooking. You can roast a whole bird at high temperature in just 1 hour. Or, try one of our jiffy one-dish broiled or baked specialties. Quick brush-on bastes and glazes can also save time— and add flavor.

MEALS IN A HURRY

Left to right: Raisin
and Almond Chicken, Roast
Chicken and Butternut Squash
and Lemon-Mint Broiled
Chicken. Recipes are on
page 53.

LEMON-MINT BROILED CHICKEN

Notice how the broiler is used. This is the correct broiling method which prevents the chicken from being charred outside. Pictured on page 51.

Makes 6 servings.

- ½ cup (1 stick) butter or margarine, softened
- 1 teaspoon salt
- ¼ teaspoon pepper
- 1 teaspoon grated lemon rind
- ½ teaspoon dried mint, crumbled
- 3 broiler-fryers, split (about 2 pounds each)
- 18 large asparagus spears (1 bunch) OR: 2 packages (10 ounces each) frozen asparagus spears
- 1 tablespoon lemon juice
  Lemon wedges
  Fresh mint or parsley

1. Mix butter or margarine, 1 teaspoon salt, ¼ teaspoon pepper, lemon rind and mint in small bowl.
2. Slide about a teaspoon of butter mixture under skin or each chicken breast.
3. Set the chickens, skin-side down, on large broiler pan; spread remaining butter mixture over chickens.
4. Broil, 4 inches from heat, 5 minutes, sprinkle lightly with salt and pepper, then lower the pan to 6 inches from heat and continue broiling 10 minutes.
5. Meanwhile, wash asparagus, break off tough ends, peel off scales, then boil in lightly salted water, 8 to 10 minutes, or until tender, or cook frozen asparagus, following label directions. Drain; keep warm while chicken broils.
6. Turn the chicken over. Brush with the butter in the bottom of broiler pan. Broil, 4 inches from heat, 5 minutes; sprinkle lightly with salt and pepper, then lower the broiler pan to 6 inches from heat. Broil another 10 minutes, brushing twice with butter from broiler pan.
7. Arrange the six chicken halves on heated serving platter with asparagus. Add lemon juice, and a pinch each of salt and pepper to juices in broiler pan; drizzle over chicken and asparagus. Garnish with wedges of lemon and mint or parsley.

Springtime Party Platter features roast Rock Cornish hens and fresh spring vegetables, ready in less than an hour. Recipe is on this page.

RAISIN AND ALMOND CHICKEN

Plump chicken breasts in a creamy rum-raisin sauce. Pictured on page 50.

Makes 8 servings.

- 3 tablespoons dark raisins
- 3 tablespoons light or dark rum
- ¼ cup (½ stick) butter or margarine
- ¼ cup slivered almonds
- 4 whole chicken breasts, halved, skinned and boned (about 12 ounces each)
- 1 teaspoon salt
- ¼ teaspoon pepper
- ¾ cup chicken broth
- 1 tablespoon cornstarch
- ½ cup light cream

1. Soak raisins in rum in small cup while preparing recipe.
2. Heat butter or margarine in a large skillet; add almonds. Cook, stirring constantly, until almonds are toasted. Remove with slotted spoon to a plate.
3. Add chicken breasts to skillet; sprinkle with salt and pepper. Cook over medium heat, turning often, 10 minutes or until firm; remove to a plate; keep warm.
4. Add broth to skillet; bring to boiling. Mix cornstarch and cream in a cup; pour into boiling liquid, stirring constantly; simmer 3 minutes. Stir in rum and raisins. Taste and add more salt and pepper, if needed.
5. Reheat the cutlets gently in the hot sauce. Arrange in heated serving dish; spoon sauce over; sprinkle with almonds and garnish with watercress. Serve with fluffy rice or thin egg noodles to soak up all the sauce.

ROAST CHICKEN AND BUTTERNUT SQUASH

Try this method of roasting young chickens at high temperature. They cook in a skimpy hour and have delicious, juicy meat. Pictured on page 50.

Roast at 375° for 1 hour.
Makes 8 servings.

- 2 small roasting chickens (3 to 3½ pounds each)
  Salt
  Pepper
- 1 teaspoon leaf tarragon, crumbled
- 2 tablespoons softened butter or margarine or vegetable oil
- 2 small butternut squash
- 3 tablespoons honey
- 3 tablespoons dry sherry

1. Sprinkle chickens inside and out with salt and pepper; place ½ teaspoon tarragon inside each; truss both chickens. Place chickens in large roasting pan; rub each with 1 tablespoon butter or oil.
2. Roast in moderate oven (375°), brushing often with pan juices, 20 minutes.
3. Meanwhile, pare squash; cut lengthwise into quarters; scrape out seeds. Parboil 5 minutes in boiling salted water. Arrange in roasting pan with chickens; baking 15 minutes.
4. Mix honey and sherry in a cup. Brush evenly over chickens and squash; continue to roast, brushing with pan drippings 15 minutes, or until juices run clear when the thigh of each bird is pierced with a skewer.
5. Arrange chickens and squash on heated serving platter.

SPRINGTIME PARTY PLATTER

Dinner tonight can be festive, yet quick with Rock Cornish hens and delicate spring vegetables. Pictured on page 52.

Roast at 375° for 50 minutes.
Makes 2 servings.

- 2 frozen Rock Cornish hens, thawed (about 1½ pounds each)
- 3 tablespoons softened butter or margarine
- 2 teaspoons seasoned salt
- ¼ teaspoon pepper
- ¼ teaspoon leaf marjoram, crumbled
- ¼ cup dry white wine or chicken broth
- 1½ pounds fresh asparagus, trimmed and cooked OR: 1 package (10 ounces) frozen asparagus spears, cooked
- 2 small yellow squash, tipped and cut into sticks, cooked
- 2 tablespoons butter or margarine, melted
- 2 tablespoons chopped parsley

1. Rub hens with a mixture of softened butter or margarine, seasoned salt, pepper and marjoram.
2. Place in a 10x16-inch plastic cooking bag and seal, following label directions. Place in a shallow roasting pan.
3. Roast in a moderate oven (375°) 50 minutes, or until skin is golden; open plastic cooking bag carefully; place hens on a heated serving platter and surround with asparagus and yellow squash. Spoon melted butter or margarine and chopped parsley over vegetables.
4. Pour juices in cooking bag into a small saucepan; bring to boiling. Combine 2 tablespoons cold water with 1 tablespoon all-purpose flour in a cup; stir into boiling liquid; cook, stirring constantly, until sauce thickens and bubbles 3 minutes.

APPLE-WINE BROILER CHICKEN

True apple flavor comes through in this easy-going chicken.

Makes 8 servings.

- 2 broiler-fryers, split (2½ to 3 pounds each)
- ½ cup (1 stick) melted butter or margarine
- 2 teaspoons salt
- 2 tablespoons apple jelly
- ¼ cup white wine

1. Brush chicken halves thoroughly with butter or margarine. Sprinkle with salt.
2. Mash apple jelly with a fork, then add wine gradually. Brush this mixture on both sides of chicken halves.
3. Place chicken, skin-side down, in broiler pan (without rack). Broil 6 to 9 inches from the heat for 20 minutes. Then turn, skin-side up, and continue broiling until chicken is evenly browned and cooked, about 20 minutes longer.
4. Cut each chicken half into quarters for serving.

STUFFED WHIRLYBIRD

Rôtisserie chicken is especially delicious with a lively fruit stuffing.

Makes 4 servings.

- 1 roasting chicken (about 4 pounds)
  Fruit Stuffing (recipe follows)
- 2 tablespoons butter or margarine
- 1 teaspoon salt
- ¼ teaspoon pepper
  Ginger-Honey Glaze (recipe follows)

1. Stuff chicken breast and body cavities with FRUIT STUFFING.
2. Secure body and neck cavities tightly closed; tie legs and wings tightly to body. Rub bird with softened butter or margarine and sprinkle with salt and pepper.
4. Place on rôtisserie spit and roast 1 hour, then begin basting with GINGER-HONEY GLAZE. Continue roasting, basting often, 30 to 45 minutes longer, or until chicken is richly browned and tender.

FRUIT STUFFING

Makes 4 cups.
- 1 can (1 pound) sliced apples
  Water
- ¼ cup (½ stick) butter or margarine
- 2 cups prepared bread stuffing mix (from an 8-ounce package)
- ½ cup chopped peanuts
- ½ cup seedless raisins

1. Drain sliced apples; add water to apple liquid to make ½ cup; bring to boiling in a large saucepan.
2. Stir in butter or margarine until melted; add ready-mix bread stuffing, sliced apples, peanuts and raisins, tossing lightly to mix.

GINGER-HONEY GLAZE: Makes about ¾ cup. Combine ½ cup soy sauce, ⅓ cup honey and 2 teaspoons ground ginger in a small saucepan. Heat, stirring constantly, to boiling.

POULTRY POINTERS

To broil chicken successfully:
- Preheat broiler for 10 minutes, or follow manufacturer's directions. (Note: If you have an electric broiler, be sure to keep the oven open a crack while broiling, or the broiler element will go off and the chicken will cook, but not broil.)
- Season chicken with salt and pepper, your favorite herbs and melted butter, margarine, vegetable oil or bottled salad dressing.
- Place chicken on rack of broiler pan and broil, 4 to 7 inches from heat, turning and basting with fat frequently, until chicken is tender, about 40 minutes. You may also wish to brush chicken with a glaze (such as GINGER-HONEY GLAZE above) during last 20 minutes.

TARRAGON CHICKEN CHAMPIGNONS

A French dish of herb-flavored chicken and fresh mushrooms.

Makes 4 servings.

- 1 broiler-fryer, cut up (3 pounds)
- 1 teaspoon seasoned salt
- ½ teaspoon freshly ground pepper
  Dash paprika
- ¼ cup peanut oil
- 1 medium-size onion, thinly sliced
- ½ pound mushrooms, sliced
- 1 teaspoon leaf tarragon, crumbled

1. Sprinkle chicken pieces with blended salt, pepper, and paprika.
2. Cook chicken slowly to a deep golden brown in oil, 15 minutes, turning to brown all sides in a large skillet; remove and keep hot.
3. Sauté onion and mushrooms until tender but not brown.
4. Return chicken to skillet, sprinkle with tarragon and cover chicken with the vegetables. Cover skillet and continue cooking, slowly, until pieces are fork-tender, about 20 minutes.

SKILLET JAMBALAYA

This version of a Southern specialty goes from skillet to table in about 40 minutes.

Makes 6 servings.

- 8 frankfurters, sliced ¼-inch thick
- 1½ cups uncooked rice
- 2 tablespoons butter or margarine
- 2 cans (1 pound each) stewed tomatoes
- 1½ cups water
- 1½ teaspoons garlic salt
- 2 cups diced cooked chicken
  OR: 2 cans (5 ounces each) boned chicken, diced
- ¼ cup diced green pepper

1. Sauté frankfurters and rice in butter or margarine in a large skillet, stirring often, until rice is golden.
2. Stir in tomatoes, water and the garlic salt; place chicken on top; cover skillet.
3. Simmer, stirring once, 30 minutes, or until rice is tender and liquid is absorbed.
4. Spoon into a serving bowl; sprinkle with green pepper.

BASIL FRIED CHICKEN

A crispy, crackly fried chicken to please all the perfectionists in the family.

Makes 4 servings.

- 1 broiler-fryer, cut up (about 2½ pounds)
- 2 eggs
- ¾ cup all-purpose flour
- 1½ teaspoons salt
- 1 teaspoon leaf basil, crumbled
- ½ teaspoon pepper
  Shortening or vegetable oil for frying

1. Dip chicken pieces in beaten eggs in a shallow dish. Shake in a mixture of flour, salt, basil and pepper in a plastic bag.
2. Dip again in egg and shake in flour mixture to form a thick coating. Place chicken pieces on wire rack for 5 minutes to allow coating to set.
3. Melt shortening or pour oil into a large heavy skillet to a 1-inch depth. Place over medium heat. Heat to 375° on a deep fat thermometer or until a cube of bread turns golden in 60 seconds.
4. Add the chicken pieces, skin-side down. Cook slowly, turning once, 20 minutes, or until chicken is golden.
5. Reduce heat; cover skillet. Cook 20 minutes longer, or until chicken is tender. Remove cover for last 5 minutes for a crunchy crust. Drain on paper towels before serving.

SCRAMBLED EGGS AND LIVERS

A perfect dish to whip up for brunch, light supper or midnight snack.

Makes 4 servings.

6 eggs
6 tablespoons milk
¾ teaspoon salt
Dash pepper
½ pound chicken livers
OR: 1 package (8 ounces) frozen chicken livers, thawed
Salt and pepper
2 tablespoons butter or margarine

1. Combine eggs, milk, salt and pepper in medium-size bowl; beat until foamy; reserve.
2. Cut chicken livers into small pieces; sprinkle with salt and pepper.
3. Melt butter or margarine in medium-size skillet; fry livers over medium heat, stirring several times, 3 to 4 minutes, or until lightly browned.
4. Add milk-egg mixture; cook over low heat, stirring several times, 3 to 4 minutes, or until eggs are set.

DEEP-DISH CHICKEN PIE

Not for dieters but guaranteed to fill up a famished family.

Bake at 425° for 30 minutes.
Makes 6 servings.

6 medium-size potatoes, pared and quartered
6 medium-size carrots, pared and quartered
1 small onion, chopped (¼ cup)
¼ cup chopped green pepper
2 tablespoons butter or margarine
1 can condensed cream of chicken soup
3 cups diced cooked chicken or turkey
Biscuit Wedge Topping (recipe follows)

1. Cook potatoes and carrots in boiling salted water in large saucepan 15 to 20 minutes, or until tender; drain, saving 1 cup of liquid.
2. While vegetables cook, sauté onion and green pepper in butter or margarine until soft in a large saucepan; stir in chicken soup and saved 1 cup liquid.
3. Spoon vegetables and chicken into an 8-cup casserole; pour sauce over.
4. Bake in hot oven (425°) 15 minutes while making BISCUIT WEDGE TOPPING; arrange biscuits on top of hot mixture. Bake 15 minutes longer, or until biscuits are golden. Serve one biscuit wedge for each.

BISCUIT WEDGE TOPPING: Makes 6 wedges. Sift 1½ cups all-purpose flour, 2 teaspoons baking powder and ½ teaspoon salt into medium-size bowl; cut in ¼ cup (½ stick) butter or margarine; add ½ cup milk all at once; stir just until blended. Turn dough out onto lightly floured pastry cloth or board; knead lightly ½ minute; roll out to the size of casserole; cut into 6 wedges; brush tops lightly with milk; sprinkle with ¼ teaspoon poppy seeds.

POULTRY POINTERS

• New Chicken Products: Besides the more familiar chicken types, new products are finding their way into supermarkets—chicken frankfurters, chicken bologna, chicken sticks, smoked chicken, chicken loaf, chicken nuggets, party packs off wings, chicken and chips (a chicken and potato combination) and frozen pouchpack chicken fricassee.

• To freeze fresh chicken, remove the store wrapping, discard the backing board or tray and rinse the chicken in cold water. Pat dry with paper towels, then wrap in plastic wrap, heavy-duty foil or freezer paper and place in your freezer. Label each package, noting which parts are included, and how many; date. It will keep up to 6 months.

BISCUITS AND CHICKEN CASSEROLE

Built-in cream sauce makes this easy-do casserole a dinner winner.

Bake at 375° for 15 minutes.
Makes 4 servings.

2 packages (10 ounces each) frozen corn, carrots and pearl onions with cream sauce
2 cans (5 ounces each) boned chicken
¼ cup chopped parsley
1 package refrigerated butterflake dinner rolls
Sesame seeds

1. Cook vegetables in a large saucepan, following label directions. Dice chicken and add to saucepan with chopped parsley. Stir; pour into a 6-cup shallow casserole.
2. Separate rolls to make 24 even pieces. Arrange, buttery-side up, on top of hot mixture; sprinkle with sesame seeds.
3. Bake in moderate oven (375°) 15 minutes, or until biscuits are golden.

ZESTY LEMON CHICKEN BREASTS

Chicken wings or a cut up chicken can be substituted for the chicken breasts.

2 whole chicken breasts, split (12 ounces each)
¼ cup (½ stick) butter or margarine
1 large lemon
1 cup sliced mushrooms
OR: 1 can (4 ounces) sliced mushrooms, drained
1 tablespoon chopped green onion
2 tablespoons dry sherry

1. Brown chicken breasts in butter or margarine in a large skillet until golden brown; lower heat; cook 20 minutes, or until tender; remove to serving platter and keep warm.
2. Cut lemon in half; juice one half and cut the second half into slices.
3. Sauté mushrooms in pan drippings with green onion until soft; stir in sherry and cook, stirring up all the cooked-on juices, until bubbly; add lemon juice and lemon slices; simmer 2 minutes; pour over chicken breasts and serve with a bottle of chilled dry white wine.

UGANDA PEANUT BUTTER CHICKEN

Africans often use peanuts in cooking. We can get the same results with peanut butter.

Makes 6 servings.

2 broiler-fryers, cut up (about 2 pounds each)
¼ cup vegetable oil
2 teaspoons salt
1 teaspoon curry powder
1 large onion, peeled and sliced
1 large sweet red pepper, halved, seeded, and cut in strips
1 large tomato, sliced thin
1½ cups uncooked rice
¼ cup crunchy peanut butter
¼ cup warm water

1. Brown chicken pieces, part at a time, in vegetable oil in a Dutch oven or large skillet; remove and reserve.
2. Stir salt and curry powder into drippings in Dutch oven; cook 1 minute. Stir in onion, red pepper, and tomato; cover. Simmer 5 minutes.
3. Return chicken to Dutch oven; cover again. Simmer 30 minutes, or until chicken is tender.
4. While chicken cooks, cook rice, following label directions; spoon onto a large deep serving platter. Arrange chicken on top; keep warm.
5. Blend peanut butter with warm water in a cup; stir into vegetable mixture in Dutch oven; bring to boiling. Spoon over chicken and rice.

PASTA TAORMINA

Here's a chicken-liver-and-chopped-onion spaghetti sauce that's as delicious as it is different.

Makes 4 servings.

½ pound chicken livers, halved
3 tablespoons olive oil or vegetable oil
1 large onion, chopped (1 cup)
1 envelope (1½ ounces) spaghetti-sauce mix
1 can (1 pound) stewed tomatoes
¼ cup water
Hot cooked pasta

1. Sauté chicken livers slowly in the oil in a medium-size saucepan just until they lose their pink color; remove and reserve.
2. Sauté onion until soft in drippings in same pan; stir in the sauce mix, tomatoes and water; simmer for 15 minutes. Add chicken livers; heat until hot. Spoon over hot cooked pasta.

BASIC BROILED CHICKEN

Note the quick flavor variations on this easy supper.

Makes 4 servings.

2 broiler-fryers, halved or quartered (about 2 pounds each)
Salt and pepper
¼ cup (½ stick) butter or margarine
OR: ¼ cup olive oil or vegetable oil

1. Sprinkle chickens with salt and pepper and brush with the melted butter or margarine or oil.
2. Place chickens, skin-side down, on rack of broiler pan.
3. Broil, 4 inches from the heat, 20 minutes, brushing occasionally with melted butter or margarine.
4. Turn chickens, brush with butter, and broil 15 to 20 minutes longer or until nicely browned.
COOK'S TIP: If chickens brown too quickly, reduce heat or move farther away from broiler unit.
SUGGESTED VARIATIONS: Try these easy versions to liven flavor in broiled chicken.
GARLIC-BROILED CHICKEN:
Warm ½ crushed clove garlic with ¼ cup melted butter or margarine 3 to 5 minutes to mellow flavors; broil chickens as directed, brushing with the garlic butter.
LEMON-BROILED CHICKEN:
Mix the juice of ½ lemon with ¼ cup melted butter or margarine; broil chickens as directed, brushing with the lemon butter.
ORANGE-BROILED CHICKEN:

Warm 2 tablespoons of orange marmalade with remaining melted butter or margarine 5 minutes; broil chickens as directed, brushing with the orange butter for the last 15 minutes of broiling.
CHILI-BROILED CHICKEN:
Warm 1 teaspoon chili powder, ½ crushed clove garlic and ⅛ teaspoon cayenne pepper with ¼ cup melted butter or margarine 3 to 5 minutes, until no raw chili powder taste remains; broil chickens as directed, brushing with the chili mixture.
CURRY-BROILED CHICKEN:
Warm 1 to 2 tablespoons of curry powder, ¼ crushed clove garlic and 1 tablespoon finely minced chutney with ¼ cup melted butter or margarine 3 to 5 minutes, until no raw curry taste remains; broil chickens as directed, brushing with the mixture.

SKILLET HUNGARIAN CHICKEN

Paprika and sour cream give an old world flavor to this time-saving chicken dish.

Makes 8 servings.

2 broiler-fryers, cut up (about 3 pounds each)
2 tablespoons butter or margarine
1 cup frozen chopped onion
2 tablespoons paprika
1 tablespoon all-purpose flour
2 teaspoons salt
¼ teaspoon pepper
1 can (8 ounces) tomatoes
1 package (1 pound) noodles
1 container (8 ounces) dairy sour cream

1. Brown chicken pieces in butter or margarine in a large skillet; remove and reserve.
2. Sauté onion in pan drippings until soft. Stir in paprika and flour; cook, stirring constantly, 1 minute. Stir in salt, pepper and tomatoes (breaking up with spoon).
3. Add chicken and giblets (except livers), turning to coat pieces well; cover skillet. Simmer 20 minutes. Turn chicken pieces add livers; simmer 15 minutes longer, or until chicken is tender.
4. Meanwhile, cook noodles, following label directions; drain; spoon onto hot serving platter. Remove chicken from skillet with slotted spoon. Arrange on platter with noodles; keep warm while finishing sauce.
5. Spoon sour cream into a medium-size bowl. Bring sauce in skillet to boiling; stir slowly into sour cream, blending well. Spoon over chicken and noodles before serving.

ROMAN FORUM CHICKEN

Flavorful red pimiento, black olives, mushrooms and white wine blend in this tempting Roman chicken-spaghetti dish.

Makes 8 servings.

2 broiler-fryers, cut up (2½ to 3 pounds each)
1 cup all-purpose flour
2 teaspoons salt
¼ teaspoon pepper
¼ cup olive oil
1 clove garlic, crushed
¼ cup chopped parsley
½ teaspoon poultry seasoning
Dash bottled red-pepper seasoning
1 cup dry white wine
¾ cup pitted black olives, sliced
1 can (6 ounces) sliced mushrooms
1 can (4 ounces) pimiento, drained and cut into large pieces
Parsley-Buttered Spaghetti (recipe follows)

1. Roll chicken pieces in flour, salt and pepper on wax paper; then brown in hot oil in a large heavy skillet.
2. Mix garlic, parsley, poultry seasoning, red-pepper seasoning and wine; pour over browned chicken; simmer a few minutes.
3. Scatter olives, mushrooms, and pimiento pieces over chicken. Cover skillet and cook over moderately low heat about 30 minutes, or until chicken pieces are fork-tender.
4. Serve hot with PARSLEY-BUTTERED SPAGHETTI and pass a bowl of grated Parmesan cheese.

PARSLEY-BUTTERED SPAGHETTI: Cook 1 package (1 pound) thin spaghetti according to package directions. Drain and toss with ¼ cup melted butter or margarine (½ stick) and with 1 cup chopped parsley.

CHICKEN SLICES WITH SUPREME SAUCE

Tasty sauce goes over slices of cooked chicken in two layers; then you can pop the whole thing under the broiler to puff and brown.

Makes 4 servings.

8 to 10 slices cooked chicken or turkey
Supreme Sauce (recipe, page 91)

1. Arrange chicken slices on a flame-proof glass-ceramic platter.
2. Spoon SUPREME SAUCE over.
3. Broil, about 4 inches from flame, for 3 to 5 minutes, or until sauce puffs and browns. Serve with a cucumber and watercress salad, if you wish.

GRAPE AND CHICKEN OMELET

Dinner in minutes can be delicious with eggs and a bit of cooked chicken on hand.

Makes 4 servings.

Filling
- 1 can condensed cream of celery soup
- 2 cups chopped cooked chicken
- ½ cup halved, seedless green grapes

Omelet
- 8 eggs
- ¼ cup water
- 1 teaspoon salt
- Dash pepper
- 2 tablespoons butter or margarine

1. Combine soup, chicken and grapes in a small saucepan. Heat and keep warm while preparing omelet.
2. Mix eggs, water, salt and pepper with fork in a large bowl. Heat 1 tablespoon of the butter or margarine in a large omelet pan or skillet until just hot enough to sizzle a drop of water. Pour in half of the omelet mixture. (Mixture should set at edges at once.)
3. With pancake turner, carefully draw cooked portions at edges toward center, so that uncooked portions flow to bottom. Tilt skillet as it is necessary to hasten flow of uncooked eggs. Slide pan rapidly back and forth over heat to keep mixture in motion and sliding freely.
4. When top is still moist and creamy-looking, spread ½ cup filling on half of omelet. With pancake turner, fold in half or roll, turning out onto heated platter with a quick flip of the wrist. Top with ½ cup filling. Keep warm or serve while preparing second omelet with remaining omelet mixture and filling. Serve with prepared refrigerated crescent rolls.

CORN CRISPED DRUMSTICKS

They look like fried chicken, but these drumsticks are actually baked with no messy clean-up.

Bake at 350° for 1 hour.
Makes 8 servings.

- 2 cups packaged corn flake crumbs
- 2 teaspoon monosodium glutamate
- 2 teaspoons salt
- ¼ teaspoon pepper
- 16 drumsticks (about 4 pounds)
- 1 small can evaporated milk

1. Combine corn flake crumbs with monosodium glutamate, salt and pepper in shallow dish.
2. Line a shallow baking sheet or pan with aluminum foil.
3. Dip drumsticks in evaporated milk, then roll immediately in seasoned corn flake crumbs. Place the drumsticks in foil-lined pan; do not crowd together.
4. Bake in moderate over (350°) 1 hour, or until tender. At the end of ½ hour, exchange side of pan on the shelf; continue to bake. No need to cover or turn chicken while cooking. Serve with DEVILED DUNKING SAUCE.

DEVILED DUNKING SAUCE: Makes 1⅔ cups. Combine ⅓ cup prepared mustard, ⅓ cup pickle relish, 1 can (8 ounces) tomato sauce, 1 tablespoon horseradish, 1 tablespoon of Worcestershire sauce and ⅛ teaspoon cayenne pepper; mix thoroughly.

HALVED CHICKEN ITALIANO

Chicken halves are simmered in an herbed tomato sauce and served over hot spaghetti.

Makes 4 servings.

- 2 broiler-fryers, split (2½ pounds each)
- 1 tablespoon vegetable oil
- 1 green pepper, halved and seeded
- 1 large onion, chopped (1 cup)
- 1 clove garlic, crushed
- 1 can (8 ounces) tomato sauce
- ½ cup dry red wine
- 1 teaspoon mixed Italian herbs, crumbled
- Dash ground cloves
- 1 package (½ pound) spaghetti
- 2 tablespoons butter or margarine
- 1 tomato, cut into wedges
- 3 tablespoons chopped parsley
- ½ teaspoon salt

1. Brown chicken in oil in large skillet. Remove halves as they brown; keep warm.
2. Chop ½ the green pepper; cut other half into strips; reserve strips. Sauté the chopped pepper, onion and garlic until soft in same skillet. Stir in tomato sauce, wine, Italian herbs and cloves. Bring to boiling. Return chicken to skillet; lower heat; cover; simmer 40 minutes, or until chicken is tender.
3. Cook spaghetti, following label directions; drain. Place on large heated platter.
4. While spaghetti is cooking, sauté pepper strips in butter or margarine in small skillet; add tomato wedges, parsley and salt; cook 2 minutes longer, or just until tomato is soft. Arrange chicken halves on hot spaghetti. Spoon sauce over. Garnish with sautéed pepper-tomato mixture on top of the sauce.

HERBED CHICKEN LIVERS

Sautéed with a delightful blend of herbs, these livers take only minutes to prepare.

Makes 4 servings.

- 1 pound chicken livers, cut in half
- 1 teaspoon salt
- ⅛ teaspoon pepper
- 1 tablespoon minced onion
- 1 tablespoon minced parsley
- ½ teaspoon leaf tarragon, crumbled
- Flour
- 2 tablespoons butter or margarine

1. Sprinkle livers with salt, pepper, onion, parsley and tarragon. Dust lightly with flour.
2. Melt butter or margarine in a large skillet over medium heat; add livers and cook about 5 minutes, turning occasionally. Serve on toast points with buttered peas with pine nuts, if you wish. Butterscotch sundaes would make a quick dessert.

ORIENTAL OMELET

The perfect choice when dinner's for two.

Makes 2 servings.

Filling
- 1 cup chopped cooked chicken
- ¼ cup drained bean sprouts
- 3 water chestnuts, thinly sliced
- 1 tablespoon soy sauce

Omelet
- 4 eggs
- ¼ cup water
- 2 tablespoons chopped green pepper
- ½ teaspoon salt
- Dash pepper
- 1 tablespoon butter or margarine

1. Combine chicken, bean sprouts, water chestnuts and soy sauce in a small bowl. Set aside.
2. Mix eggs, water, green pepper, salt and pepper with a two-tined fork in a small bowl.
3. Heat butter or margarine in a large skillet or omelet pan until just hot enough to sizzle a drop of water. Pour in egg mixture. (Mixture should set at edges at once.)
4. With pancake turner, carefully draw cooked portions at edges toward center, so that uncooked portions flow to bottom. Tilt skillet as it is necessary to hasten flow of uncooked eggs. Slide pan rapidly back and forth over heat to keep mixture in motion and sliding freely.
5. When top is still moist and creamy-looking, arrange filling on half of omelet. With pancake turner, fold in half or roll, turning out onto heated platter with a quick flip of the wrist.

QUICK CACCIATORE

An easy way to make this Italian favorite.

Makes 4 servings.

1 medium size onion, chopped
   (½ cup)
3 tablespoons vegetable oil
1 broiler-fryer, cut up (about 3
   pounds)
½ teaspoon salt
⅛ teaspoon pepper
1 clove garlic, minced
1 can (1 pound) tomatoes
1 tablespoon vinegar
½ teaspoon leaf rosemary, crumbled
½ teaspoon sugar

1. Sauté onion in 1 tablespoon oil in large skillet about 5 minutes; remove and reserve.
2. Sprinkle chicken with salt and pepper; brown in same pan with remaining 2 tablespoons oil and garlic.
3. Return onion to pan; add remaining ingredients; cover tightly. Simmer 30 minutes, or until chicken is tender.

CANADIAN CHICKEN WITH CREAM SAUCE

Broiled chicken breasts are served in Canadian bacon and blanketed with sauce.

Makes 6 servings.

6 chicken cutlets
¼ cup (½ stick) butter or margarine, melted
1 can (about 11 ounces) chicken gravy
¼ cup light cream
1 teaspoon lemon juice
2 or 3 drops bottled red-pepper seasoning
12 slices Canadian-style bacon (about ½ pound)

1. Place chicken cutlets, rounded side down, on greased broiler rack; brush with half the melted butter or margarine; broil about 10 minutes; turn; brush again with remaining butter or margarine; broil 10 to 12 minutes longer, or until golden-brown and tender when pierced with a fork.
2. While chicken cooks, combine chicken gravy, cream, lemon juice and red-pepper seasoning in a small saucepan; heat, stirring often, just to boiling.
3. Arrange bacon slices in single layer in shallow pan; 2 to 3 minutes before chicken is done, slide pan into hot oven (hot from broiling) to cook bacon and crisp any fat edges.
4. Put 2 slices bacon on each dinner plate; top with half a chicken breast; spoon about ¼ cup heated sauce over.

VERACRUZ CHICKEN

Serve this dish to guests with adventurous palates. The sauce is a hot one, heady with spices and tart with orange.

Makes 6 servings.

1 tablespoon peanut oil or vegetable oil
3 whole chicken breasts, split (about 12 ounces each)
3 tablespoons butter or margarine
½ teaspoon salt
   Pepper
⅓ cup brandy
2 cloves garlic, thinly sliced
1 can (4 ounces) green chili peppers, seeded and chopped
   Few drops bottled red-pepper seasoning
1 can (6 ounces) frozen concentrate for orange juice
½ cup pine nuts (optional)

1. Heat butter or margarine and the oil in a skillet and sauté chicken breasts until golden. Season with salt and a few dashes of pepper, pour brandy over and carefully set aflame.
2. When flames have died down, add garlic, chili peppers and red-pepper seasoning. Blend in orange juice concentrate simmer 20 to 25 minutes, turning chicken breasts several times.
3. When chicken breasts are tender, remove to a hot platter and pour sauce over. Sprinkle with pine nuts. Garnish with red pepper and orange slices, if you wish. Serve with a pitcher of chilled Sangria.

POULTRY POINTERS

Refrigerated biscuits make the perfect quick topper for casseroles. Brush with softened butter or margarine and sprinkle with sesame seeds, poppy seeds, mixed Italian herbs or grated Parmesan cheese. Place on bubbling-hot casserole and bake in hot oven (425°) 10 minutes, or until golden brown.

Storing Frozen Birds:
• Hard-frozen poultry may go right from your shopping cart into your freezer without rewrapping.
• Do not allow it to thaw at all.
• If it has thawed in the store or in getting it home, cook it promptly and then freeze it, if you wish.
• Never refreeze thawed, uncooked chicken.
• If you are making a stew, chicken can go right into the pot from the freezer.
• If you're using it for fried, broiled barbecued or roasted dishes, thaw it first. It will cook more evenly.

PEANUT COATED CHICKEN

Try this chicken with a difference.

Bake at 375° for 40 minutes.
Makes 4 servings.

1 broiler fryer, cut up (about 3 pounds
1 teaspoon salt
¼ teaspoon pepper
¾ cup all-purpose flour
1 egg, beaten
1 cup orange marmalade
1 teaspoon dry mustard
2 cloves garlic, crushed
1½ cups peanuts, finely chopped

1. Season chicken with salt and pepper. Toss in flour in a plastic bag.
2. Combine egg, marmalade, mustard and garlic in a pie plate. Dip chicken in egg mixture to coat, then roll in chopped peanuts on wax paper. Place in single layer in shallow baking pan.
3. Bake in moderate oven (375°) 40 minutes, or until golden.

CHICKEN BAKED WITH BARBECUE SAUCE

Whip the sauce together in no time, spoon it over chicken, pop the dish in the oven, and forget it while it cooks to savory tenderness.

Bake at 375° about 1 hour.
Makes 6 servings.

2 broiler-fryers, cut up (about 2½ pounds each)
   Butter or margarine
   Barbecue Sauce (recipe follows)

1. Arrange chicken pieces in a single layer in a well-buttered large shallow baking pan.
2. Spoon BARBECUE SAUCE over chicken so pieces are well coated. (If you have any leftover sauce, it will keep in a covered jar in the refrigerator.)
3. Bake in a moderate oven (375°) about 1 hour, or until chicken is fork-tender.

BARBECUE SAUCE

Makes 2½ cups.
2 cans (8 ounces each) tomato sauce
1 medium-size onion, chopped
   (½ cup)
1 clove garlic, minced
¼ cup soy sauce
2 tablespoons sugar
1 teaspoon dry mustard
⅛ teaspoon cayenne pepper

Combine tomato sauce, onion, garlic, soy sauce, sugar, dry mustard and cayenne pepper in a bowl.

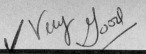 *Very Good*

SOY BAKED CHICKEN

Chicken quarters absorb piquant flavors from the soy-sherry sauce which glazes the chicken as it bakes.

Bake at 375° for 50 minutes.
Makes 4 servings.

¼ cup water
¼ cup soy sauce
¼ cup dry sherry
¼ cup corn syrup
2 teaspoons seasoned salt
1 broiler-fryer, cut up (about 3 pounds)

1. Combine water, soy sauce, sherry, corn syrup and seasoned salt in a small bowl.
2. Arrange chicken, skin-side down, in a shallow baking pan. Brush generously with part of the sauce.
3. Bake in moderate oven (375°) 20 minutes; turn; baste with remaining sauce; bake 30 minutes longer, or until chicken is tender and golden.

SHREDDED CHICKEN AND VEGETABLES

A little meat goes a long way in this vegetable-chicken combo.

Makes 4 servings.

1 whole chicken breast (14 ounces), split, skinned and boned
2 tablespoons vegetable oil
1 clove garlic, minced
3 carrots, pared and thinly sliced
2 small zucchini, sliced
1 cup sliced green beans
6 water chestnuts
2 teaspoons salt
⅛ teaspoon pepper
3 tablespoons soy sauce
1 cup water
1 tablespoon cornstarch
1 tablespoon dry sherry
4 cups hot cooked rice (1 cup raw)
2 tablespoons toasted sliced almonds

1. Cut chicken into thin shreds. Heat oil in a wok or large skillet. Add chicken; quickly stir-fry until the color turns from pink to white.
2. Add garlic, carrots, zucchini, beans, water chestnuts, salt, pepper, soy sauce and ¾ cup of the water. Cover; reduce heat; simmer until vegetables are crisply tender, about 5 minutes (do not overcook).
3. Combine cornstarch, sherry and remaining ¼ cup of the water in a cup. Add to skillet; cook and stir gently just until sauce is thickened and bubbly. Spoon hot rice onto serving platter; spoon mixture over; sprinkle with toasted almonds.

CHICKEN IN ORANGE SAUCE

This luscious dish can be made the day before.

Makes 4 servings.

1 broiler-fryer, cut up (about 3 pounds)
½ cup (1 stick) butter or margarine
¼ cup all-purpose flour
2 tablespoons brown sugar
1 teaspoon salt
½ teaspoon ground ginger
1 teaspoon pepper
1½ cups orange juice
½ cup water
2 California oranges, pared and sectioned

1. Brown chicken slowly in butter or margarine in a large glass-ceramic casserole; remove and reserve.
2. Blend flour, brown sugar, salt, ginger and pepper into drippings in casserole; cook, stirring constantly, just until mixture bubbles. Stir in orange juice and water slowly; continue cooking and stirring until sauce thickens; boil 1 minute; remove casserole from heat.
3. Return chicken to casserole; cool. Cover and refrigerate.
4. About 45 minutes before serving time, reheat chicken and sauce just to boiling, then simmer, covered, 30 minutes. Lay orange sections around chicken; continue cooking 15 minutes longer, or until chicken is tender. Serve with fluffy hot rice.

POULTRY POINTERS

Time-Saving Tips:
• Turkey time? Try one of the new prestuffed and self-basting turkeys. Roasting the big family-size bird was never easier!
• For carefree mealtimes when serving turkey and goose, follow the roasting times in recipe and add 1 hour. Subtract this total from the time you plan to serve the bird and start to roast then. Should the bird need an extra 30 minutes to finish roasting, your dinner time won't be delayed, yet an extra 30 minutes of resting time won't affect the bird and bubbly-hot gravy will ensure a hot entrée.
• For stuffing in minutes to serve with any poultry dish, look at the assortment of packaged stuffing mixes on the supermarket shelf. For a distinctive touch, stir in 1 tablespoon orange rind, 1 teaspoon lemon rind, ¼ cup chopped parsley, ¼ cup finely chopped walnuts, almonds or peanuts or 2 tablespoons chopped celery leaves.

CHICKEN SCALLOPINE

Garnish with lemon and serve on buttered noodles.

Makes 4 servings.

8 chicken cutlets
1 teaspoon salt
2 tablespoons butter or margarine
1 tablespoon lemon juice
2 tablespoons chopped parsley
1 tablespoon chopped chives
¼ teaspoon leaf marjoram, crumbled

1. Place chicken cutlets between 2 pieces of aluminum foil; pound with side of cleaver or rolling pin to flatten. Sprinkle with salt.
2. Melt butter or margarine over medium heat in a large skillet. Add chicken; cook about 10 minutes, until lightly browned. Turn; sprinkle with lemon juice, parsley, chives and marjoram. Cook about 10 minutes, until chicken is tender.
3. Serve on buttered noodles.

MAKE-AHEAD CHICKEN CASSEROLE

This meal-in-one dish understands a busy household and caters to its cook.

Bake at 350° for 1 hour.
Makes 4 servings.

1 cup creamed cottage cheese
1½ cups dairy sour cream (from a 16-ounce container)
6 tablespoons grated Parmesan cheese
1½ teaspoons salt
¼ teaspoon bottled red-pepper seasoning
¼ cup sliced pitted ripe olives
1 package (8 ounces) spinach or regular medium-size egg noodles, cooked
2½ cups diced cooked chicken

1. Mix cottage cheese, sour cream, 4 tablespoons Parmesan cheese, salt and red-pepper seasoning in a large bowl. Stir in olives, noodles and diced chicken.
2. Turn into a greased 8-cup casserole. Sprinkle with remaining 2 tablespoons Parmesan cheese. Cover and refrigerate.
3. One hour before serving, place in moderate oven (350°). Bake, covered, for 35 minutes.
4. Uncover and bake 25 minutes more. Serve with an antipasto salad.
SUGGESTED VARIATION: Diced cooked turkey can be substituted for the chicken in this recipe.

Chapter 6 continued on page 117.

MEALS IN A HURRY

CHAPTER 7
PRIZE RECIPES FROM AROUND THE WORLD

Every national cuisine has its distinctive way with chicken. The recipes in this chapter represent some of the very best dishes of six continents, from spicy Mexicali Chicken and Arroz con Pollo Criollo to exotic Japanese Tempura and Chicken Kiev.

FRENCH CHICKEN BROIL

A zesty splash of lime and tarragon seasons tender broiled chicken.

Makes 6 servings.

- 3 broiler-fryers, split (about 2 pounds each)
- ½ cup lime juice
- ½ cup vegetable oil
- 1 tablespoon grated onion
- 2 teaspoons leaf tarragon , crumbled
- 1 teaspoon seasoned salt
- ¼ teaspoon seasoned pepper

1. Place split chickens, skin-side down, on rack in broiler pan.
2. Mix lime juice, vegetable oil, onion, tarragon, and seasoned salt and pepper in a small bowl. Brush generously over chickens.
3. Broil 4 inches from heat, turning every 10 minutes and brushing with more lime mixture, 40 minutes, or until the chickens are tender and richly browned. Remove to a heated large serving platter.

ROMEO SALTA'S CHICKEN SCARPARIELLO

"Scarpariello" in Italian means the shoe repair man. This might be a poor man's dish, but when you make it and taste it, you'll see it's fit for a king. (Pictured, page 61.)

Makes 6 to 8 servings.

- 2 broiler-fryers (2 ½ pounds each)
- 2 tablespoons olive oil
- 4 tablespoons butter
- 2 teaspoons salt
- ½ teaspoon freshly ground black pepper
- 1 clove garlic, minced
- 2 tablespoons chopped chives or green onions
- ¾ cup diced mushrooms
- 1 ½ cups dry white wine
- ½ cup chicken broth
- ½ pound chicken livers, cut in half
- 2 tablespoons minced parsley

1. To prepare recipe as Romeo Salta does: Have the chickens chopped up, bones and all, into small bite-size pieces, or use cut up chickens.

2. Heat the oil and 2 tablespoons butter in a large skillet; sauté the chicken in it until browned. Sprinkle with salt and pepper. Mix in the garlic and chives or green onions, then add the mushrooms, wine and broth.
3. Bring to boiling and cook over medium heat 30 minutes, or until chicken is tender.
4. Melt the remaining butter in a separate skillet; sauté the livers in it 5 minutes, or until very little pink remains. Season with a little salt and pepper. Add to the chicken; cook 5 minutes longer; top with parsley before serving.

Restaurateur Romeo Salta's Chicken Scarpariello (foreground) is a grand mingling of chicken, wine, herbs and mushrooms. Recipe is on this page. For the classic Italian side dishes, turn to page 94.

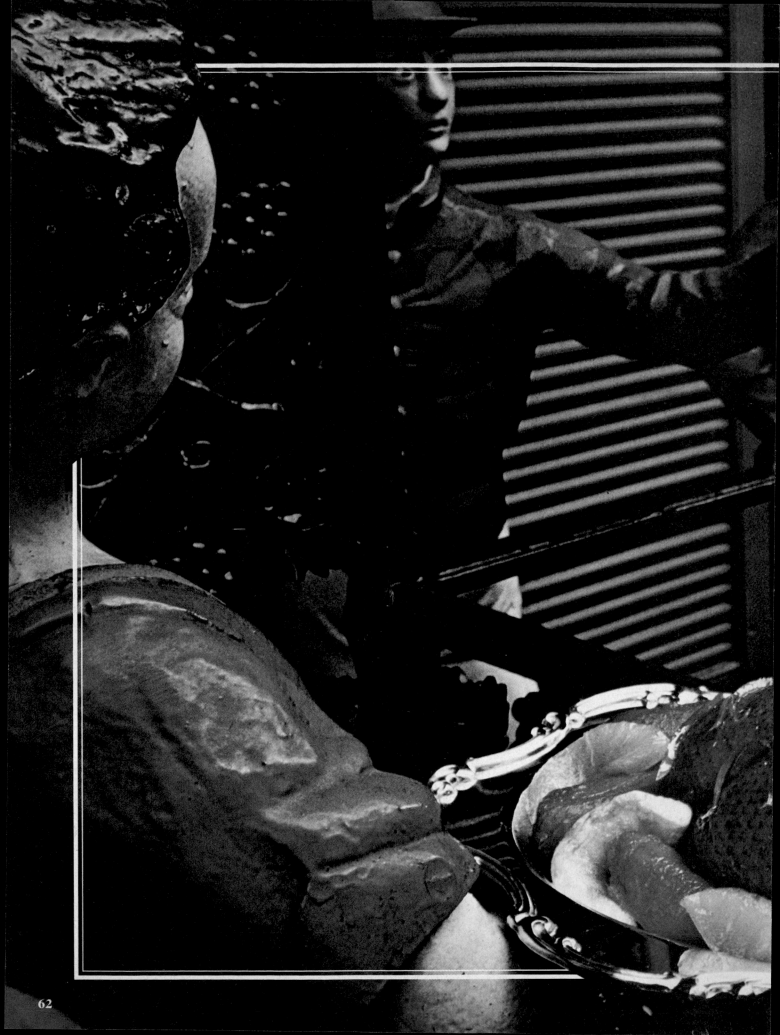

From New
York's "21"
restaurant
comes orange-
glazed Long
Island Duck
Bigarade. Recipe,
page 65.

Italian Parsley

Rosemary

Sage

Savory

Tarragon

Parsley

Oregano

Mint

Marjoram

Chives

Chervil

Celery

Capers

Bay Leaf

Thyme

Basil

Garlic

Turkey

Giblet broth is the most flavorful liquid for the gravy. Add 1 tablespoon chopped fresh herb or 1 teaspoon dried leaf herb to broth.

Goose

Bake a casserole of savory stuffing along with the bird, adding 2 tablespoons chopped fresh herb or 1½ teaspoons dried leaf herb.

Duckling

Baste with a blend of dry red wine and 2 tablespoons chopped fresh or 1½ teaspoons dried leaf herb for a moist, flavorful bird.

Rock Cornish Hen

Oven braised hens are especially moist and tender. Use 1 teaspoon chopped fresh herb or ¼ teaspoon dried leaf herb for each hen.

Capon

Serve this elegant bird with a cream sauce seasoned with 1 teaspoon chopped fresh herb or ½ teaspoon dried leaf herb.

Chicken

Try 1 tablespoon chopped fresh herb or 1 teaspoon dried leaf herb in your favorite baste for a broiler-fryer or roaster.

DIETER'S CHICKEN EN ASPIC

A masterpiece, and fun to make: Chilled chicken breasts in a gelatin glaze decorated with vegetable flowers.

Makes 6 servings at 196 calories each.

- 3 chicken breasts, split (about 12 ounces each)
- 2 envelopes or teaspoons instant chicken broth
- 1½ cups water
- 1 tablespoon leaf tarragon
- 1 tablespoon instant minced onion
  Few sprigs parsley
- 1 envelope unflavored gelatin
- 6 carrot slices
- 2 green onion tops, cut in strips
  Fresh spinach leaves

1. Combine chicken breasts, instant chicken broth and water in a large saucepan. Tie tarragon, onion and parsley in a cheesecloth; add to saucepan; cover. Simmer 30 minutes, or until chicken is tender. Remove from broth and cool until easy to handle; pull off skin; chill. Chill broth until fat rises to top, then skim off.
2. Soften gelatin in ½ cup of the broth in a small saucepan; heat, stirring constantly, until gelatin dissolves; remove from heat. Stir in remaining broth.
3. Place chicken breasts in a single layer on a wire rack set in a shallow baking pan.
4. Measure ½ cup of the gelatin mixture; set cup in a small bowl of ice and water; chill just until as thick as unbeaten egg white. Brush over chicken breasts to coat. (Keep remaining gelatin at room temperature.)
5. Arrange a flower in gelatin on each chicken breast, using a carrot slice for blossom and a long strip of green onion top for stem and short pieces for leaves. Chill until firm.
6. Measure out another ½ cup of the gelatin mixture and chill until thickened; brush over decorations on chicken; chill until firm. Chill remaining gelatin mixture; spoon over chicken a third time to make a thick coating, then chill several hours.
7. When ready to serve, arrange chicken on a spinach-lined large platter. Garnish with cherry tomatoes.

Exotic Tandoori Chicken is steeped in a spiced lemon-yogurt marinade, then roasted. Just 230 calories per serving. Recipe is on this page.

POULTRY POINTERS

Calorie-Saving Tips:
- Choose lean birds (chicken, turkey, game hen) instead of the fattier ones (duckling, goose).
- Pick young birds (broiler-fryers, for example) over the older; they have less fat and fewer calories.
- Choose light meat instead of dark (chicken breasts are particularly slimming).
- For ease in carving poultry, always allow the bird to rest about 20 minutes so that the juices will be absorbed. Place bird on a heated platter and cover with a "tent" of aluminum foil to keep it warm while making gravy, if you wish.

TANDOORI CHICKEN

In India a chicken is marinated in yogurt and exotic herbs before roasting, delicious as well as low in calories. (Photograph on page 76.)

Roast at 350° for 1 hour, 30 minutes. Makes 6 servings at 230 calories each.

- 1 roasting chicken (about 3½ pounds)
- 1 teaspoon saffron (optional)
- 1 tablespoon hot water
- 1 container (8 ounces) plain yogurt
- ¼ cup lime juice or lemon juice
- 2 cloves garlic, crushed
- 1½ teaspoons salt
- 1 teaspoon ground ginger
- ½ teaspoon ground cumin
- ½ teaspoon turmeric
  Dash cayenne pepper
  Watercress
  Lemon wedges

1. Skewer neck of chicken to body; push tail inside bird and secure body cavity closed; tie legs together and draw string up and under wings and knot. Place in a large oval glass casserole.
2. Soak saffron in hot water for 5 minutes in a small bowl; stir in yogurt, lime or lemon juice, garlic, salt, ginger, cumin, turmeric, and cayenne. Spoon over chicken, coating evenly; cover casserole with plastic wrap. Marinate chicken for at least 4 hours, or overnight.
3. Roast in moderate oven (350°) 1 hour, 30 minutes, basting often with yogurt mixture, or until drumstick moves easily at joint; remove string.
4. Arrange on a heated serving platter with watercress and lemon wedges. Serve with a crisp salad of broken greens and sliced fresh mushrooms and cucumbers and a lemon-lime low-calorie drink, if you wish.

ROAST CHICKEN WITH WILD RICE

Tender chickens are stuffed with wild rice and mushrooms, then coated with a low-calorie orange glaze.

Bake at 375° for 1 hour, 15 minutes. Makes 8 servings at 281 calories each.

- 1 can (6 ounces) mushroom stems and pieces
- 1 package (6 ounces) long grain and wild rice mix
- 1 tablespoon instant minced onion
- 1 can (13¾ ounces) chicken broth plus mushroom liquid and water to make 2½ cups
- 2 broiler-fryers (about 2½ pounds each)
- 2 tablespoons thinly slivered orange peel
- ¼ cup orange juice
- ½ cup diet maple syrup
- ¼ teaspoon ground ginger

1. Drain mushrooms, reserving liquid. Combine rice mix and onion in a medium-size saucepan; stir in chicken broth, reserved mushroom liquid and water. Cook, following label directions. Stir in mushrooms.
2. Lightly stuff chickens with rice mixture; secure with poultry skewers.
3. Place chickens, breast sides up, on rack in large shallow baking pan; tuck wings under or tie across backs.
4. Roast in moderate oven (375°) for 1 hour, 5 minutes, or until just tender. Drain excess fat.
5. Combine orange peel, juice, maple syrup and ground ginger in a small bowl. Brush glaze over chickens; roast 10 minutes longer, or until well glazed. Remove cord and skewers.

LOW-CAL CHICKEN TERIYAKI

A delicious calorie-counter's supper, Japanese-style.

Makes 6 servings at 159 calories each.

- 3 whole chicken breasts, split (about 12 ounces each)
- ½ cup lemon juice
- ¼ cup water
- 3 tablespoons soy sauce
- ¼ teaspoon ground ginger
- 1 teaspoon garlic salt

1. Marinate chicken breasts in a sauce made by combining lemon juice, water, soy sauce, ground ginger and garlic salt in a glass or ceramic bowl for at least 3 hours, or overnight; remove breasts and reserve marinade.
2. Barbecue chicken about 30 minutes, or until tender, on the hibachi or under your broiler; baste frequently with marinade.

DIET CHICKEN CACCIATORE

Spaghetti sauce mix in an envelope gives a zesty flavor to baked chicken breasts.

Bake at 350° for 1 hour.
Makes 6 servings at 177 calories each.

- **3 whole chicken breasts, split (about 12 ounces each)**
- **1 Bermuda onion, cut in 6 slices**
- **1 envelope (1½ ounces) spaghetti sauce mix**
- **1 can (1 pound) tomatoes**

1. Brown chicken breasts in a large nonstick skillet; arrange in single layer in an 8-cup shallow casserole. Top each breast with an onion slice.
2. Blend spaghetti sauce mix into drippings in skillet; stir in tomatoes; bring to boiling, stirring constantly. Spoon around chicken breasts and onions; cover casserole.
3. Bake in moderate oven (350°) 1 hour, or until chicken breasts are tender. Serve with Italian green beans, if you wish.

SWEET AND SOUR CHICKEN

The Oriental way to diet—delicious.

Makes 4 servings at 306 calories each.

- **2 whole chicken breasts (about 12 ounces each)**
- **3 tablespoons teriyaki sauce or soy sauce**
- **1 tablespoon vegetable oil**
- **2 medium-size yellow squash, trimmed and sliced**
- **1 package (9 ounces) frozen cut green beans**
- **2 cups water**
- **2 tablespoons lemon juice**
- **1 can (8½ ounces) pineapple chunks in pineapple juice**
- **2 tablespoons cornstarch**
- **1 can (5 ounces) water chestnuts, sliced**
- **Granulated or liquid low-calorie sweetener**

1. Pull skin from chicken breasts; cut meat from bones; cut into thin strips.
2. Marinate chicken with teriyaki sauce or soy sauce in a bowl for 15 minutes.
3. Heat oil in a wok or large skillet; remove chicken from sauce; brown quickly in hot oil. Add yellow squash and green beans. Sauté, stirring gently, 3 minutes, or just until shiny-moist. Add remaining teriyaki sauce or soy sauce, water, lemon juice; cover; steam 5 minutes.
4. While vegetables steam, drain liquid from pineapple into small cup; stir in cornstarch to make a smooth paste.

5. Add pineapple and sliced water chestnuts to skillet; bring just to boiling. Stir in cornstarch mixture; cook, stirring constantly, until mixture thickens and bubbles 1 minute. Stir in your favorite low-calorie sweetener, using the equivalent of 1 tablespoon sugar. Serve with Chinese noodles, if you wish (70 calories per ⅓ cup for noodles).

BARBECUE CHICKEN

Broiled chicken with a flavorful tomato basting sauce.

Makes 4 servings at 259 calories each.

- **1 broiler-fryer, cut up (2½ pounds)**
- **¾ cup tomato juice**
- **1 small onion, grated**
- **2 tablespoons tarragon vinegar**
- **1 tablespoon prepared mustard**
- **1 tablespoon Worcestershire sauce**
- **½ teaspoon salt**
- **¼ teaspoon pepper**

1. Place chicken, skin-side down, in a single layer on rack in broiler pan.
2. Combine tomato juice, onion, vinegar, mustard, Worcestershire sauce, salt and pepper in a small bowl. Brush some over chicken.
3. Broil, 8 inches from heat, basting often with sauce, 20 minutes; turn skin-side up. Continue broiling, basting often with sauce, 20 minutes longer, or until chicken is richly browned and tender when pierced with a fork.
4. Serve with cooked rice, if you wish (92 calories per ½ cup serving).

CORN CRISPED FRIED CHICKEN

Who says you can't have fried chicken on a diet?

Bake at 375° for 1 hour.
Makes 6 servings at 251 calories each.

- **2 broiler-fryers, cut up (about 2 pounds each)**
- **½ cup skim milk**
- **1 cup packaged corn flake crumbs**
- **1½ teaspoons onion salt**
- **¼ teaspoon pepper**
- **1 teaspoon paprika**

1. Wash chicken pieces; pat dry. Pour milk into a shallow dish. Combine the corn flake crumbs, onion salt, pepper and paprika in a plastic bag.
2. Dip chicken pieces in the milk; shake pieces, a few at a time, in crumb mixture in bag to coat well.
3. Arrange chicken, skin-side up, in a single layer on a nonstick pan.
4. Bake in moderate oven (375°) 1 hour, or until tender.

CHICKEN MARENGO, DIET STYLE

Mushrooms and herbs add the gourmet touch without extra calories.

Makes 8 servings at 252 calories each.

- **2 broiler-fryers, cut up (about 2½ pounds each)**
- **1 can condensed tomato soup**
- **½ pound mushrooms**
- **Instant garlic powder**
- **1 teaspoon salt**
- **½ teaspoon leaf thyme, crumbled**
- **1 can (1 pound) small boiled onions**

1. Place chicken pieces, skin-side down, in a nonstick skillet. Brown slowly over moderate heat. (Chicken will brown in its own fat.) Turn; brown other side; drain fat.
2. Add the soup, mushrooms, garlic powder, salt, thyme, and onion liquid.
3. Cover; simmer over low heat for 45 minutes, or until chicken is tender. Add onions. Uncover; continue cooking until sauce thickens, about 10 minutes.

FRENCH CHICKEN IN SHERRY SAUCE

Chicken breasts are a dieter's delight! No need to strip the skin if you follow our fat-reducing technique for oven-browning. Add wine sauce for a quick main course that's quite Continental!

Bake at 375° for 45 minutes.
Makes 6 servings at 217 calories each.

- **3 whole chicken breasts, split (about 10 ounces each)**
- **½ teaspoon salt**
- **1 medium-size onion, sliced**
- **¼ cup chopped green pepper**
- **1 cup sliced mushrooms**
- **Sauce**
- **1 cup orange juice**
- **¼ cup dry sherry**
- **½ cup water**
- **1 tablespoon firmly packed brown sugar**
- **1 teaspoon salt**
- **¼ teaspoon pepper**
- **1 teaspoon grated orange rind**
- **1 tablespoon all-purpose flour**
- **2 teaspoons chopped parsley**
- **Paprika**
- **1 California orange, peeled and sliced**

1. Place chicken breasts, skin-side up, on rack of broiler pan. Broil 2 inches from heat for 10 minutes, or until skin is brown and crackly. Do not turn.
2. Place browned chicken breasts in a shallow 8-cup casserole. Sprinkle with ½ teaspoon salt. Add onion, green pepper and mushrooms.
3. Make sauce. Combine orange juice, sherry, water, brown sugar, 1

78

MAKE THE MOST OF THE BIRD

Cutting and carving guides, supermarket tips & helpful kitchen aids

ALL THE TRIMMINGS

Dress up a chicken or turkey dinner with
some of the stuffings, gravies, glazes and side dishes in this special
section. Or, sample our collection of tempting appetizers
and soups. There are time-saving tips as
well, plus over 100 more recipes.

Appetizers

GOOSE LIVER PÂTÉ

Chefs always know how to make the most out of every part of the bird. This is a grand way to use goose liver.

Makes 8 servings.

    3 tablespoons goose drippings or
        butter or margarine
    1 cup sliced mushrooms
    ½ pound chicken livers
    1 large goose liver, quartered
    1 teaspoon instant minced onion
    ½ teaspoon salt
    ½ teaspoon sugar
    1 envelope or teaspoon instant
        chicken broth
    2 cups finely chopped ham

1. Melt goose drippings or butter or margarine in a large skillet. Sauté mushrooms 2 to 3 minutes. Add livers, onion, salt, sugar and instant broth. Cover and simmer 6 to 8 minutes, or just until livers lose their pink color.
2. Pour into an electric blender container. Cover and process on high until smooth. Stir in ham. Spread into an oiled 3-cup terrine or serving bowl. Cover and refrigerate several hours or overnight.
3. Serve with cocktail rye bread or crackers. Garnish with chopped hard-cooked egg, chopped pistachio nuts or finely chopped green onion, if you wish.

PÂTÉ MAISON

Prepare the chicken livers, add the seasonings and cream and you're ready to bring out the appetizer tray.

Makes 1⅓ cups.

    ¼ cup (½ stick) butter or margarine
    1 pound chicken livers
    ½ cup frozen chopped onion
    1 teaspoon salt
    ¼ teaspoon dry mustard
    ¼ teaspoon ground thyme
    ¼ teaspoon freshly ground pepper
    ⅛ teaspoon ground mace
    ¼ cup light cream

1. Heat butter or margarine in a large skillet. Add chicken livers and onion; cook over medium heat, stirring frequently, for 5 to 8 minutes or until livers are done and onion is tender.
2. Force livers with onion through strainer or food mill. Blend in salt, mustard, thyme, pepper, mace and cream. Turn into serving container or mold. Serve with sliced French bread.

PÂTÉ-CHEESE MOLD

Stuffed olives crown a pretty double-molded spread of chicken and cheese.

Makes 25 servings.

Chicken Layer
    1 envelope unflavored gelatin
    1 envelope or teaspoon instant
        chicken broth
    1 cup water
    1 tablespoon lemon juice
    3 large stuffed green olives, sliced
    2 cups ground cooked chicken
    ¼ cup mayonnaise or salad dressing
    ¼ cup sweet mustard relish
Cheese Layer
    1 envelope unflavored gelatin
    ¼ cup water
    2 wedges (1⅓ ounces each)
        Camembert cheese
    ¼ pound blue cheese
    ¼ teaspoon curry powder
    1 egg, separated
    1 container (8 ounces) dairy sour
        cream
        Green food coloring

1. Make chicken layer: Soften gelatin with instant broth in water in a small saucepan. Heat, stirring constantly with a spoon, just until gelatin dissolves. Measure ¼ cup into a 6-cup mold; stir in lemon juice. (Keep remaining gelatin mixture at room temperature.)
2. Set mold in a pan of ice and water to speed setting; chill just until syrupy-thick. Arrange stuffed olives in gelatin to make a pretty pattern. Chill until sticky-firm.
3. Mix chicken with remaining gelatin mixture, mayonnaise or salad dressing and relish in a medium-size bowl; spoon over sticky-firm olive layer in mold. Continue chilling in same pan of ice and water until sticky-firm while making cheese layer.
4. Make cheese layer: Soften gelatin in water in a small saucepan; heat slowly just until gelatin dissolves.
5. Beat Camembert and blue cheeses until well-blended in a medium-size bowl; beat in curry powder, egg yolk and the dissolved gelatin.
6. Beat egg white in a small bowl until it stands in firm peaks. Fold into cheese mixture, then fold in sour cream. Tint mixture light green with a drop or two of food coloring.
7. Spoon over sticky-firm chicken layer in mold; cover with wax paper, aluminum foil or plastic wrap. Chill in refrigerator several hours, or until firm. (Overnight is best.)
8. When ready to unmold, run a sharp-tip, thin-blade knife around top of mold, then dip mold *very quickly*

in and out of a pan of hot water. Cover mold with a serving plate; turn upside down; gently lift off mold. Surround with your choice of crisp crackers.

TURKEY LIVER PÂTÉ

Save livers from your turkeys and freeze until you have enough for this pâté.

Makes 12 servings.

    2 cups water
    ½ stalk celery with leaves
    1 small onion, peeled and quartered
    1 bay leaf
        Salt
    4 turkey livers
    ⅓ cup butter or margarine, softened
    1 to 2 tablespoons dry sherry or
        Madeira
        White pepper
        Pinch nutmeg
    2 tablespoons chopped pistachio
        nuts
    1 clove garlic, cut in half

1. Simmer water with celery, onion, bay leaf and a pinch of salt for 10 minutes. Simmer turkey livers for 7 minutes, or until cooked on outside but still pink inside. Drain and trim off bits of fat and connective tissue.
2. Purée livers but do not liquefy them in container of an electric blender on high; lower speed. Blend in softened butter or margarine and when thoroughly mixed, add wine, salt and white pepper to taste, nutmeg and nuts. Check seasonings. Rub inside of small bowl with cut sides of garlic. Discard garlic and pack pâté into bowl. Cover and chill at least 5 hours, but preferably 24. Soften at room temperature about 15 minutes before serving. Melba toast, Scandinavian crisp breads or French bread are best as bases.
SUGGESTED VARIATION: ½ pound chicken livers can be substituted for the turkey livers in this recipe and chicken broth can be used in place of wine; if you wish.

DUNKING CHICKEN

Fine finger food for picnic or patio meals —crackly crisp outside, juicy inside.

Makes 6 servings.

    2 broiler-fryers, cut-up (about 2½
        pounds each)
    1 cup all-purpose flour
    2 teaspoons salt
    ½ teaspoon pepper
        Bacon drippings
        Orange Curry Dunk (recipe, p.83)
        Zippy Tomato Dunk (recipe, p.83)

1. Shake chicken pieces in mixture of flour, salt and pepper in a plastic bag to coat well.
2. Heat bacon drippings in large skillet or electric fry pan. It'll take about 1 cup, for fat should be about ½ inch deep. (If you like, use part shortening.)
3. Place chicken in a single layer in hot fat; cover tightly. Cook over *low heat* 20 minutes, or until golden; turn; cover again and cook 20 minutes to brown other side. Remove browned chicken and set aside while cooking any remaining pieces, adding more drippings, if needed, to keep fat ½ inch deep.
4. Drain fat from pan leaving just enough to keep chicken from sticking; return all chicken to pan. Cover; cook, turning once or twice, over very low heat 10 minutes longer, or until chicken is tender.
5. Serve hot or cold, with the two dunking sauces.

ORANGE CHICKEN HORS D'OEUVRES

A glamorous appetizer served with a zesty orange sauce.

Bake at 400° for 15 minutes.
Makes 24 balls.

  2 cups ground cooked chicken
  ½ cup soft white bread crumbs (1 slice)
  1 teaspoon salt
  ¼ teaspoon pepper
  1 teaspoon grated onion
  1 egg
  1 tablespoon dry white wine
     Orange Sauce (recipe, page 91)

1. Combine chicken, bread crumbs, salt, pepper, onion, egg and wine in a medium-size bowl. Form into balls ¾ to 1 inch in diameter. Place on greased baking sheet.
2. Bake in hot oven (400°) for 15 minutes.
3. Place balls in small chafing dish; add ORANGE SAUCE and keep warm; serve with cocktail picks. Or serve on cocktail picks, with a bowl of ORANGE SAUCE as a dip.

ORANGE CURRY DUNK

Makes about 1½ cups.

  1 cup orange marmalade
  ⅓ cup vinegar
  ¼ cup granulated sugar
  2 tablespoons brown sugar
  1 tablespoon curry powder
  1 tablespoon Worcestershire sauce
  1 teaspoon salt
  ½ teaspoon ground ginger

1. Combine orange marmalade, vinegar, granulated sugar, brown sugar, curry powder, Worcestershire sauce, salt and ginger in saucepan.
2. Bring to boiling, then simmer, stirring constantly, until marmalade is melted and sauce is blended. Serve warm or cold.

ZIPPY TOMATO DUNK

This zesty sauce is a natural with finger food like fried chicken wings.

Makes 1½ cups.

  1 can (8 ounces) tomato sauce
  ½ cup finely chopped green pepper
  ½ cup finely chopped celery
  2 tablespoons vinegar
  2 tablespoons light molasses
  1 tablespoon Worcestershire sauce
  ¼ teaspoon bottled red-pepper seasoning

1. Combine tomato sauce, green pepper, celery, vinegar, molasses, Worcestershire and red-pepper seasoning in small saucepan.
2. Bring to boiling, then simmer, stirring constantly, 5 minutes, or until vegetables are softened and sauce is well blended.

Soups

BASIC CHICKEN BROTH

It is well worthwhile to make homemade chicken broth.

Makes 12 cups.

  2 broiler-fryers (3 to 3½ pounds each)
  2 medium-size carrots, pared and chopped
  1 large parsnip, pared and chopped
  1 large onion, chopped (1 cup)
  2 stalks celery
     Handful celery leaves
  3 sprigs parsley
  1 leek, trimmed and washed well
 12 cups cold water
  2 tablespoons salt
 12 peppercorns

1. Combine chicken with giblets, but not the livers, carrots, parsnip, onion and celery in a large kettle; tie celery leaves; parsley and leek together with a string; add to kettle. Add cold water to cover chicken and vegetables.
2. Heat slowly to boiling; skim; add salt and peppercorns; reduce heat; cover kettle. Simmer very slowly 1 to 1½ hours, or until meat falls off the bones. Remove meat and vegetables from broth; discard the greens.

3. Strain broth through cheesecloth into a large bowl. (There should be about 12 cups.) Use this delicious broth in any of our recipes calling for chicken broth.
4. When cool enough to handle, remove and discard skin and bones from chicken; cut meat into bite-size pieces; use in recipes that call for cooked chicken in this book. To store in refrigerator, up to 3 to 4 days, keep in covered container. To freeze, pack in 1 or 2 cup portions in plastic bags or plastic freezer containers.
5. To store broth in refrigerator, up to 4 days, leave fat layer on surface of broth until ready to use, then lift fat off and discard, or use in other cooking. To freeze, transfer broth to plastic freezer containers, allowing space on top for expansion. Freeze until ready to use (3 to 4 months maximum).

TOBAGO CHICKEN-AVOCADO SOUP

An elegant hot soup, rich with cream and avocado.

Makes 4 to 6 servings.

  3 tablespoons all-purpose flour
  3 tablespoons melted butter or margarine
  ⅓ cup heavy cream
 2½ cups chicken broth
  2 tablespoons finely minced green pepper
  1 cup chopped peeled avocado
  ½ teaspoon salt
  ⅛ teaspoon leaf basil, crumbled
     Lemon slices

1. Stir flour into melted butter or margarine in saucepan. Add cream, 1½ cups of the chicken broth, and minced green pepper. Stir over medium heat until mixture bubbles. Reduce heat and simmer 3 minutes.
2. Blend avocado with remaining 1 cup chicken broth until smooth in an electric blender. Add to pan with the salt; heat slowly; add the basil. Serve hot with the lemon slices.

CHICKEN-LEMON SOUP

Here's a cool and tangy opener for a warm-weather supper.

Makes 4 servings.

  1 envelope (2 to a package) chicken-noodle soup mix
  1 cup thinly sliced celery
  4 teaspoons lemon juice
  2 hard-cooked eggs, finely diced

1. Prepare soup mix, following label directions; cook 5 minutes; add celery and cook 2 minutes longer.
2. Remove from heat; stir in lemon juice; pour into bowl; cover; chill.
3. Serve in cups or small bowls, with diced hard-cooked eggs sprinkled over the top.

CHUNKY CHICKEN-BEEF SOUP

An entire broiler-fryer and plenty of beef go into this made-from-scratch soup.

Makes 8 servings.

    1½ pounds chuck steak, cut into
        ½-inch cubes
      1 large onion, chopped (1 cup)
      1 broiler-fryer (about 2 ½ to 3
        pounds)
      1 cup chopped celery
      2 teaspoons salt
      1 teaspoon seasoned salt
      ½ teaspoon pepper
      ½ teaspoon leaf rosemary, crumbled
      ½ teaspoon leaf thyme, crumbled
      1 bay leaf
     10 cups water
      2 cups uncooked medium noodles

1. Brown beef in its own fat in a kettle or Dutch oven; stir in onion and sauté lightly until it is soft.
2. Add chicken, celery, salt, seasoned salt, pepper, rosemary, thyme, bay leaf and water to kettle; bring to boiling; cover. Simmer 1 hour, or until chicken is tender; remove from kettle. Continue cooking beef 20 minutes, or until tender; remove bay leaf.
3. While beef finishes cooking, pull skin from chicken and take meat from bones; cut meat into cubes. Return to kettle; bring to boiling.
4. Stir in noodles. Cook 10 minutes, or until noodles are tender.
5. Ladle into soup plates. Sprinkle with chopped parsley.

BRUNSWICK CHOWDER

Chicken, canned soup and vegetables add up to this satisfying meal in a bowl.

Makes 12 servings.

      1 broiler-fryer, quartered (about
        2 ½ pounds)
      5 teaspoons seasoned salt
        Water
      1 large onion, chopped (1 cup)
      2 tablespoons butter or margarine
      2 packages (10 ounces each) frozen
        Fordhook lima beans
      2 cans condensed tomato-rice soup
      2 cups thinly sliced celery
      2 cans (1 pound each) cream-
        style corn

1. Combine chicken, 3 teaspoons of the salt and 4 cups water in a kettle; cover. Simmer 45 minutes, or until chicken is tender. Take meat from bones; dice. Strain broth into a 4-cup measure; add water, if needed, to make 4 cups.
2. Sauté onion in butter or margarine until soft in same kettle; add lima beans, tomato-rice soup, 2 ½ cups water and celery; cover. Simmer 15 minutes, or until beans are tender. Stir in chicken, broth, corn and remaining 2 teaspoons seasoned salt.
3. Bring slowly just to boiling. Ladle into heated soup bowls.

CORN 'N' CHICKEN CHOWDER

Canned chicken soup, canned corn, canned milk—by the time the kids wash up, soup's all ready.

Makes 6 servings.

      1 medium-size onion, chopped
        (½ cup)
      2 tablespoons butter or margarine
      2 cans condensed chicken noodle
        soup
    1¼ cups water
      1 can (about 1 pound) cream-
        style corn
      1 small can evaporated milk
      ¼ teaspoon pepper
      2 tablespoons chopped parsley

1. Sauté onion in butter or margarine just until soft in medium-size saucepan.
2. Stir in chicken noodle soup, water, cream-style corn, evaporated milk, and pepper. Bring just to boiling.
3. Pour into heated soup bowls or mugs; sprinkle with parsley.

CHOWDER DIAMOND HEAD

Ginger, pineapple and coconut make this an enchanting South Seas soup. It would be the perfect choice of a soup to accompany a light supper.

Makes 6 servings.

      1 cup sliced celery
      1 small onion, chopped (¼ cup)
      2 tablespoons butter or margarine
      ½ teaspoon ground ginger
      2 cans condensed cream of
        chicken soup
    1⅓ cups water
    1⅓ cups milk
      1 can (5 ounces) boned chicken,
        diced
      1 can (8¼ ounces) crushed
        pineapple, drained
        Shredded coconut

1. Sauté celery and onion in butter or

margarine until soft in a large heavy saucepan or Dutch oven; add ginger, blending thoroughly.
2. Stir in soup, water and milk. Add chicken and pineapple. Heat, stirring frequently, until bubbly-hot.
3. Ladle into soup bowls. Sprinkle with coconut. Serve with hot buttered rolls, if you wish.

MACARONI-CHICKEN CHOWDER

Clock watchers can have this hearty soup on the table in minutes.

Makes 4 servings.

      2 cans (13¾ ounces each) chicken
        broth
    1½ cups diced cooked chicken or
        turkey
      1 cup cooked peas and carrots
      1 cup diced celery
      ¼ cup frozen chopped onion
      ¼ teaspoon leaf rosemary, crumbled
        Pinch leaf tarragon, crumbled
      ½ teaspoon salt
      ¼ teaspoon pepper
      1 cup cooked macaroni shells or
        other pasta

1. Combine broth, chicken, peas and carrots, celery, onion, rosemary, tarragon, salt and pepper in a large saucepan.
2. Cover and simmer 15 minutes. Add macaroni and simmer 5 minutes longer. Serve with a sprinkling of chopped parsley and chowder crackers, if you wish.

CHICKEN CHOWDER

Soup mixes are just the beginning!

Makes 6 servings.

      3 cups water
      1 envelope (2 to a package) chicken
        noodle soup mix
      1 envelope (2 to a package) cream of
        mushroom soup mix
      ½ cup sliced carrots
      ¼ cup sliced celery
      ¼ cup chopped green pepper
      1 can (5 ounces) boned chicken,
        diced
      3 cups light cream

1. Bring water to boiling in a large saucepan; stir in soup mixes until blended, then carrots, celery and green pepper.
2. Bring to boiling; simmer 10 minutes.
3. Stir in chicken and cream; heat very slowly, just until bubbly.
4. Ladle into heated soup plates or bowls. Serve with your favorite crisp crackers or rye toast.

OLD-FASHIONED GOOSE GIBLET SOUP

English cooks often choose a hearty goose and barley soup as the perfect ending to a holiday bird.

Makes 6 servings.

    2 tablespoons goose drippings or
        butter or margarine
    1 large onion, sliced
        Goose giblets and neck
    5 cups water
    1 teaspoon salt
    ½ teaspoon celery salt
    1 can (1 pound) tomatoes
    1 cup pearl barley
    1 envelope or teaspoon instant
        chicken broth
    ½ teaspoon leaf thyme, crumbled
    1 cup diced cooked goose

1. Melt fat or butter or margarine in a Dutch oven or large kettle. Sauté onion until soft. Add giblets and neck, water, salt and celery salt.
2. Bring to boiling; reduce heat; cover and simmer 1 hour. Remove meat with a slotted spoon. Cut meat off neck and finely chop giblets; return meat to kettle.
3. Add tomatoes, barley, instant chicken broth and thyme. Return to boil, cover and simmer 1 hour; add cooked goose. Serve in heated soup bowls and top with sieved hard-cooked egg, if you wish.

CHICKEN SOUP WITH DUMPLINGS

A creamy-thick soup with tender little chicken balls and vegetables.

Makes 6 servings.

Chicken Dumplings
    1 cup diced cooked chicken
    1 cooked chicken liver (optional)
    1 egg
    ⅓ cup all-purpose flour
    ¼ cup milk
    1 teaspoon salt
        Dash pepper
        Dash ground nutmeg
    1 tablespoon chopped parsley
    1 cup water
    6 cups Basic Chicken Broth (recipe,
        page 83)
Soup
    ¼ cup sliced green onion
    ¼ cup chicken fat, butter or
        margarine
    ¼ cup all-purpose flour
    1 package (10 ounces) frozen mixed
        vegetables
    ½ teaspoon salt
    1½ cups diced cooked chicken

1. Make Chicken Dumplings: Combine chicken, liver, egg, flour, milk, salt, pepper and nutmeg in blender;

blend at high speed until smooth. Turn into small bowl, stir in parsley; cover bowl.
2. Bring water and 1 cup of the chicken broth to boiling in large saucepan. Shape chicken mixture, one-half at a time, into ¾-inch balls with a teaspoon. Drop one by one into boiling broth. Simmer gently, uncovered, 8 to 10 minutes; remove with a slotted spoon; keep warm. Repeat with second half.
3. Make Soup: Sauté onion in chicken fat, or butter or margarine in kettle or Dutch oven, until soft but not brown, 3 to 4 minutes; stir in flour; gradually add remaining chicken broth; stirring constantly; bring to boiling; add vegetables and salt; cover. Cook 10 minutes, or until vegetables are tender.
4. Add chicken dumplings, cooking broth and chicken; heat 5 minutes. Ladle into soup bowls; serve with crusty bread.

CUCUMBER-CHICKEN CUP

Float a spoonful of sour cream on top.

Makes 4 servings.

    2 cans condensed chicken broth
    2½ cups water
    1 large cucumber, pared and
        shredded
    ⅓ cup dairy sour cream
        Dillweed

1. Combine chicken broth and water in a medium-size saucepan; bring to boiling. Stir in cucumber and salt to taste, if needed. Heat until bubbly.
2. Ladle into soup cups or small bowls. Float a spoonful of sour cream on each; sprinkle dillweed over cream. Serve with small wheat crackers.

CREME D'OIE

A cream of goose soup that uses up the last delicious tidbits of the bird.

Makes 6 servings.

    2 large leeks, washed and chopped
    1 cup chopped celery
    ¼ cup (½ stick) butter or margarine
    2 tablespoons all-purpose flour
    8 cups Basic Chicken Broth (recipe,
        page 83)
        OR: 8 envelopes or teaspoons
        instant chicken broth and 8 cups
        water
        Carcass of goose plus neck and
        giblets
    2 cups heavy cream
    3 egg yolks
        Salt and pepper

1. Sauté leeks and celery in butter or margarine in a large kettle until golden. Stir in flour and brown lightly, stirring constantly.
2. Add BASIC CHICKEN BROTH or instant chicken broth and water, carcass, neck and giblets of goose. Bring to boiling; lower heat; cover.
3. Simmer 2 hours or until mixture is rich with flavor. Strain liquid into a large saucepan and discard bones and dice any tidbits of goose.
4. Beat cream and egg yolks together in a large bowl with a wire whisk; whisk in about 2 cups of the hot broth; return to saucepan. Heat gently, stirring often, just until hot; taste and season with salt and pepper; add goose tidbits. Serve immediately.
COOK'S TIP: You can substitute 6 green onions for leeks in recipe.

GARDEN PATCH SOUP

An easy-to-make soup that's ready to serve in about 30 minutes.

Makes 6 servings.

    1 medium-size onion, chopped (½
        cup)
    2 medium-size potatoes, peeled and
        chopped
    1 can (1 pound) whole-kernel corn,
        drained
    1 package (10 ounces) frozen lima
        beans, cooked and drained
    2 cans (13¾ ounces each) chicken
        broth
    1 can (26 ounces) tomato juice
    1 cup diced cooked chicken
    1½ teaspoons salt
    ¼ teaspoon pepper
    1 tablespoon butter or margarine
    1 tablespoon Worcestershire sauce

1. Combine onion, potatoes, corn, lima beans, chicken broth, tomato juice, chicken, salt, pepper, butter or margarine and Worcestershire sauce in a kettle.
2. Bring slowly to boiling; lower heat; cover kettle; simmer 30 minutes, or until vegetables are tender. Serve with wedges of process American cheese and crackers for a complete meal.

HOT SENEGALESE SOUP

This creamy soup is an exotic but very easy version of an honored specialty.

Makes 6 servings.

    2 cans condensed cream of chicken
        soup
    3 cups milk
    ½ teaspoon curry powder
    2 tablespoons toasted coconut

1. Combine soup, milk and curry powder in medium-size saucepan; heat just until bubbly-hot, then beat with wire whip until creamy smooth.
2. Pour into 8 small bowls or cups, dividing evenly; sprinkle with coconut.

COLD CURRIED CHICKEN SOUP

This is one of the most delicious of all iced summer soups.

Makes 6 servings.

3 tart apples, pared, cored and sliced (apples must be tart)
1 large onion, peeled and sliced
1 tablespoon butter or margarine
2 teaspoons curry powder
2 teaspoons salt
    Freshly ground pepper
3 drops bottled red-pepper seasoning
3 cups chicken consommé or broth
1 cup dry white wine
1 cup light cream
½ cup very finely diced cooked chicken or turkey
    Paprika

1. Cook apples and onion in butter or margarine in a large saucepan over low heat, stirring often, until soft. Do not let them brown.
2. Stir in curry powder and cook 3 minutes longer. Add salt, pepper, red-pepper seasoning, chicken consommé or broth and wine. Simmer, covered, 10 minutes, stirring frequently.
3. Purée in blender or press through a fine sieve. Chill thoroughly.
4. Just before serving, stir in cream and chicken; sprinkle with paprika. Serve icy cold.

COLD CUCUMBER SOUP WITH CHICKEN

Cold soups add the perfect touch to a summer salad supper.

Makes 4 servings.

1 cucumber, peeled, seeded and diced
½ cup apple cider
½ cup dairy sour cream
½ cup heavy cream
1 cup diced cooked chicken
½ teaspoon salt
    Dash white pepper
2 sprigs fresh dill, finely chopped (2 teaspoons)
    Chopped chives

1. Purée cucumber with cider in the container of an electric blender until smooth. Mix with sour cream, heavy cream and chicken in a glass bowl. Add salt and pepper. Stir in dill; cover

bowl with plastic wrap; chill.
2. Serve in chilled soup cups and garnish with chives.

CHILLED CHICKEN CREAM

Celery seeds give canned cream soup an exceptional flavor.

Makes 4 servings.

1 can condensed cream of chicken soup
1 cup light cream
½ cup milk
1 teaspoon lemon juice
½ teaspoon celery seeds

1. Combine cream of chicken soup, cream, milk, lemon juice and celery seeds in the container of an electric blender; cover; process on high until creamy-smooth. Or combine in a large bowl and beat with an electric mixer until very smooth. Chill 4 hours, or overnight.
2. Pour into mugs or cups. Garnish each with a celery-stick stirrer and serve with tiny croutons to sprinkle over, or a dash of paprika, if you wish.

MULLIGATAWNY SOUP

A classic soup with origins in the West Indies, it's richly flavored with exotic curry.

Makes 6 servings.

3 large carrots, pared and sliced
2 stalks celery, sliced
6 cups Basic Chicken Broth (recipe, page 83)
3 cups diced cooked chicken
1 large onion, chopped (1 cup)
¼ cup (½ stick) butter or margarine
1 apple, pared, quartered, cored and chopped
5 teaspoons curry powder
1 teaspoon salt
¼ cup all-purpose flour
1 tablespoon lemon juice
2 cups hot cooked rice
¼ cup chopped parsley
6 lemon slices

1. Cook carrots and celery in 1 cup BASIC CHICKEN BROTH in a medium-size saucepan 20 minutes, or until tender. Add chicken; heat just until hot; cover; keep warm.
2. Sauté onion until soft in butter or margarine in Dutch oven; stir in apple, curry powder and salt; sauté 5 minutes longer, or until apple is soft; add flour. Gradually stir in remaining chicken broth; bring to boiling, stirring constantly; reduce heat; cover; simmer 15 minutes.
3. Add vegetables and chicken with the broth they were cooked in; bring

just to boiling. Stir in lemon juice.
4. Ladle into soup plates or bowls; pass hot cooked rice and chopped parsley and lemon slices. Good with crusty French bread.

COMPANY SOUP

Garnish this tasty soup with bacon, green onions and cucumbers.

Makes 6 servings.

3 cans (13¾ ounces each) chicken broth
¼ cup dry white wine
1½ cups chopped cooked chicken
1 package (10 ounces) frozen green peas, cooked and drained
1 can (5 ounces) water chestnuts, sliced
⅓ cup sliced ripe olives
1½ teaspoons salt
⅛ teaspoon pepper
1 teaspoon leaf tarragon, crumbled
    Chopped cooked bacon
    Sliced green onions
    Cucumber slices

1. Combine chicken broth, wine, chicken, peas, water chestnuts, olives, salt, pepper and tarragon in a large saucepan.
2. Bring slowly to boiling; lower heat, simmer 15 minutes to blend flavors.
3. Ladle into soup bowls and pass tiny bowls of bacon, green onions and cucumber to sprinkle on top.

Stuffings

APPLE AND CHESTNUT STUFFING

Stuffs a 16-pound turkey or bake in a casserole to serve with roast goose.

Bake at 375° for 15 minutes.
Makes 10 cups.

1 pound fresh chestnuts
    OR: 1 can (10 ounces) water packed chestnuts
½ cup (1 stick) butter or margarine
1 large onion, chopped (1 cup)
1 large apple, grated (1 cup)
2 cups water
2 packages (8 ounces each) herb-seasoned stuffing mix

1. Wash fresh chestnuts; cut slits in each shell; place in a shallow baking pan. Bake in moderate oven (375°) 15 minutes. Remove from pan; when cool enough to handle, shell and skin.
2. Cook, covered, in boiling salted water to cover, in a medium-size saucepan, about 15 minutes, or until tender; drain; chop fine. (Or, drain and chop canned chestnuts.)
3. Melt butter or margarine in a large

saucepan; sauté onion until soft; stir in apple and chestnuts; sauté 2 minutes. Add water; heat to boiling. Stir in prepared stuffing mix.

ORANGE PECAN STUFFING

Excellent for a goose or two ducklings. Or bake it in a separate casserole.

Makes 6 cups.

  2 large California oranges
  1 large onion, diced (1 cup)
  1 cup chopped celery
  ½ cup (1 stick) butter or margarine
  4 cups cubed white bread (8 slices)
  1 cup chopped pecans
  ¼ cup chopped parsley
  1 teaspoon salt
  ¼ teaspoon pepper
  ¼ teaspoon leaf thyme, crumbled

1. Grate 1 tablespoon rind from one orange; reserve. With a sharp knife, cut skin (through white) from both oranges. Section both over a large bowl. (You should have 1 cup fresh orange sections.) Reserve.
2. Sauté onion and celery in butter or margarine until soft in a large skillet.
3. Add orange sections, rind, bread cubes, pecans, parsley, salt, pepper and thyme to skillet, toss lightly until evenly moist.

SPICY CORN BREAD STUFFING

Golden cornbread combines with spicy sausage and crunchy celery for a delightful difference in stuffing.

Makes 10 cups.

  1 package (8 ounces) cornbread
       stuffing mix
  1 pound bulk sausage
  2 large onions, chopped (2 cups)
  2 cups sliced celery
  ½ teaspoon leaf sage, crumbled
  ½ teaspoon leaf thyme, crumbled
  1 teaspoon salt
       Dash pepper
  1 cup chicken broth

1. Pour stuffing mix into a large bowl.
2. Cut sausage into 8 slices. Brown 5 minutes on each side in a medium-size skillet, then break into small pieces. Cook 1 minute longer, or until no trace of pink remains; combine with crumbled cornbread mix.
3. Pour drippings from skillet into a cup; measure and return 4 tablespoons. Add onions and celery; sauté until tender. Stir in sage, thyme, salt, pepper and chicken broth. Bring to boiling, scraping off browned bits from skillet. Pour over sausage mixture; toss lightly until evenly moist.

SAVORY STUFFING

Simple, yet delicious. It's made with ingredients you have on hand.

Makes 2 cups.

  ½ cup chopped celery leaves
  2 tablespoons chopped onion
  ¼ cup (½ stick) butter or margarine
  ½ cup water
  2 cups prepared bread stuffing mix
       (½ of an 8-ounce package)

1. Sauté celery leaves and onion in butter or margarine in medium-size saucepan. Add water; bring mixture to boiling.
2. Stir in bread stuffing; toss with fork just until moistened.

OYSTER STUFFING

This recipe will stuff the neck of a 16-pound turkey or a 4-pound roasting chicken.

Makes about 3 cups.

  ¼ cup (½ stick) butter or margarine
  1 medium-size onion, chopped
       (½ cup)
  ½ pint oysters
       OR: 1 can (8 ounces) oysters
       Water
  1 package (6 ounces) herb-flavor
       stuffing mix

1. Melt butter or margarine in medium-size saucepan; sauté onion until soft.
2. Drain liquid from oysters into a 2-cup measure; add enough water to make 1¾ cups. Chop oysters.
3. Add oyster liquid to saucepan; bring to boiling; cover saucepan; lower heat. Simmer 6 minutes. (If using fresh oysters, add to saucepan for the last 2 minutes of cooking.)
4. Remove saucepan from heat; stir in stuffing mix and the can of oysters, if used. Cover saucepan; allow to stand 5 minutes.

VEGETABLE AND SAUSAGE STUFFING

Excellent for Rock Cornish hens.

Makes about 3 cups.

  ¼ pound bulk sausage or link
       sausage
  ½ cup grated carrot
  1 green pepper, halved, seeded and
       chopped
  1⅓ cups water
  1 package (6 ounces) stuffing mix

1. Sauté sausage in a large skillet, breaking up with a fork, until lightly

browned. Add carrot and green pepper; continue cooking over low heat until pepper is tender.
2. Add water to sausage-vegetable mixture with stuffing mix. Bring to boiling. Toss to blend well.

PECAN-FRUIT STUFFING AND GRAVY

Raisins and crunchy pecans make this stuffing special.

Makes 3 cups.

  ¼ cup dry sherry
  ¼ cup golden raisins
  1 cup sliced green onions
  ½ cup chopped celery
  ¼ cup (½ stick) butter or margarine
  1½ cups soft bread crumbs (3 slices)
  1 small apple, cored and chopped
  1 small orange, peeled and chopped
  ¼ cup chopped pecans
  1 teaspoon leaf marjoram,
       crumbled
  ½ teaspoon salt
  ⅛ teaspoon pepper

1. Heat sherry in small saucepan; add raisins; allow to stand for 15 minutes.
2. Sauté green onions and celery in butter until soft, in a large skillet.
3. Stir in bread crumbs, apple, orange, pecans, marjoram, salt, pepper and raisins.

SAUSAGE AND APPLE STUFFING

A Southern stuffing to fill big birds.

Bake at 250° for 10 minutes.
Makes 10 cups.

  8 cups cubed white bread (16 slices)
  1 pound bulk sausage
  1 large onion, chopped (1 cup)
  ½ cup water
  2 large apples, pared, quartered,
       cored and chopped
  1 teaspoon salt

1. Spread bread cubes on large cooky sheets; place in very slow oven (250°) 10 minutes to dry slightly; remove from oven to large bowl.
2. Remove casing from sausage; cut into 8 thick slices. Brown 5 minutes on each side in a medium-size skillet, then break into small pieces. Cook 1 minute longer, or until no trace of pink remains. Transfer sausage with slotted spoon to bowl.
3. Pour off drippings from skillet; measure and return 2 tablespoons. Add onion; sauté until tender. Stir in water and apples; bring to boiling. Pour over sausage and bread mixture; add salt; toss lightly until the entire mixture is evenly moist throughout.

YORKTOWN WALNUT STUFFING

A rich bread stuffing with crispy nuts for crunch.

Bake at 250° for 10 minutes
Makes 12 cups.

- **12 cups cubed white bread (24 slices)**
- **1 cup light cream**
- **6 eggs, separated**
- **2 cups chopped walnuts**
- **½ cup (1 stick) butter or margarine, melted**
- **1 teaspoon salt**
- **½ teaspoon ground nutmeg**
- **⅛ teaspoon pepper**

1. Spread bread cubes on large cooky sheets; place in very slow oven (250°) 10 minutes to dry; remove from oven.
2. Combine cream and egg yolks in a large bowl; beat until foamy; add bread, walnuts, butter or margarine, salt, nutmeg and pepper.
3. Beat egg whites in a medium-size bowl just until they form soft peaks; add to bread mixture; fold in until well blended and smooth.

HAWAIIAN STUFFING

Try coconut and pineapple for a truly tangy stuffing for Rock Cornish hens.

Makes about 2½ cups.

- **1½ cups soft white bread crumbs (3 slices)**
- **⅓ cup flaked coconut**
- **¼ cup finely chopped celery**
- **¼ cup drained crushed pineapple**
- **1 tablespoon grated orange peel**
- **2 tablespoons melted butter or margarine**

Combine bread crumbs, coconut, celery, pineapple, orange peel and butter or margarine in a medium-size bowl; toss lightly to blend.

RAISIN-NUT STUFFING

Apples and raisins add the perfect touch to a roast goose or 10-pound turkey.

Makes 7 cups.

- **1 can (1 pound) sliced apples**
  Water
- **½ cup (1 stick) butter or margarine**
- **1 package (8 ounces) prepared bread stuffing mix**
- **1 cup chopped peanuts**
- **½ cup seedless raisins**

1. Drain apples and add water to apple liquid to make 1 cup. Bring to boiling in large saucepan. Stir in butter or margarine until melted.
2. Add prepared stuffing, apples, peanuts and raisins; toss lightly to mix fruits with stuffing mix.

POULTRY POINTERS

A Variety of Bread Toppings
A golden coating of crumbs can give your casserole the final touch. It's also a good way to use up the tag-ends of bread not used for stuffing.
- **Soft Bread Crumbs:** Tear slices of bread into small pieces with a three-tined fork, Or, place one slice at a time, quartered, in an electric-blender container; cover; whirl at high speed 15 seconds.
- **Dry Bread Crumbs:** Put dry bread slices through a food chopper fitted with a fine blade. (A neat trick is to tie a plastic bag on the blade end of the grinder so that the crumbs will drop directly into the bag as they are ground—no mess.) Or, place slices of dry bread in a plastic bag and seal; crush with a rolling pin. Or, fastest trick of all, whirl dry bread pieces in an electric-blender container at high speed for 30 seconds. For fine crumbs: Sift the ground crumbs through a fine sieve. Store the fine crumbs and the coarse (those left behind in the sieve) separately in plastic containers.
- **Bread Crumbs:** Melt 2 tablespoons butter or margarine in a skillet; add 1 cup of dry bread crumbs and stir-fry until crumbs are golden-brown. Makes 1 cup.
- **Soft Bread Cubes:** Stack two or three slices of bread on a cutting board and cut into strips of desired width, then cut across the strips to form cubes of even size.
- **Toasted Bread Cubes:** Spread soft bread cubes in a jelly-roll pan and place in slow oven (300°). Toast, shaking occasionally, 20 minutes, or until golden-brown on all sides.
- **Croutons:** Brown soft bread cubes, about 1 cup at a time, in 2 tablespoons olive oil or vegetable oil in a large, heavy skillet over moderately high heat, stirring and turning often until evenly golden-brown.
- **Garlic Croutons:** Sauté 1 crushed clove garlic in oil until golden; remove before browning croutons.

FRUITED RICE STUFFING

This stuffing is well suited for a small turkey, a goose or especially a capon.

Makes 5 cups.

- **2¼ cups water**
- **1 envelope or teaspoon instant chicken broth**
- **½ teaspoon salt**
- **⅛ teaspoon powdered saffron**
- **1 cup uncooked rice**
- **1 cup sliced celery**
- **¼ cup sliced green onion**
- **¼ cup (½ stick) butter or margarine**
- **¼ cup chopped parsley**
- **1 tablespoon grated lemon rind**
- **¼ cup raisins**
- **¼ cup sliced kumquats**

1. Combine water, instant broth, salt and saffron in a large saucepan. Bring to boiling. Stir in rice; reduce heat; cover. Simmer 20 minutes.
2. Sauté celery and onion in butter or margarine until soft in small skillet, about 5 minutes. Stir in parsley, lemon rind, raisins and kumquats. Add to rice; toss to mix.

JARDINIÈRE DRESSING

Makes 1½ cups or enough to stuff one 2½ pound chicken.

- **1 medium-size onion, chopped (½ cup)**
- **½ cup finely chopped celery**
- **½ cup finely chopped carrots**
- **2 tablespoons butter or margarine**
- **1 cup soft bread crumbs (2 slices)**
- **½ teaspoon leaf savory, crumbled**
- **½ teaspoon salt**
  Dash pepper

1. Sauté onion, celery and carrots until soft in butter or margarine in a large skillet. Stir in bread crumbs, savory, salt and pepper until well blended.
2. Cool before stuffing bird.

FRUITED GIBLET DRESSING

Try this apple and giblet stuffing with a 2½ pound whole chicken.

Makes 1½ cups.

- **1 large apple, pared, cored and chopped**
- **2 tablespoons butter or margarine**
  Chopped giblets
- **1½ cups soft bread crumbs (3 slices)**
- **3 tablespoons giblet broth**
- **½ teaspoon salt**
- **¼ teaspoon ground allspice**
  Dash pepper

Sauté apple until soft in butter or margarine in a large skillet. Stir in chopped giblets and cook 2 minutes. Stir in bread crumbs, broth, salt allspice and pepper until blended.

WHOLE-WHEAT BREAD STUFFING

Delicious choice for a goose or small turkey.

Makes 5 cups.

4 cups whole-wheat or cracked-wheat bread cubes (8 slices)
1 teaspoon leaf sage, crumbled
1 teaspoon leaf savory, crumbled
½ teaspoon salt
¼ teaspoon pepper
¼ teaspoon ground nutmeg
¼ pound mushrooms, chopped
1 cup chopped celery
1 cup chopped carrot
1 medium-size onion, chopped (½ cup)
1 clove garlic, crushed
⅓ cup butter or margarine
¼ cup chopped parsley
2 tablespoons water

1. Combine bread cubes, sage, savory, salt, pepper and nutmeg in a large bowl.
2. Sauté mushrooms, celery, carrot, onion and garlic until soft, in butter or margarine in a large skillet, about 10 minutes; stir in parsley. Add to bread mixture; toss to mix well. Stir in water; mix.

PENNSYLVANIA DUTCH POTATO STUFFING

Perfect for a small turkey or a goose.

Makes 4 cups.

1½ pounds potatoes
½ teaspoon salt
¼ teaspoon pepper
1 large onion, diced (1 cup)
½ cup (1 stick) butter or margarine
4 cups cubed white bread (8 slices)
½ cup chopped parsley
½ teaspoon poultry seasoning

1. Pare and dice potatoes. Cook, covered, in boiling salted water to cover in a large saucepan until fork-tender. Measure and reserve ½ cup of the potato water; drain and discard remaining water. Toss potatoes over low heat in pan to dry.
2. Mash potatoes in a large bowl. Add the ½ cup reserved potato water, salt and pepper; beat until fluffy-smooth. Reserve.
3. Sauté onions in butter or margarine in a small skillet until lightly browned. Add onions, bread cubes, parsley and poultry seasoning to potato mixture; mix until moist.

APRICOT-WALNUT STUFFING

Try this California favorite.

Makes 4 cups.

1 medium-size onion, chopped (½ cup)
¼ cup (½ stick) butter or margarine
½ cup chopped dry apricots
1 envelope instant chicken broth OR: 1 chicken bouillon cube
⅓ cup water
6 slices white bread, cubed (3 cups)
½ cup chopped walnuts

1. In a large skillet, sauté onion in butter or margarine until soft; stir in apricots, chicken broth or bouillon cube and water. Heat to boiling, crushing bouillon cube if used.
2. Add cubed bread and walnuts; toss until evenly moist.

APPLE AND CORNBREAD STUFFING

Excellent for a goose or two ducklings . Or heat in separate casserole.

Makes 3 cups.

1 large onion, chopped (1 cup)
1 cup chopped celery
½ cup (1 stick) butter or margarine
1 package (8 ounces) cornbread stuffing mix
1 jar (8 ounces) applesauce
½ teaspoon leaf thyme, crumbled
½ teaspoon marjoram, crumbled
¼ teaspoon lemon-pepper seasoning
⅓ cup boiling water

1. Sauté onion and celery in butter or margarine until soft in a large skillet.
2. Add cornbread stuffing mix, applesauce, thyme, marjoram, lemon-pepper seasoning and boiling water to skillet; toss lightly until evenly moist.

BROWN RICE STUFFING

Different and delicious.

Makes about 10 cups.

9 cups water
1 tablespoon salt
3 cups brown rice (1½ boxes, 12 ounces each)
2 cups chopped celery
1 medium-size onion, grated
½ cup (1 stick) butter or margarine
½ cup chopped parsley
2 teaspoons salt
1½ teaspoons poultry seasoning

1. Combine water and the 1 tablespoon salt in a kettle. Bring to boiling. Stir in rice; lower heat; cover. Simmer 45 minutes, or until rice is tender.

Drain; place in a large bowl.
2. Sauté celery and onion in butter until soft in a medium-size skillet. Stir in parsley, the remaining 2 teaspoons salt and poultry seasoning.
3. Pour over rice; stir lightly until evenly mixed.

GOURMET STUFFING

Here is the perfect way to use those chicken livers that come with whole birds.

Makes 2 cups.

3 chicken livers
¼ cup (½ stick) butter or margarine
2 cups soft white bread crumbs (4 slices)
2 tablespoons frozen chopped onion
1 tablespoon water
1 teaspoon Worcestershire sauce
½ teaspoon salt

1. Sauté livers in butter or margarine, stirring often, in skillet 5 minutes, or until livers lose their pink color.
2. Remove livers and chop, then add to bread crumbs in medium-sized bowl. Sauté onion just until soft in same pan.
3. Stir water, Worcestershire sauce and salt into onions in skillet; pour over crumb mixture. Toss lightly to mix well. (Mixture will be crumbly.)

WILD RICE STUFFING

Choose this stuffing for a duckling or the neck cavity of a 12-pound turkey.

Makes 3 cups.

¼ cup (½ stick) butter or margarine
¼ pound mushrooms, chopped OR: 1 can (3 or 4 ounces) chopped mushrooms
1 package (6 ounces) white and wild rice mix
2½ cups boiling water
⅓ cup chopped parsley
¼ cup pine nuts

1. Melt butter or margarine in a large heavy saucepan; sauté the chopped mushrooms until soft. (Or, drain liquid from canned mushrooms into a 2-cup measure and use as part of the 2½ cups of water. Sauté chopped canned mushrooms in butter.)
2. Stir white and wild rice into saucepan; sauté for 2 minutes. Blend in boiling water and packet of seasoning; cover saucepan; lower heat to simmer.
3. Cook 25 minutes, or until liquid is absorbed; stir in chopped parsley and pine nuts.

HILO STUFFING

Macadamia nuts add a gourmet touch to this rice stuffing that's perfect with duckling.

Makes 4 cups.

- 1 cup uncooked long-grain rice
- ¼ cup (½ stick) butter or margarine
- 1 medium-size onion, chopped (½ cup)
- 2 envelopes instant chicken broth OR: 2 chicken bouillon cubes
- 2½ cups water
- ½ cup chopped macadamia nuts (from a 6-ounce jar)
- ½ cup flaked coconut

1. Sauté rice in butter or margarine in a saucepan, stirring often, just until golden.
2. Stir in onion, instant broth or bouillon cubes and water; bring to boiling, crushing cubes, if using, with a spoon; cover. Simmer 20 minutes, or until rice is tender and liquid is absorbed.
3. Sprinkle with nuts and coconut; toss lightly to mix.

BREAD AND BUTTER STUFFING

Easy, economical and perfect for a capon.

Makes 3 cups.

- 3 cups (6 slices) small dry bread cubes (To make dry bread cubes: Spread cubes out on baking sheet; bake in a very slow oven (250°) 15 minutes, or until cubes are dry but not brown.)
- 1 small onion, finely chopped (¼ cup)
- 2 tablespoons chopped parsley
- 1½ teaspoons leaf basil, crumbled
- ¼ teaspoon salt
- ⅛ teaspoon pepper
- 1 egg
- ¼ cup (½ stick) melted butter or margarine

1. Combine bread cubes, onion, parsley, basil, salt, pepper and egg in medium-size bowl.
2. Sprinkle melted butter or margarine over bread mixture; toss with fork until blended.

FRENCH PÂTÉ STUFFING

Use this elegant mixture to stuff the neck cavity of a 12-pound bird, or to stuff a roasting chicken.

Makes 3 cups.

- 1 cup finely chopped mushrooms
- 2 tablespoons butter or margarine

- 1½ cups soft bread crumbs (3 slices)
- ½ cup milk
- 2 tablespoons chopped parsley
- ½ teaspoon leaf rosemary, crumbled
- ½ teaspoon salt
- ⅛ teaspoon pepper
- 1 egg
- 1 turkey liver or 3 chicken livers
- ½ pound ground pork

1. Sauté mushrooms in butter or margarine until soft in a small skillet. Set aside to cool.
2. Combine bread crumbs, milk, parsley, rosemary, salt, pepper and egg in a medium-size bowl.
3. Chop liver finely on a chopping board; add to bread mixture. Stir in ground pork; beat well with a wooden spoon. Add mushrooms and mix.

Sauces

BASIC POULTRY GLAZES

ORANGE-HONEY GLAZE: Makes about 1½ cups. Mix 1 can (6 ounces) thawed frozen concentrate for orange juice with ¾ cup of honey and 1 teaspoon Worcestershire sauce. Use to baste a large turkey, applying glaze about every 10 minutes during the last half hour of cooking.

PINEAPPLE-CURRY GLAZE: Makes about 1¼ cups. Mix 1 cup pineapple preserves, ¼ cup dill pickle juice (from jar of pickles) and 1 teaspoon of curry powder. Spread on quartered chicken pieces during last half hour of cooking.

CURRANT JELLY GLAZE: Makes about 1¼ cups. Soften 1 cup currant jelly with 2 tablespoons hot water; stir in 2 tablespoons prepared mustard and ¼ teaspoon ground cloves. Brush glaze over a turkey or duckling during final half hour of cooking.

GINGER-MARMALADE GLAZE: Makes ½ cup. Blend together ½ cup orange marmalade, 1 teaspoon sweet-pickle juice (from jar of pickles) and ⅛ teaspoon each ground ginger and allspice. Brush glaze over broiling chicken for last 5 minutes of cooking.

BASIC BARBECUE SAUCE

Good on all broiled or grilled poultry.

Makes 3 cups.

- 1 cup light molasses
- 1 cup prepared mustard
- 1 cup cider vinegar

Combine molasses, mustard and the vinegar in 4-cup jar with tight-fitting lid; shake well to mix. Store the sauce in refrigerator.

SUGGESTED VARIATIONS:
Ginger Sauce: Mix 1 cup Basic Barbecue Sauce with ½ cup of ginger marmalade and 1 teaspoon ground ginger. Makes 1½ cups.

Zing Sauce: Mix 1 cup Basic Barbecue Sauce with ¼ cup catsup, ¼ cup vegetable oil and 2 tablespoons Worcestershire sauce. Makes 1½ cups.

Italian Herb Sauce: Mix 1 cup Basic Barbecue Sauce with ½ cup chili sauce and ½ teaspoon crumbled leaf oregano. Makes 1½ cups.

CREAMY GRAVY

Still have cooked turkey or chicken, but no gravy left? Here's a flavorful answer.

Makes about 2 cups.

- 2 tablespoons finely chopped scallions or chives
- 3 tablespoons butter or margarine
- ¼ cup all-purpose flour
- 1 can (13¾ ounces) chicken broth
- ½ cup light cream
- 1 tablespoon chopped parsley
  Salt and pepper

Sauté scallions or chives in butter or margarine in a medium-size saucepan. Cook, stirring constantly, until bubbly; stir in flour; add chicken broth. Cook over low heat, stirring constantly, until gravy thickens. Add cream and parsley; simmer 3 minutes. Taste and season with salt and pepper.

CURRY SAUCE

You never need to wonder what to do with the last of the bird when you can turn it into an exotic dish so easily with this sauce.

Makes 6 cups.

- 2 large onions, chopped (2 cups)
- 2 cloves garlic, minced
- 3 tablespoons vegetable oil
- 2 tablespoons curry powder
- 2 teaspoons ground allspice
- 2 teaspoons salt
- 1 teaspoon ground coriander
- 2 jars (about 8 ounces each) junior prunes (baby-pack)
- 2 jars (about 8 ounces each) junior apples-and-apricots (baby-pack)
- 1½ cups water
- ¼ cup lemon juice
- ½ cup chopped bottled chutney

1. Sauté onion and garlic in vegetable oil until soft in a large heavy saucepan; stir in curry powder, allspice, salt and the coriander. Continue cooking, stirring constantly, about 2 minutes.
2. Stir in fruits, water and lemon juice. Simmer, uncovered, stirring often, 30 minutes to season and blend flavors; remove from heat, then stir in chutney.
3. Heat your choice of cooked and diced poultry in the sauce to spoon over rice, noodles or wheat pilaf.

CHUTNEY FRUIT SAUCE

Canned peaches blend with onion and spices for this savory spread. Especially good with curries or cold roast turkey.

Makes 2 cups.

 1 can (1 pound, 13 ounces) sliced cling peaches
 1 small onion, chopped (¼ cup)
 ¼ teaspoon ground cumin
 ⅛ teaspoon ground allspice
 ½ teaspoon Worcestershire sauce
 ¼ teaspoon bottled red-pepper seasoning
 2 tablespoons lemon juice

1. Drain syrup from peaches into a cup. Measure 2 tablespoonfuls and combine with the cling peaches, onion, cumin, allspice, Worcestershire sauce and the red-pepper seasoning in container of an electric blender; cover. Whirl at high speed 1 minute, or until smooth; pour into a small saucepan.
2. Bring to boiling, then simmer, stirring often, 5 minutes to blend flavors; remove from heat.
3. Stir in the lemon juice and chill.

MORNAY SAUCE

Swiss cheese seasons this classic; Parmesan goes into its variation. Delicious over Chicken Divan.

Makes 1⅓ cups.

 1 tablespoon butter or margarine
 1 tablespoon all-purpose flour
 ⅛ teaspoon white pepper
 1 small can evaporated milk
 ⅔ cup water
 1 envelope or teaspoon instant chicken broth
 1 egg yolk
 ½ cup shredded Swiss cheese

1. Melt butter or margarine in a small saucepan; stir in flour and pepper. Cook, stirring constantly, until bubbly. Stir in the evaporated milk, water and instant chicken broth; continue cooking and stirring until the mixture thickens and bubbles 3 minutes.
2. Beat egg yolk slightly in a small bowl; slowly beat in half of the hot mixture, then beat back into remaining mixture in pan. Cook, stirring constantly, 1 minute. (Do not boil.) Stir in cheese until melted.
SUGGESTED VARIATION: For PARMESAN SAUCE: Prepare recipe above, using ¼ cup of grated Parmesan cheese. Stir in ¼ cup chopped parsley.

SUPREME SAUCE

Whipped cream folded into this sauce adds the gourmet touch.

Makes ¾ cup

 2 tablespoons butter or margarine
 2 tablespoons all-purpose flour
 1 envelope or teaspoon instant chicken broth
 ½ cup milk
 ¼ cup heavy cream

1. Melt butter or margarine in a small saucepan; stir in flour and instant broth. Cook, stirring constantly, just until bubbly.
2. Stir in milk; continue cooking and stirring until sauce thickens and bubbles 3 minutes; remove from heat.
3. Beat cream until stiff in a small bowl; fold into sauce.

POULTRY GIBLET GRAVY

With broth ready ahead of time, gravy goes together quickly.

Makes about 4 cups.

    Giblets
 1 medium-size onion, chopped (½ cup)
    Few celery leaves
 1 teaspoon salt
 1 bay leaf
 4 cups water
 ½ cup fat from roast poultry
 ½ cup all-purpose flour
    Salt and pepper

1. Combine giblets except liver, onion, celery leaves, 1 teaspoon salt, bay leaf and 4 cups water in a large saucepan. Simmer 1 hour and 40 minutes; add liver, simmer 20 minutes longer, or until meat is tender.
2. Strain broth; measure; add water, if necessary, to make 4 cups. Reserve.
3. Chop giblets fine and stir into broth. Cool, then chill until ready to make gravy.
4. After poultry has been removed from roasting pan, remove rack, if used; tip pan and let fat rise in one corner. Pour all fat into a cup leaving juices in pan. Measure ½ cup fat and return to pan; blend in flour with a wire whip. Cook, stirring constantly, just until bubbly.
5. Stir in giblet broth and giblets; continue cooking and stirring, scraping baked-on juices from bottom and sides of pan, until gravy thickens and bubbles 3 minutes.
6. Taste and season with salt and pepper.

ORANGE SAUCE

Great over duckling or small roasting chickens.

Makes about 2 cups.

 ½ cup currant jelly
 ½ teaspoon grated onion
 ¼ teaspoon bottled red-pepper seasoning
 ¾ teaspoon salt
 ½ teaspoon dry mustard
 ¼ teaspoon ground ginger
 1 tablespoon chopped fresh dill
 1½ cups orange juice
 2 tablespoons cornstarch
 ¼ cup cold water

1. Heat currant jelly, onion, red-pepper seasoning, salt, dry mustard, ginger, dill and orange juice in a small saucepan until boiling.
2. Blend cornstarch with cold water and stir into mixture in saucepan. Cook, stirring constantly, until mixture thickens and bubbles 1 minute.

FLUFFY HOLLANDAISE SAUCE

Here's the real thing, and with our meticulous instructions it's easy to make.

Makes 2 cups.

 ½ cup (1 stick) butter or margarine
 ¼ cup hot water
 4 egg yolks
 2 tablespoons lemon juice
 ¼ teaspoon salt
    Dash cayenne pepper

1. Melt butter or margarine in top of a double boiler over simmering water; stir in hot water. Remove top from heat and set on work surface.
2. Add unbeaten egg yolks to butter all at once; beat with electric mixer or rotary beater 2 to 3 minutes, or until mixture is almost double in volume. Stir in lemon juice, salt and cayenne.
3. Place over simmering water again; cook, stirring constantly, 5 minutes, or until thickened. (Be sure water in lower part of double boiler does not touch the bottom of the upper part

or boil at any time during cooking. Overheating can curdle the sauce.)
4. Remove sauce from heat; let stand, uncovered, until serving time. To reheat: Place over simmering water again and stir lightly for 2 to 3 minutes. (In reheating, sauce may lose some of its fluffiness, but it will keep its golden-rich creaminess.)
SUGGESTED VARIATIONS: Try these other versions of Hollandaise on poultry and side dishes.

MOUSSELINE SAUCE: Makes 2 cups. This sauce is light and fluffy and so good on spinach, cauliflower, broccoli and asparagus and sliced chicken or turkey casseroles. Prepare half of the recipe for FLUFFY HOLLANDAISE SAUCE. Fold in 1 cup whipped cream. Heat over simmering water, stirring lightly once or twice just until hot.

FIGARO SAUCE: Makes 1 cup. Delicious as a sauce for leftover roast goose or duckling. Prepare half of the recipe for FLUFFY HOLLANDAISE SAUCE. Lightly fold in 1 tablespoon of bottled barbecue sauce.

SPRINGTIME SAUCE: Makes 2 cups. Great over baked potatoes stuffed with cubed chicken and peas. Prepare half of the recipe for FLUFFY HOLLANDAISE SAUCE. Lightly fold in 1 cup of whipped cream and 2 teaspoons finely cut chives.

PEANUT SAUCE

Peanut butter is the base of this mild sauce. Serve with broiled chicken.

Makes 1¼ cups.

- 1 small onion, chopped (¼ cup)
- 2 tablespoons peanut oil or vegetable oil
- ¼ teaspoon ground cardamom OR: seeds from 4 cardamom pods, crushed
- ½ cup cream-style peanut butter
- ¼ cup firmly packed brown sugar
- ¼ cup soy sauce
- ¼ cup lemon juice
- ¼ teaspoon bottled red-pepper seasoning

1. Sauté onion in oil just until soft in a small skillet; stir in cardamom. Let cool slightly.
2. Blend peanut butter with brown sugar in a small bowl; stir in soy sauce, lemon juice and red-pepper seasoning, then the cooled onion mixture.
3. Let stand at room temperature until serving time. If sauce becomes too thick, add a little hot water.

VELOUTÉ SAUCE

Excellent with chicken croquettes.

Makes 2 cups.

- ¼ cup (½ stick) butter or margarine
- ¼ cup all-purpose flour
- ⅛ teaspoon pepper
- 1 can (13¾ ounces) chicken broth
- ¼ cup water
- 1 teaspoon lemon juice

1. Melt butter or margarine in small saucepan; remove from heat.
2. Blend in flour and pepper; gradually stir in broth and water.
3. Cook over low heat, stirring constantly, until sauce thickens and bubbles 3 minutes; stir in lemon juice.

CAPE COD SAUCE

A spicy cranberry sauce for roast turkey or chicken. Any left over? Simply store in a covered jar in the refrigerator.

Makes about 2½ cups.

- 1 can (1 pound) jellied cranberry sauce
- ½ cup sugar
- 1 tablespoon curry powder
- 1 teaspoon salt
- 1 teaspoon ground cardamom
- ½ teaspoon ground ginger
- ½ cup cider vinegar
- 2 tablespoons dark molasses
- 1 tablespoon Worcestershire sauce

1. Break up cranberry sauce with a fork in a medium-size saucepan; blend in sugar, curry powder, salt, cardamom, ginger, vinegar, molasses and Worcestershire sauce.
2. Bring to boiling; simmer 5 minutes, stirring often; remove from the heat; beat until blended.

GUACAMOLE SAUCE

Serve this versatile avocado sauce over hearts of lettuce and slices of cold turkey.

Makes 2 cups.

- 1 medium-size avocado, peeled and pitted
- 1 large tomato, peeled, chopped and drained
- ¼ cup mayonnaise or salad dressing
- ¼ cup lemon juice
- 1 teaspoon grated onion
- 1 teaspoon salt
- ⅛ teaspoon bottled red-pepper seasoning

1. Mash avocado in a small bowl.
2. Blend in tomato, mayonnaise or salad dressing, lemon juice, onion, salt and the red-pepper seasoning.

Cover tightly and chill. (The sauce will keep its bright green color for several hours before serving.)

SWEET SOUR SAUCE

You can have the flavors of Polynesian restaurant at home, when you combine this sauce with chicken and vegetable dishes.

Makes about 2 cups.

- ⅓ cup firmly packed brown sugar
- 3 tablespoons cornstarch
- 1 cup pineapple juice
- 3 tablespoons cider vinegar
- 3 tablespoons soy sauce

Combine brown sugar, cornstarch, pineapple juice, vinegar and soy sauce in a small saucepan. Cook, stirring constantly, until sauce thickens and bubbles 1 minute.

CUMBERLAND SAUCE

It's slightly sweet, slightly spicy and delicious with roast chicken or goose.

Makes 1 cup.

- ⅔ cup currant jelly
- 1 tablespoon grated lemon rind
- ¼ cup lemon juice
- 1 teaspoon grated onion
- 1 teaspoon dry mustard
- ½ teaspoon ground ginger

1. Combine jelly, lemon rind and lemon juice, onion, mustard and ginger in a small saucepan.
2. Heat slowly, stirring constantly, just until the jelly melts and sauce is blended. Serve warm.

STROGANOFF SAUCE

Use to top chicken cutlets or to dress up leftover turkey.

Makes 3 cups.

- 1 small onion, chopped (¼ cup)
- 1 tablespoon butter or margarine
- 1 can (10¾ ounces) chicken gravy
- 1 can (3 or 4 ounces) sliced mushrooms, drained
- 1 container (8 ounces) dairy sour cream

1. Sauté onion in butter or margarine just until soft in a small saucepan; stir in the chicken gravy and the mushrooms. Heat, stirring constantly, just to boiling; remove from heat.
2. Stir ½ cup of the hot sauce into sour cream in a small bowl; stir into remaining sauce in saucepan. Heat and stir just until hot. Serve with noodles and cooked turkey.

Accompaniments

MASHED BUTTERNUT SQUASH AND YAMS

Yams were grown in our southern colonies, principally Virginia, while squash, especially the large winter Hubbard, was grown throughout the New England colonies. They make a delicious combination in the following recipe. Photo on page 19.

Makes 8 servings.

```
2  pounds butternut squash
2  pounds yams or sweet potatoes
¼  cup (½ stick) butter or margarine,
     melted
1  teaspoon salt
½  teaspoon ground ginger
¼  teaspoon pepper
```

1. Pare squash, cut in half, remove seeds, cut into 1-inch pieces.
2. Pare yams or sweet potatoes, cut into 1-inch pieces.
3. Combine squash and yams, boiling water and salt in a large saucepan. Bring to boiling; lower heat; cook 25 minutes or until vegetables are tender. Drain.
4. Whip vegetables with butter or margarine, salt, ginger and pepper in a large bowl with a wire whisk or at high speed with an electric mixer until smooth and fluffy. Serve hot.
COOK'S TIP: To prepare in advance, place squash and yams in a buttered 8-cup casserole; cover; refrigerate. To heat: Place covered in a moderate oven (325°) for 50 minutes.

ORANGE-LEMON CRANBERRY RELISH

A lightly spiced, refreshing accompaniment to a holiday meal. Two centuries ago, oranges were transplanted to Florida by the Spanish settlers. Photo on page 18.

Makes 5 cups.

```
4  cups (1 pound) fresh or frozen
     cranberries
1  large orange, quartered and
     seeded
1  lemon, quartered and seeded
1½ cups sugar
1  teaspoon ground cinnamon
½  teaspoon ground cloves
```

1. Wash cranberries; drain and remove any stems. Put cranberries, orange and lemon quarters through coarse blade of food chopper.
2. Add sugar, cinnamon and cloves to cranberry mixture in a large bowl; mix thoroughly. Cover. Refrigerate several hours or overnight.

MAPLE-BUTTER GLAZED CARROTS

In Colonial days maple syrup was the popular native-grown sweetener in the years before refined sugar. Molasses, which was very strong and dark, had to be imported from the West Indies. Pictured on page 19.

Makes 8 servings.

```
1  cup water
1  teaspoon salt
2  pounds carrots, pared, cut in half
     crosswise
¼  cup maple syrup
¼  cup (½ stick) butter or margarine
1  teaspoon leaf marjoram, crumbled
1  teaspoon salt
¼  teaspoon pepper
```

1. Bring water and 1 teaspoon salt to boiling in a medium-size heavy saucepan. Add carrots; return to boiling; cover. Simmer 15 to 20 minutes or until carrots are just tender. Drain thoroughly.
2. Cook maple syrup, butter, marjoram, salt and pepper in a large skillet over low heat 2 or 3 minutes or until bubbly and caramel-like in consistency.
3. Add carrots. Toss gently to coat in the maple butter. Cook over high heat, tossing gently, until carrots are glazed and liquid is absorbed.
4. Keep warm in covered skillet, if prepared ahead.

HARVEST PUMPKIN SOUP

The American Indians were already growing crops of pumpkin, squash and corn when the colonists arrived. The colonists used pumpkin and squash not only for pies but as a vegetable and for soups. Pictured on page 19 at the back of table.

Makes 8 servings.

```
1  large onion, sliced
2  tablespoons butter or margarine
2  cans (13¾ ounces each) chicken
     broth
1  can (1 pound) pumpkin
1  teaspoon salt
¾  teaspoon ground cinnamon
¼  teaspoon ground nutmeg
⅛  teaspoon pepper
1  cup light cream
```

1. Sauté onion in butter in a large saucepan until soft, about 5 minutes. Add 1 can chicken broth; bring to boiling; cover; simmer 10 minutes.
2. Place ½ cup of the onion mixture in container of electric blender; cover. Whirl until smooth. Add remaining onion broth mixture and whirl until smooth. Return to saucepan.
3. Add remaining can of chicken broth, pumpkin, salt, cinnamon, nutmeg and pepper to saucepan. Stir until smooth. Bring to boiling; cover. Lower heat; simmer 10 minutes.
4. Slowly stir in cream; heat just until thoroughly hot. Garnish with CINNAMON-SUGAR TOAST TRIANGLES.

CINNAMON-SUGAR TOAST TRIANGLES: Blend 3 tablespoons softened butter or margarine with 1 tablespoon sugar and ½ teaspoon ground cinnamon in a small bowl. Spread generously on 4 slices of cracked wheat or whole-wheat bread. Place on a cooky sheet. Bake in a hot oven (400°) 8 minutes. Cut each bread slice into 4 triangles.

STUFFED ONIONS

Corn was a staple in the diet of the colonists, who had been taught by the Indians how to grow it. Combined with sausage, it makes an excellent filling for sweet onions. Pictured on page 18.

Bake at 400° for 20 minutes.
Makes 8 servings.

```
8  large sweet Spanish onions, peeled
½  pound bulk pork sausage
1  cup soft white bread crumbs
     (2 slices)
2  tablespoons chopped parsley
1  can (8 ounces) whole-kernel corn,
     drained
2  tablespoons butter or margarine
½  teaspoon paprika
```

1. Cut a slice from top of each onion; with a small knife, scoop out enough to leave a cavity about 1 to 1½ inches deep. Reserve scooped-out onion. Place onions in large kettle or saucepan with enough salted water to just cover; bring to boiling. Lower heat; simmer, covered, 20 minutes or until just tender. (Do not overcook.) Drain well.
2. Chop enough of the reserved onion to make ½ cup. Sauté sausage meat until brown in small skillet, break into small pieces with fork; drain off excess fat. Add chopped onion; sauté, stirring often until soft, 6 to 8 minutes. Remove from heat; stir in breadcrumbs, parsley and corn.
3. Melt butter or margarine in a shallow casserole in oven; stir in paprika. Brush onto onions to coat well, then fill onions with sausage mixture; arrange in same dish. Cover loosely with aluminum foil.
4. Bake in hot oven (400°) 15 minutes; uncover and bake 5 minutes longer or until heated through and filling is lightly browned.

REFRIED BEANS

Mashed beans are mixed with bacon fat and fried in a skillet until thick and delicious. This is the classic Mexican side dish.

Makes 6 servings.

2 cans (1 pound each) pinto beans, drained
½ cup bacon fat
Shredded Cheddar cheese

1. Mash beans well in a medium-size bowl; stir in bacon fat.
2. Cook in a large heavy skillet over medium heat, stirring constantly, until beans thicken and fat has been absorbed. Serve with shredded Cheddar cheese.

FRIED SWEET POTATO SHREDS

Just a few sprinkled over turkey and pilaf add a pleasingly crunchy contrast.

Makes 8 servings.

2 large sweet potatoes
Shortening or vegetable oil for frying

1. Pare sweet potatoes, then shred finely; pat dry on paper towels.
2. Melt enough shortening or pour in enough oil to make a 2-inch depth in a small saucepan; heat to 350° on a deep-fat thermometer, or until a cube of bread turns golden in 1 minute.
3. Fry shredded potatoes, a heaping tablespoonful at a time, 1 to 2 minutes, or until crisp. Lift out with a slotted spoon; drain well on paper towels. Serve warm.

TURKEY TIME PEARS

A festive addition to poultry platters that's delicious to eat, as well.

Bake at 325° for 30 minutes.
Makes 8 servings.

1 can (1 pound) jellied cranberry sauce
½ cup orange juice
4 fresh Bartlett pears

1. Melt cranberry jelly in a small saucepan over low heat; blend in orange juice.
2. Halve pears lengthwise; remove core with melon baller or half-teaspoon measure and cut out remainder towards stem and blossom ends. About ½ hour before turkey is done, arrange pears, cut-sides up in roasting pan around turkey or in separate baking pan. Spoon cranberry glaze liberally over pears.
3. Bake in slow oven (325°) 30 minutes, spooning on any remaining glaze during baking. Garnish turkey platter with pears, and, if desired, twisted orange slices.

VEGETABLE BOUQUET

Add a Victorian touch with this bouquet that is eatable too. Pictured on page 40.

Makes 1 bouquet.

1 pound fresh green peas
1 bunch radishes, washed and trimmed
Cauliflower
Parsley

Measure an 18-inch piece of florist's wire and thread on green peas to a 10 inch length; turn to form a circle and twist wires to secure. Measure a 14 inch piece of florist's wire and thread on radishes, root-ends up, to make a 7-inch length; turn to form a circle and twist wires to secure. Place radish ring inside pea pod ring and place a 4-inch cauliflower flowerette in center. Wrap a paper doily around "bouquet" using extra wire to secure in place; place in a low glass bowl and tuck parsley springs around edge to hide wire.

HERBED PILAF

Pan-toasted rice and bulgur wheat make this delectable accompaniment for poultry.

Makes 8 servings.

1 cup uncooked long-grain rice
¼ cup peanut oil or vegetable oil
1 large onion, chopped (1 cup)
1 cup chopped celery
4 envelopes instant chicken broth OR: 4 chicken bouillon cubes
1 teaspoon leaf rosemary, crumbled
4 cups water
1 cup bulgur wheat pilaf (from a 12-ounce package)

1. Sauté rice, stirring constantly, in oil until golden in an electric frypan set at 375°; remove with a slotted spoon. Stir onion and celery into drippings in pan; sauté just until soft.
2. Stir in chicken broth or bouillon cubes, rosemary, and water; bring to boiling, crushing cubes, if using, with a spoon. Stir in bulgur wheat and browned rice; cover. Lower frypan heat to 200°.
3. Simmer, stirring once or twice, 1 hour, or until liquid is absorbed and wheat and rice are fluffy-tender.

COOK'S TIP: This recipe can be made in a large heavy saucepan on a surface burner, if you wish.

GOLDEN SPICED PEACHES

Jiffy-quick to fix and so good with turkey.

Makes 8 servings.

1 can (1 pound) cling peach halves
1 tablespoon mixed pickling spices

1. Drain syrup from peaches into a small saucepan; stir in pickling spices. Bring to boiling, then simmer 5 minutes.
2. Strain syrup over peaches; cover; chill several hours or overnight to blend flavors.

ARTICHOKE HEARTS

A quick side-dish that is a most satisfactory accompaniment for chicken. Pictured on page 61.

Bake at 350° for 30 minutes.
Makes 4 servings.

2 cans (7 ½ ounces each) artichoke hearts
1 cup soft Italian bread crumbs
½ cup grated Romano cheese
½ teaspoon salt
¼ teaspoon pepper
½ teaspoon leaf oregano, crumbled
¼ cup olive oil

1. Place artichoke hearts in baking pan. Combine bread crumbs, cheese, salt, pepper and oregano. Cover artichokes with crumb mixture. Pour olive oil over. Sprinkle with a few drops of water.
2. Bake in moderate oven (350°) until bread crumbs are golden brown, about 30 minutes.

CROSTINI SALVATORE
(Italian Canapes)

Savory little appetizers that go together so fast. Pictured on page 61.

Bake at 350° for 5 minutes.
Makes 4 servings.

4 thin slices French or Italian bread, toasted and cut in half
8 thin slices mozzarella cheese
8 thin slices of prosciutto
8 thin slices tomato
8 roast pepper strips
1 tablespoon butter
¼ teaspoon leaf oregano, crumbled

1. Put bread on a small cooky sheet. Place mozzarella, prosciutto, tomato and roast pepper on bread, in that order. Put small piece of butter on each and sprinkle with oregano.
2. Bake in moderate oven (350°) 5 minutes, or until heated through and cheese melts.

WINTER GARDEN SALAD TRAY

Marinated vegetables make an easy, yet colorful addition to the buffet table. This has a Scandinavian look.

Makes 12 servings.

- **5 medium-size carrots**
- **1 package (10 ounces) frozen lima beans**
- **1 can (1 pound) whole green beans, drained**
- **2 cans (3 or 4 ounces each) whole mushrooms, drained**
- **1 envelope (about 1 ounce) Italian salad-dressing mix**
- **1 envelope (about 1 ounce) onion salad-dressing mix**
  Vegetable oil
  Vinegar
- **1 large cucumber**
- **1 large sweet onion**
- **¼ cup cider vinegar**
- **¼ cup water**
- **1 teaspoon salt**
- **¼ teaspoon pepper**
- **1 jar (about 1 pound) sliced pickled beets, drained**

1. Pare carrots, then cut into 3-inch-long sticks. Cook, covered, in small amount boiling salted water in small saucepan 10 minutes, or until crisply tender; drain. Cook lima beans, following label directions; drain.
2. Place carrots, limas, green beans, and mushrooms in separate piles in large shallow dish.
3. Prepare Italian and onion salad-dressing mixes with oil, vinegar, and water, following label directions for each, then combine and mix well. Pour over vegetables; cover. Chill at least an hour to season and blend flavors.
4. Score rind of cucumber with a fork; slice cucumber thin. Peel and slice onion, then separate into rings. Place each in separate piles in shallow dish. Mix the ¼ cup vinegar, water, salt, and pepper in a cup; pour over vegetables; cover. Chill at least an hour to season and blend flavors.
5. When ready to serve, spoon up vegetables, 1 at a time, with slotted spoon; let dressings drain back into dishes. Arrange each, along with pickled beets, in separate piles or rows on a large shallow platter or tray. (Save any Italian-onion salad dressing that's left over in vegetable dish for salad for another meal.)
SUGGESTED VARIATIONS: This recipe can be your guide to an assortment of delicious vegetable platters. Substitute cooked zucchini, yellow squash or asparagus spears for the carrots, lima beans and green beans, if you wish.

Chapter 1 (from page 10)

CHUTNEY CHICKEN

Choose this when you want an exotic company dish.

Bake at 350° for 1 hour.
Makes 4 servings.

- **1 broiler-fryer (about 3 pounds)**
- **1 teaspoon salt**
- **1 can (8¼ ounces) crushed pineapple**
- **½ cup chopped chutney**
- **½ cup coarsely chopped pecans**
- **¼ cup prepared mustard**

1. Cut up chicken, following directions on page 103. Sprinkle with salt. Place, skin-side up, in a single layer in an 8-cup shallow casserole, just before baking.
2. Mix together pineapple, chutney, pecans and mustard in a small bowl; spoon over chicken.
3. Bake in moderate oven (350°) for 1 hour, or until chicken is tender and well glazed.

ONION ROAST CHICKEN

You can be sure of a moist and flavorful bird, when you use plastic cooking bags.

Roast at 350° for 1 hour.
Makes 4 servings.

- **1 broiler-fryer (about 3 pounds)**
- **¾ teaspoon salt**
- **¼ teaspoon pepper**
- **1 teaspoon leaf rosemary, crumbled**
- **1 can (1 pound) small boiled onions, drained**
- **2 tablespoons butter or margarine**
- **½ cup cold water**
- **¼ cup all-purpose flour**

1. Rub chicken inside and out with salt, pepper and rosemary.
2. Place onions and butter in cavity of the chicken. Tie legs with string to secure onions.
3. Place in a 10x16-inch plastic cooking bag and seal, following label directions. Place in a shallow roasting pan.
4. Bake in a moderate oven (350°) 1 hour, or until skin is golden.
5. Open plastic cooking bag carefully; place chicken on heated platter; keep warm.
6. Pour juices in cooking bag into a medium-size saucepan; bring to boiling. Stir cold water into flour in a cup until smooth. Stir into bubbling juices; cook, stirring constantly, until mixture bubbles 3 minutes. Add a little bottled gravy coloring, if you wish. Pass in heated gravy boat.

OLD-FASHIONED CHICKEN PIE

It's so good, it's no wonder this dish has been around for ages.

Bake at 400° for 30 minutes.
Makes 8 servings.

- **2 broiler-fryers (about 2½ pounds each)**
  Water
- **2 teaspoons salt**
- **¼ teaspoon pepper**
- **2 cups sliced carrots**
- **1 package (10 ounces) frozen peas**
- **¼ cup (½ stick) butter or margarine**
- **⅓ cup all-purpose flour**
- **1½ cups biscuit mix**
- **½ cup dairy sour cream**
- **1 egg**
- **2 teaspoons sesame seeds**

1. Place chickens in a large heavy skillet or Dutch oven; add 2 cups water, salt, pepper and carrots. Bring to boiling; reduce heat; cover; simmer 45 minutes. Add peas; simmer 15 minutes longer, or until chicken is tender. Remove chicken; cool.
2. Skim fat from chicken broth-vegetable mixture; reserve 2 tablespoons fat. Melt butter or margarine with reserved chicken fat in a medium-size saucepan; stir in flour; cook, stirring constantly, just until bubbly. Stir in chicken broth-vegetable mixture; continue cooking and stirring until gravy thickens and bubbles 3 minutes.
3. When chickens are cool enough to handle, pull off skin and slip meat from bones; cut meat into bite-size pieces; stir into gravy; pour into an 8x8x2-inch baking dish.
4. Combine biscuit mix and sour cream in a small bowl; stir to form a stiff dough; turn out onto a lightly floured board; knead a few times; roll out dough to ¼-inch thickness; trim to make an 8½-inch square; cut into 8 strips, each about one inch wide.
5. Using 4 of the strips, make a lattice design on top of the chicken mixture, spacing evenly and attaching ends firmly to edges of the dish. Place remaining strips, one at a time, on edges of dish, pinching dough to make a stand-up rim; flute rim. (Or, roll out dough to a 9-inch square and place over chicken mixture; turn edges under, flush with rim; flute to make a stand-up rim. Cut slits near center.)
6. Combine egg with 1 tablespoon water in a cup; mix with a fork until well blended; brush mixture over strips and rim; sprinkle with seeds.
7. Bake in hot oven (400°) 30 minutes, or until chicken mixture is bubbly-hot and crust is golden. Serve immediately.

COUNTRY CHICKEN FRICASSEE

Serve this fricassee with homemade gravy over hot biscuits.

Makes 6 servings.

- **1 stewing chicken (about 5 pounds)**
- **½ cup sliced celery**
- **1 large onion, sliced**
- **2 medium-size carrots, pared and sliced**
- **1 bay leaf**
- **½ teaspoon peppercorns**
- **1 tablespoon salt**
- **4 cups water**
- **2 tablespoons butter or margarine**
- **½ cup all-purpose flour**
- **1 can (3 or 4 ounces) sliced mushrooms, drained**

1. Cut chicken into serving-size pieces, following directions on page 103. Place chicken in kettle or Dutch oven; add celery, onion, carrots, bay leaf, peppercorns, salt and water to cover. Bring to boiling; reduce heat; cover. Simmer 1 hour, 30 minutes, or until chicken is tender.
2. Remove chicken to heated deep serving dish; keep hot while making gravy.
3. Strain broth into a large bowl; let stand until fat rises to top. Skim off fat, then measure 6 tablespoons back into kettle; reserve broth.
4. Heat the butter or margarine with the chicken fat until melted. Blend flour into fat; cook, stirring constantly, just until bubbly. Stir in 4 cups of the broth and mushrooms.
5. Cook, stirring constantly, until gravy thickens and bubbles 1 minute. Pour over the chicken.

PARTY CHICKEN AMANDINE

A creamy chicken dish topped with almonds, festive enough for all occasions.

Makes 12 servings.

- **Simmered Chicken (recipe follows)**
- **½ cup (1 stick) butter or margarine**
- **1½ pounds mushrooms, sliced**
- **⅔ cup all-purpose flour**
- **3 cups light cream**
- **1½ teaspoons salt**
- **¼ teaspoon bottled red-pepper seasoning**
- **Rice Ring (recipe follows)**
- **½ cup toasted slivered almonds**

1. Prepare SIMMERED CHICKEN. Melt butter or margarine in a large saucepan over low heat. Add mushrooms and cook, stirring occasionally, 10 minutes. Add flour; stir to blend.

2. Add reserved chicken broth and cream. Cook, stirring constantly, until mixture thickens and bubbles 3 minutes.
3. Stir in salt, red-pepper seasoning, chicken; heat until bubbly. Turn mixture into RICE RING; sprinkle with almonds.

Van Dak.

SIMMERED CHICKEN

- **3 broiler-fryers (2½ pounds each)**
- **3 cups water**
- **3 small onions, sliced**
- **6 celery leaves**
- **3 bay leaves**
- **2 teaspoons monosodium glutamate**
- **2 teaspoons salt**

1. Put chickens in large kettle with tight-fitting lid. Add water, onion, celery leaves, bay leaves, monosodium glutamate and salt; cover. Bring to a boil; reduce heat and simmer 1 hour, or until tender.
2. Remove from heat; strain stock and reserve. (You should have 3 cups.) Remove meat from bones in as large pieces as possible. (You should have 6 cups.)

RICE RING: Press 12 cups hot cooked rice into 12-cup ring mold. Turn out on large platter.

DAPPLED DUMPLING FRICASSEE

Kettle chicken cooked tender, served with gravy and topped with parsley-sprigged dumplings.

Makes 6 servings.

- **1 stewing chicken (about 5 pounds)**
- **4½ cups cold water**
- **1 large onion, sliced**
- **1 cup chopped celery and leaves**
- **1 medium-size carrot, pared and sliced**
- **2 teaspoons salt**
- **¼ teaspoon pepper**
- **⅓ cup all-purpose flour**
- **Dappled Dumplings (recipe follows)**

1. Cut up stewing chicken, following directions on page 103. Combine chicken, 4 cups water, onion, celery and leaves, carrot, salt and pepper in a large kettle or Dutch oven. Cover; bring to boiling; lower heat; simmer 1½ to 2 hours, or until chicken is fork-tender.
2. Remove from broth; cool slightly, slip off skin, if you wish. Strain and measure broth; add water, if needed, to make 4 cups. Press vegetables through strainer into broth in kettle; bring to boiling.

3. Stir ½ cup cold water into flour in cup to make a smooth paste; stir into hot broth. Cook, stirring constantly, until gravy thickens and bubbles 3 minutes. Season with salt and pepper to taste, if needed.
4. Return chicken to gravy in kettle; bring slowly to boiling while stirring up DAPPLED DUMPLINGS.
5. Drop dough in 12 mounds on top of steaming chicken. Cook, covered, 20 minutes. (No peeking, or the dumplings won't puff properly.)
6. Arrange chicken and dumplings on a heated serving platter; pass gravy.

DAPPLED DUMPLINGS: Makes 12 dumplings. Sift 2 cups all-purpose flour, 1 tablespoon baking powder and 1 teaspoon salt into medium-size bowl. Cut in 2 tablespoons shortening with pastry blender until mixture is crumbly. Stir in ¼ cup chopped parsley and 1 cup milk just until flour is moistened. (Dough will be soft.) You can substitute parsley flakes.

ARROZ CON POLLO

Chicken with rice, Spanish style, includes tomatoes, onion, mushrooms, pimiento—and a nip of garlic.

Bake at 350° for 1 hour.
Makes 4 servings.

- **1 broiler-fryer, cut up (about 3 pounds)**
- **¼ cup olive oil or vegetable oil**
- **1 cup uncooked rice**
- **1 large onion, chopped (1 cup)**
- **2 cloves garlic, minced**
- **6 strands saffron, crushed**
- **2 cans (about 1 pound each) tomatoes**
- **1 can (3 or 4 ounces) chopped mushrooms**
- **1 can (about 4 ounces) pimiento, diced**
- **2 tablespoons chopped parsley**
- **1½ teaspoons salt**
- **¼ teaspoon pepper**

1. Brown chicken on all sides in hot oil in large heavy skillet; drain on paper towels; place in 12-cup casserole.
2. Sauté rice in same pan, stirring often, about 5 minutes, or until golden-brown; add onion and garlic; sauté over low heat 10 minutes.
3. Stir in saffron, tomatoes, mushrooms, diced pimiento, parsley, salt and pepper; bring to boiling.
4. Pour hot tomato mixture over chicken in casserole; cover.
5. Bake in moderate over (350°) 30 minutes; uncover; bake 30 minutes longer, or until chicken is tender.

POULTRY POINTERS

- To save money on cooking fuel, roast two 3-pound chickens, rather than one 6 pound roasting chicken. They usually cost less than the roaster and will be cooked in about half the time.
- Sauces and gravies will be higher in nutrition, as well as flavor, if you substitute vegetables as potatoes, carrots, green beans or peas for all or part of the liquid in the sauce or gravy recipe. Taste before seasoning with salt and pepper.
- To get a golden crisp skin on poultry roasted in a plastic cooking bag, carefully slit the bag across the top for the last 20 minutes of cooking time.
- Chefs never waste a bit of the bird, not even the baked-on pan juices. Deglaze the skillet or roasting pan after cooking poultry by adding wine, broth or water to the pan bring to boiling, stirring all the time, to loosen all the bits of cooked-on juices. This liquid can be poured over the poultry as is, or it can be the basis of a sauce or gravy to serve with the bird.

BRUNSWICK CHICKEN

A chicken dish from Colonial days.

Bake at 350° for 1 hour, 30 minutes.
Makes 8 servings.

- 2 broiler-fryers (about 3 pounds each)
- ½ cup all-purpose flour
- 1 envelope (1 ounce) herb salad-dressing mix
- ¼ cup vegetable shortening
- 1 large onion, chopped (1 cup)
- 1 can (1 pound, 12 ounces) tomatoes
- 1 package (10 ounces) frozen whole-kernel corn, thawed
- 1 package (10 ounces) frozen Fordhook lima beans, thawed

1. Cut-up chickens, following directions on page 103. Shake chicken in mixture of flour and salad-dressing mix in a plastic bag to coat well; reserve remaining seasoned flour. Brown, a few pieces at a time, in shortening in large skillet; arrange in a 12-cup casserole.
2. Sauté onion in same pan; blend in seasoned flour; stir in tomatoes. Bring to boiling, stirring constantly.
3. Spoon corn and lima beans around chicken in casserole; pour tomato sauce over; cover.
4. Bake in moderate oven (350°) 1 hour, 30 minutes, or until tender.

BRIDIE'S REALLY GREAT CHICKEN

This oven-baked chicken is one of Bridie Donohue's specialties. It is quick to prepare and a treat to eat.

Bake at 375° for 1 hour.
Makes 4 servings.

- 1 broiler-fryer (about 3 pounds)
- 1 leek, washed and thinly sliced (1 cup)
  OR: 1 large onion, chopped (1 cup)
- 1 can condensed golden mushroom soup
- 3 tablespoons butter or margarine
- 1 can (3 or 4 ounces) chopped mushrooms
- ¼ cup dry white wine or water

1. Cut chicken into serving-size pieces, following directions on page 103. Arrange in single layer in a 13x9x2-inch baking dish. Sauté leek or onion in butter or margarine until soft in a large skillet; stir in soup, mushrooms and liquid and wine or water; stir to blend well. Spoon over chicken pieces.
2. Bake in moderate oven (375°) 1 hour, or until chicken is tender and richly browned. Serve with oven-baked acorn squash and baked potatoes, if you wish.

CRISSCROSS CHICKEN PIE

This would be grandmother's idea of a stick-to-the-ribs dinner.

Bake at 400° for 20 minutes, then at 350° for 25 minutes.
Makes 6 servings.

- 1 broiler-fryer (3 pounds)
- 3 cups water
  Handful celery leaves
- 2 teaspoons salt
- 6 peppercorns
  Curry Cream Sauce (recipe follows)
- 1 package (10 ounces) frozen peas, cooked and drained
- 1 pimiento, chopped
- 2 cups sifted all-purpose flour
- ⅓ cup shortening
- ⅔ cup milk

1. Simmer chicken with water, celery leaves, 1 teaspoon of the salt and peppercorns in kettle 1 hour, or until tender. Remove from broth and cool.
2. Strain broth into a 4-cup measure; add water, if needed, to make 3 cups. Make CURRY CREAM SAUCE.
3. Slip skin from chicken, then remove meat from bones. (It comes off easily while still warm.) Cut into bite-size pieces; toss with peas, pimiento and 2 cups of CURRY CREAM SAUCE in medium-size bowl.
4. Sift flour and remaining 1 tea-

spoon salt into medium-size bowl; cut in shortening with pastry blender until mixture is crumbly; stir in milk with a fork just until dough holds together.
5. Turn out onto lightly floured pastry cloth or board; knead lightly 5 or 6 times. Roll out ⅔ of dough to rectangle, 16x12 inches; fit into a 10x6x2-inch baking dish. Spoon filling into shell.
6. Roll out remaining pastry to a rectangle about 14x7 inches; cut into 9 long strips, each about ¾-inch wide, with knife or pastry wheel. Lay 5 strips lengthwise over filling. Halve remaining 4 strips; weave across long strips to make a crisscross top. Trim overhang to 1 inch; fold under; flute.
7. Bake in hot oven (400°) 20 minutes; reduce heat to moderate (350°). Bake 25 minutes longer, or until golden. Cut into 6 servings. Serve with remaining hot CURRY CREAM SAUCE.

CURRY CREAM SAUCE: Makes about 4½ cups. Melt ⅓ cup butter or margarine over low heat in medium-size saucepan. Stir in ⅓ cup all-purpose flour, 1 teaspoon salt, 1 teaspoon curry powder and ⅛ teaspoon pepper. Cook, stirring all the time, just until mixture bubbles. Stir in 3 cups chicken broth slowly; continue cooking and stirring until sauce thickens and bubbles 3 minutes. Stir in 1 tall can evaporated milk.

SAN ANGEL POLLO RANCHERO

Ranch-house chicken, Mexican-style, is not plain or rustic, but spicy and sophisticated.

Roast at 375° for 1 hour, 30 minutes.
Makes 12 servings.

- 3 broiler-fryers (2½ to 3 pounds each)
- 3 cups dry white wine
- 3 cloves garlic, minced
- 2 teaspoons salt
- 1 teaspoon leaf marjoram, crumbled
- 1 teaspoon pepper
- ⅓ cup lard or butter or margarine, melted
  Refried Beans (recipe, page 94)

1. Soak chicken in a marinade of wine, garlic, salt, marjoram and pepper in a large plastic bag for 4 hours, turning frequently. Remove; pat dry.
2. Brush chickens with melted lard or butter or margarine.
3. Roast in moderate oven (375°) 1 hour, 30 minutes, basting often with pan drippings and marinade.
4. Serve on REFRIED BEANS.

PAPRIKASH CHICKEN

The delicious combining of paprika-flavored chicken in sour cream with noodles is one of Hungary's great contributions to the world of food.

Makes 8 servings.

- 2 broiler-fryers (about 3 pounds each)
- 1 large onion, chopped (1 cup)
- 2 tablespoons butter or margarine
- 2 tablespoons paprika
- 1 tablespoon all-purpose flour
- 1 tablespoon salt
- ¼ teaspoon pepper
- 1 can (8 ounces) tomatoes
- 1 package (1 pound) noodles
- 1 container (8 ounces) dairy sour cream
- 1 tablespoon chopped parsley

1. Cut the chicken into serving-size pieces, following cutting directions on page 103.
2. Sauté onion in butter or margarine until soft in a large skillet. Stir in paprika and flour; cook, stirring constantly, 1 minute. Stir in salt, pepper and tomatoes, breaking with spoon.
3. Add chicken and giblets (except livers), turning to coat pieces well; cover. Simmer 30 minutes. Turn chicken pieces; add livers; simmer 15 minutes longer, or until tender.
4. Meanwhile, cook noodles, following label directions; drain; spoon onto hot serving platter. Remove chicken from skillet with a slotted spoon. Arrange on platter with noodles; keep warm while making sauce.
5. Spoon sour cream into medium-size bowl. Bring sauce in skillet to boiling; stir slowly into sour cream, blending well. Garnish with parsley.

CREOLE JAMBALAYA

Rice from the fields of southwestern Louisiana is the backbone of this one-dish meal —a favorite as old as New Orleans itself.

Makes 8 servings.

- 1 broiler-fryer (about 2½ pounds)
- 2 cups water
- 3 teaspoons salt
- ¼ teaspoon pepper
- 1 bay leaf
- 2 large onions, chopped (2 cups)
- 1 large clove garlic, crushed
- ¼ cup (½ stick) butter or margarine
- 2 cups cubed cooked ham
- 1 can (1 pound, 12 ounces) tomatoes
- 1 large green pepper, halved, seeded, and chopped
- ½ teaspoon leaf thyme, crumbled
- ¼ teaspoon cayenne pepper
- 1 cup uncooked rice

1. Place chicken in a large kettle or Dutch oven; add water, salt, pepper, and bay leaf; bring to boiling; reduce heat; cover.
2. Simmer 45 minutes, or until chicken is tender; remove chicken from broth; reserve. When cool enough to handle, remove meat from bones; cut into cubes; reserve.
3. Pour broth into a 2-cup measure; remove bay leaf; add water, if necessary, to make 2 cups; reserve.
4. Sauté onions and garlic in butter or margarine until soft in same kettle; add ham, tomatoes, green pepper, thyme, cayenne, and reserved chicken and broth. Bring to boiling; stir in rice; reduce heat; cover. Simmer 20 minutes, or until rice is tender and most of the liquid is absorbed.
5. Serve in large bowls. Sprinkle generously with chopped parsley and serve with crusty French bread.

STUFFED CRÊPES

You don't have to wait for a special occasion to serve crêpes.

Bake at 400° for 40 minutes.
Makes 8 individual casseroles.

- 2 broiler-fryers (about 2½ pounds each)
- 3 cups water
- 1 medium-size onion, sliced
- Handful celery leaves
- 3 teaspoons salt
- 6 peppercorns
- ⅓ cup liquid margarine
- ⅓ cup all-purpose flour
- 1 tall can evaporated milk
- ¼ teaspoon white pepper
- ⅔ cup grated Parmesan cheese
- Crêpes (recipe follows)

1. Combine chickens, water, onion, celery leaves, 2 teaspoons of the salt and peppercorns in a large kettle. Bring to boiling; lower heat; cover kettle. Simmer 45 minutes, or until chickens are tender.
2. Remove chickens from broth; strain and reserve broth. Slip skin from chicken; remove meat from bones; cut into tiny pieces; place in a medium-size bowl; reserve.
3. Combine liquid margarine and flour in a large saucepan. Cook, stirring constantly, 3 minutes, over medium heat. Stir in reserved broth, evaporated milk, remaining 1 teaspoon salt and pepper.
4. Cook, stirring constantly, until mixture thickens and bubbles 3 minutes. Add 1½ cups of sauce to chicken. Stir ⅓ cup of the cheese into remaining sauce and reserve.

5. Unroll one crêpe at a time and spread with ¼ cup of chicken mixture. Place 2 filled crêpes in each of 8 individual freezer-to-oven casseroles or 1-cup disposable aluminum pans. Pour ¼ cup of reserved sauce over each set of crêpes and sprinkle with part of remaining Parmesan cheese.
6. Cover each dish with heavy-duty aluminum foil; label, date and freeze.
7. To bake: Remove crêpes from freezer and loosen foil around container.
8. Bake in hot oven (400°) 30 minutes, then remove foil and bake 10 minutes longer, or until sauce is bubbly-hot and browned.
HOSTESS TIP: Crêpes can be layered in a 12-cup shallow freezer-to-oven casserole. Bake, covered, 45 minutes; uncover and bake 15 minutes longer.

CRÊPES

Makes sixteen 8-inch crêpes.

- 4 eggs
- 2 cups milk
- 2 teaspoons liquid margarine
- 1½ cups sifted all-purpose flour
- 1 teaspoon salt
- Liquid margarine

1. Beat eggs until foamy in a medium-size bowl; stir in milk and the 2 teaspoons liquid margarine. Beat in flour and salt until smooth.
2. Heat an 8-inch skillet or crêpe pan until very hot. Brush lightly with liquid margarine. Pour in batter, a scant ¼ cup at a time; quickly tilt pan so batter spreads and covers bottom.
3. Cook over medium to medium-high heat until edges of crêpe brown; turn and cook about 1 minute longer, or until bottom browns.
4. Turn crêpe out onto cooky sheet by flipping pan upside down; roll up crêpe, jelly-roll fashion. Repeat with remaining batter to make 16 crêpes.

GINGER CRISP CHICKEN

Secret of this favorite is double cooking: First baking, then frying. The ginger in the golden crust gives it a slightly spicy flavor.

Bake at 350° for 1 hour.
Makes 8 servings.

- 2 broiler-fryers, (about 2½ pounds each)
- 2 teaspoons salt
- 1 teaspoon leaf rosemary, crumbled
- ½ cup water
- Ginger Batter (recipe follows)
- Shortening or vegetable oil for frying

1. Cut up chickens,, following directions on page 103. Place chicken pieces in a single layer in a large shallow baking pan; sprinkle with the salt and rosemary; add water; cover with aluminum foil.
2. Bake in moderate oven (350°) for 1 hour.
3. While chicken cooks, make GINGER BATTER.
4. Remove chicken from pan; drain chicken thoroughly on paper towels.
5. Melt enough shortening or pour in enough vegetable oil to make a depth of ½ inch in a large skillet or electric deep-fat fryer. Heat until hot (350° in electric fryer).
6. Dip chicken pieces, 2 or 3 at a time, into GINGER BATTER; hold over bowl to let excess drip back.
7. Fry in hot shortening 3 minutes, or until golden-brown. Lift out with a slotted spoon; drain well. Keep warm on a hot platter.

GINGER BATTER

Makes about 1½ cups.
- 1¼ cups all-purpose flour
- 1 teaspoon baking powder
- 1 teaspoon salt
- ½ teaspoon ground ginger
- 1 egg
- 1 cup milk
- ¼ cup vegetable oil

1. Sift flour, baking powder, salt and ginger into a medium-size bowl.
2. Add egg, milk and oil, all at once. Beat until smooth.

POULTRY POINTERS

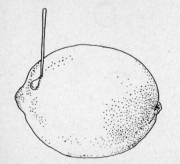

• A few drops of lemon juice are often all that a chicken recipe requires for a special taste. To obtain just a few drops, insert a wooden pick into a lemon; remove pick and squeeze just the amount you need. Then return pick to the hole to keep the rest of the juices in.
• Dieters can add all the squirts of lemon they wish to add flavor to chicken, with few calories.

Money-Saving Tips:
• You'll save most by buying whole birds and either roasting them whole or cutting them up yourself—not as difficult a task as it may seem. (You'll find illustrated, step-by-step directions to cut up chicken on page 103.)
• Watch for specials on 5-pound boxes of drumsticks or breasts. Compared to the same quantity in smaller packages, savings can amount to as much as $1.
• Buy chicken wings and backs. Simmered into soups or stews, or cooked *en casserole* in the company of vegetables and rice or pasta, they are savory and succulent.
• When buying turkey, remember that the bigger the bird, the more meat there will be in proportion to bone. Half of a 20-pound bird, for example, will be meatier than a 10-pound bird —and thus less expensive per serving.
• Use our leftover poultry recipes.

COUNTRY ROAST CHICKEN

Cornbread stuffing makes this an extra special roast.

Bake at 375° for 1 hour, 30 minutes.
Makes 8 servings.

- 2 broiler-fryers (about 3 pounds each)
- 1 cup water
- ½ teaspoon salt
- 1 package (8 ounces) cornbread-stuffing mix
- 1 medium-size onion, chopped (½ cup)
- ½ cup sliced celery
- ½ cup (1 stick) butter or margarine
- ¼ cup bacon drippings
  OR: ¼ cup (½ stick) butter or margarine, melted

1. Remove giblets and necks from chickens and place (except livers) with water and salt in a small saucepan; cover. Simmer 45 minutes. Add livers; cover; simmer 15 minutes longer; remove from heat; cool.
2. Remove giblets and necks from broth; reserve broth. Chop giblets and the meat from necks; place in a large bowl; stir in stuffing mix.
3. Simmer reserved broth until reduced to ½ cup; reserve.
4. Sauté onion and celery in the ½ cup butter or margarine for 5 minutes in a medium-size skillet. Add with reserved broth to stuffing mixture in bowl; toss until evenly moistened.
5. Stuff neck and body cavities of chickens lightly with stuffing. Skewer neck skin to back; close body cavities and tie legs to tails. Place chickens on

rack in roasting pan. Brush with part of bacon drippings or butter or margarine.
6. Roast in moderate oven (375°) basting every 30 minutes with bacon drippings or butter or margarine, 1 hour, 30 minutes or until tender.
7. To serve, place on heated serving platter. Cut chickens into quarters with poultry shears and serve with a casserole of oven baked carrots.

BUTTERMILK FRIED CHICKEN

A crunchy chicken topped with a creamy buttermilk gravy.

Makes 4 servings.

- 1 broiler-fryer (about 2½ pounds)
- 2½ cups buttermilk
- 1 cup all-purpose flour
- 1½ teaspoons salt
- ½ teaspoon laf rosemary, crumbled
- ¼ teaspoon pepper
  Shortening or vegetable oil for frying

1. Cut chicken into serving-size pieces, following cutting directions on page 103.
2. Pour ½ cup of the buttermilk into a shallow dish. Combine flour, salt, rosemary and pepper in a plastic bag.
3. Dip chicken pieces in buttermilk; shake in flour mixture to coat well. Dip again in buttermilk and flour mixture to build a thick coating. Place chicken pieces on wire rack for 15 minutes to allow coating to set. Reserve remaining flour mixture.
4. Melt enough shortening, or pour enough oil, into a large heavy skillet with a cover to ½-inch depth. Place over medium heat. Heat to 360° on a deep fat thermometer, or until a 1-inch cube of bread turns golden in 60 seconds. Add the chicken pieces skin-side down. Cook slowly, turning once, 20 minutes, or until chicken is golden.
5. Reduce heat; cover skillet. Cook 20 minutes longer, or until chicken is tender. Remove cover for last 5 minutes for a crunchy crust. Place chicken on platter; keep hot.
6. Pour off all fat into a cup. Return 3 tablespoons to skillet; blend in 3 tablespoons of the reserved flour mixture; cook, stirring constantly just until bubbly. Gradually add remaining 2 cups buttermilk; continue cooking and stirring, scraping to loosen browned bits in pan, until gravy is thickened and bubbles 3 minutes. Taste; season with additional salt and pepper, if you wish. Spoon over chicken and serve with hot biscuits, if you wish.

BATTER-FRIED CHICKEN

A Deep South style of fried chicken you'll want to try for supper.

Bake at 375° for 45 minutes.
Makes 12 servings.

 3 broiler-fryers, cut up (about 3
    pounds each)
¼ cup water
 2 teaspoons salt
    Vegetable oil for frying
    Batter for Chicken (recipe follows)

1. Place chicken pieces in a large shallow baking pan; add water and sprinkle with salt. Cover with aluminum foil.
2. Bake in moderate oven (375°) 45 minutes. Remove chicken pieces from liquid; dry well.
3. Heat a 1-inch depth of oil to 350° in a heavy skillet.
4. Dip chicken pieces in BATTER FOR CHICKEN; drain off excess. Fry 2 or 3 pieces at a time, until golden brown, about 3 minutes. Drain.

BATTER FOR CHICKEN

Makes enough to coat 3 chickens.

1¼ cups all-purpose flour
 1 teaspoon baking powder
 ½ teaspoon salt
 1 egg
 1 cup milk
 ¼ cup vegetable oil

Sift flour, baking powder and salt into a large bowl. Add egg, milk and oil; beat until smooth.

MEDITERRANEAN CHICKEN

A savory skillet dish that's quickly prepared.

Makes 4 servings.

 1 broiler-fryer, quartered (about
    3 pounds)
1½ teaspoons salt
 ¼ teaspoon pepper
 3 tablespoons butter or margarine
 1 medium-size onion, chopped
    (½ cup)
 ½ cup chicken broth
 1 medium-size eggplant, pared
    and cubed
 2 medium-size tomatoes, peeled
    and chopped
 1 teaspoon mixed Italian herbs,
    crumbled
 ¼ cup grated Parmesan or Romano
    cheese

1. Sprinkle chicken with 1 teaspoon of the salt and pepper. Heat butter or margarine in a large skillet; add chicken and brown on both sides. Remove from skillet.
2. Add onion and sauté until tender. Add broth, scraping brown particles from bottom of skillet. Add eggplant and tomatoes; sprinkle with Italian herbs and remaining ½ teaspoon salt. Add chicken; spoon some of the vegetable mixture over chicken.
3. Cover; simmer 30 minutes, until chicken is tender. Serve sprinkled with grated Parmesan or Romano cheese. Serve with a rich red wine and hot linguini, if you wish.

QUICK CHICKEN LIVERS STROGANOFF

Sour cream sauce turns chicken livers into a Continental dish.

Makes 6 servings.

 1 pound chicken livers
 2 tablespoons butter or margarine
 ½ teaspoon leaf oregano, crumbled
 ½ teaspoon Worcestershire sauce
 1 medium-size onion, chopped (½
    cup)
 2 tablespoons all-purpose flour
 ½ teaspoon salt
    Dash pepper
 1 can (6 ounces) sliced mushrooms
 ¼ cup dairy sour cream

1. Halve chicken livers.
2. Brown livers slowly in butter or margarine seasoned with oregano and Worcestershire sauce; remove. Add onion to pan; sauté until soft.
3. Blend in flour, salt and pepper; stir in mushrooms and liquid. Heat, stirring constantly, to boiling; return livers; cover. Simmer 3 minutes.
4. Stir about ¼ cup liver mixture into sour cream in a small bowl, then stir back into the skillet. Heat very slowly just until hot. Serve over fluffy rice and garnish with bacon slices.

SOUTHERN FRIED CHICKEN

Time-honored, crusty chicken with cream gravy.

Makes 6 servings.

 2 broiler-fryers, cut up (about 2
    pounds each)
 3 cups light cream
 2 cups all-purpose flour
2½ teaspoons salt
 ¼ teaspoon pepper
    Shortening or vegetable oil for
    frying

1. Place chicken pieces in a single layer in a large shallow dish; pour 1 cup of the cream over top; chill at least 20 minutes.
2. Shake chicken pieces, a few at a time in mixture of flour, salt and pepper in a plastic bag to coat well. Dip each again in remaining cream in dish; shake again in flour mixture. Reserve remaining seasoned flour.
3. Melt enough shortening or pour enough vegetable oil into a large heavy skillet to make a depth of ½-inch; heat. Add chicken pieces, skin-side down. Brown slowly, turning once, then continue cooking 30 minutes, or until tender. Remove; keep warm while making gravy.
4. Pour all drippings from skillet into a small bowl; measure 2 tablespoonfuls and return to pan. Stir in 2 tablespoons of the seasoned flour. Cook, stirring constantly, until bubbly. Stir in remaining 2 cups cream; continue cooking and stirring, until gravy thickens and bubbles 3 minutes.

HAWAIIAN CHICKEN

The chicken is glazed with a fruit sauce.

Bake at 375° for 1 hour.
Makes 8 servings.

 2 broiler-fryers, quartered (about 3
    pounds each)
 2 teaspoons salt
 1 tablespoon melted butter or
    margarine
 1 can (1 pound) sliced pineapple
 2 cans (1 pound, 1 ounce each) yams
    in syrup
 3 tablespoons cornstarch
 ¼ cup lemon juice
 ½ teaspoon dry mustard
 ½ teaspoon ground ginger
 2 teaspoons instant minced onion
 ½ cup currant jelly

1. Sprinkle chicken quarters with 1½ teaspoons of the salt. Place, skin-side up, in 12-cup shallow casserole. Brush with melted butter or margarine.
2. Bake in moderate oven (375°) for 45 minutes.
3. Drain syrup from pineapple and yams into a medium-size saucepan. Add cornstarch, lemon juice, remaining ½ teaspoon salt, dry mustard, ginger and instant minced onion. Stir until cornstarch is well blended. Add currant jelly. Cook, stirring constantly, until mixture thickens and bubbles 1 minute. Remove from heat.
4. When chicken has baked for 45 minutes, remove from oven. Add drained pineapple slices and yams. Pour sauce over all. Return to oven and bake 15 minutes longer.

TENNESSEE CLUB CHICKEN

Southern-fried chicken breasts and ham, in a milky sauce lightly touched with sherry.

Bake at 350° for 45 minutes.
Makes 8 servings.

- **4 chicken breasts (about 12 ounces each)**
- **8 small thin slices cooked ham**
- **½ cup all-purpose flour**
- **1 ½ teaspoons salt**
- **¼ teaspoon pepper**
- **¼ cup (½ stick) butter or margarine**
- **2 ½ cups milk**
- **½ cup dry sherry**

1. Halve chicken breasts; wash and pat dry. Cut a pocket in thin side of each. Place breasts on wax paper.
2. Sauté ham slices quickly in a large skillet; cool slightly. Tuck one into pocket in each half chicken breast.
3. Mix ¼ cup of the flour, 1 teaspoon of the salt and pepper in a cup; sprinkle over chicken to coat evenly.
4. Melt butter or margarine in pan; add chicken breasts and brown slowly; place in a 12-cup shallow casserole.
5. Blend remaining ¼ cup flour and ½ teaspoon salt into drippings in pan; cook, stirring constantly, just until bubbly. Stir in milk; continue cooking and stirring, scraping brown bits from bottom of pan, until sauce thickens and bubbles 3 minutes; stir in sherry. Pour over chicken breasts; cover.
6. Bake in moderate oven (350°) 45 minutes, or until chicken is tender.
7. Arrange chicken on a heated deep serving platter; spoon sauce over top. Garnish with parsley, if you wish.

SAN FERNANDO PEPPER CHICKEN

Seasoned pepper—a spunky blend—flavors this Southwest chicken dish that's served with a mushroom gravy.

Bake at 350° for 1 hour.
Makes 6 servings.

- **¼ cup (½ stick) butter or margarine**
- **2 broiler-fryers, cut up (about 2 pounds each)**
- **1 ½ teaspoons seasoned pepper**
- **2 teaspoons salt**
- **Savory Mushroom Gravy (recipe follows)**

1. Melt butter or margarine in large shallow baking pan. Roll chicken pieces, one at a time, in butter or margarine to coat well; then arrange, skin-side down, in single layer in pan.
2. Combine seasoned pepper and salt in a small cup; sprinkle half evenly over the chicken.

3. Bake in moderate oven (350°) 30 minutes; turn; sprinkle remaining seasoning mixture over. Bake 30 minutes longer, or until chicken is tender.
4. Arrange on heated serving platter; keep warm in a slow oven while making gravy. Serve gravy separately.

SAVORY MUSHROOM GRAVY:
Makes 2 cups. Pour off all chicken drippings from pan; return ¼ cup. Stir in 1 can condensed cream of mushroom soup. Blend in ½ cup water. Cook slowly, stirring constantly, 8 to 10 minutes, until thickened.

SAUTÉED CHICKEN LEGS ISABEL

A bit expensive with those delicious artichokes and mushrooms, but it's worth it, once in a while.

Makes 6 servings.

- **3 tablespoons vegetable oil, butter or margarine**
- **6 large drumsticks with thighs (about 3 pounds)**
- **1 teaspoon salt**
- **¼ teaspoon pepper**
- **1 box (9 ounces) frozen artichokes, thawed**
- **½ pound mushrooms**
- **½ cup chicken broth (optional)**
- **½ cup dry sherry**
- **½ cup light cream**
- **4 teaspoons cornstarch**

1. Heat the oil in a large skillet. Brown the drumsticks well on all sides. Sprinkle with ½ teaspoon of the salt and ⅛ teaspoon of the pepper. Cover and cook gently for 25 minutes.
2. Uncover the pan. Add the artichokes and mushrooms. Sprinkle with remaining salt and pepper. Cover the pan again and continue cooking another 20 to 25 minutes, or until a skewer inserted at thick part of thigh moves freely.
3. Remove the drumsticks to a heated serving platter. Surround them with the mushrooms and artichokes. Keep warm.
4. There should be about ½ cup of juices in the pan. Skim fat. Should there be less, add enough chicken broth to the pan to make ½ cup. Add the sherry and reduce to about ¾ cup.
5. Mix the cream with the cornstarch until smooth in a cup; stir into skillet; cook, stirring constantly until sauce thickens and bubbles 1 minute. Taste; add additional seasoning, if you wish and spoon over the drumsticks. Serve with a salad of watercress topped with sieved hard-cooked egg and a dry white wine.

PENNSYLVANIA CHICKEN

Tender chicken breasts are served with mushrooms, noodles and a creamy gravy in the delicious Pennsylvania Dutch tradition.

Makes 6 servings.

- **3 whole chicken breasts, split (about 12 ounces each)**
- **2 cups water**
- **1 slice onion**
- **Handful celery leaves**
- **1 teaspoon salt**
- **4 peppercorns**
- **1 package (1 pound) noodles**
- **½ pound mushrooms, sliced**
- **2 tablespoons butter or margarine**
- **1 can (about 11 ounces) chicken gravy**

1. Combine chicken breasts, water, onion, celery leaves, salt and peppercorns in large saucepan. Simmer, covered, 20 minutes.
2. While chicken simmers, cook noodles in large amount boiling salted water, following label directions; drain; place in 10-cup casserole.
3. Sauté mushrooms in butter or margarine in a large skillet; arrange in clusters on top of noodles. (Keep casserole warm in heated oven while browning chicken and heating gravy.)
4. Drain chicken breasts (strain broth and save for soup). Brown chicken quickly in same pan, adding more butter or margarine, if needed; place on noodles.
5. Stir chicken gravy into pan; bring to boiling; pour over chicken.

BUDAPEST CHICKEN LIVERS

A delicious dinner with little work for you.

Bake at 375° for 30 minutes.
Makes 4 servings.

- **1 pound chicken livers**
- **1 cup quick-cooking rice**
- **1 medium-size onion, finely chopped (½ cup)**
- **½ cup dairy sour cream**
- **1 envelope or teaspoon instant chicken broth**
- **½ teaspoon leaf thyme, crumbled**
- **½ teaspoon salt**
- **¼ teaspoon pepper**
- **¾ cup tomato juice**

1. Place chicken livers in a 10x16-inch plastic cooking bag in a shallow baking pan; combine rice, onion, sour cream, chicken broth, thyme, salt and pepper in a large bowl. Stir in tomato juice. Pour over chicken livers.
2. Close and seal cooking bag, following label directions.
3. Bake in moderate oven (375°) 30 minutes, or until livers are tender.

WESTERN CHICKEN AND ICEBERG

All along the Pacific Coast, cooks have been using shredded lettuce for years to catch poultry sauces at lots less calories than rice or noodles.

Bake at 350° for 1 hour.
Makes 4 servings.

    1 large head iceberg lettuce
    8 drumsticks (about 2 pounds)
    ¼ cup bottled barbecue sauce
    ¼ cup teriyaki sauce
    3 California oranges
    1 small red onion, sliced
    ¼ cup ripe olives, halved (optional)

1. Core, rinse and thoroughly drain lettuce; chill in disposable plastic bag or plastic crisper.
2. Place chicken in shallow casserole; drizzle with barbecue and teriyaki sauces; cover.
3. Bake in moderate oven (350°) 45 minutes, basting occasionally. Uncover chicken and bake about 15 minutes longer or until fork-tender.
4. Cut lettuce lengthwise into halves; place cut-sides down on board and chop coarsely. (You will get about 8 cups.) Cut oranges into sections, catching juice. Toss lettuce with oranges and juice, onion and olives; mound on serving platter. Stand hot chicken against mound. Pour drippings into gravy boat, skim off excess fat and serve drippings alongside as a dressing. Serve with a bottle of California dry white wine.

STUFFED DRUMSTICKS NAPOLI

Each golden leg contains a zippy salami stuffing.

Makes 8 servings.

    8 drumsticks with thighs (about 4
         pounds)
    1 piece (4 ounces) salami
    ½ cup all-purpose flour
    2 teaspoons salt
    1 teaspoon paprika
    1 teaspoon leaf oregano, crumbled
    ⅛ teaspoon pepper
    ½ cup vegetable oil

1. Cut through chicken legs at joints to separate drumsticks and thighs, then cut an opening along bone of each drumstick and in meaty part of each thigh to make a pocket for a salami strip.
2. Cut salami into 16 strips; stuff 1 strip into each piece of chicken.
3. Shake pieces, a few at a time, in mixture of flour, salt, paprika, oregano and pepper in a plastic bag to coat evenly.

4. Cook pieces slowly in vegetable oil in a large skillet 20 minutes; turn; cover loosely. Cook 20 minutes longer, or until tender and crisply golden. Serve warm or cold.

KENTUCKY BURGOO

A delicious soup-stew for cold days—easy on the budget, too.

Makes 6 servings.

    12 chicken wings (about 1½ pounds)
     1 medium-size onion, chopped
          (½ cup)
     5 cups water
     1 can (1 pound) stewed tomatoes
     2 tablespoons bottled steak sauce
     ⅛ teaspoon cayenne pepper
     1 tablespoon salt
     ½ pound ground beef
     2 cans (1 pound each) mixed
          vegetables
     1 small head cabbage, shredded
     2 cups instant mashed potato flakes
     ¼ cup chopped parsley

1. Cut apart chicken wings at joints with a sharp knife. Combine with onion, water, tomatoes, steak sauce, cayenne and salt in a large heavy kettle or Dutch oven. Bring to boiling; reduce heat; cover. Simmer 30 minutes.
2. Shape ground beef into 18 little meatballs.
3. Add mixed vegetables and cabbage to kettle, bring to a boil; add meatballs; reduce heat; cover. Simmer 10 minutes. Stir in potato flakes. Remove from heat.
4. Sprinkle with parsley. Spoon into soup bowls. Serve with hot corn bread, if you wish.

CORN FLAKE CHICKEN

You can give this chicken its corn flake coating ahead of time and refrigerate it, oven-ready, till baking time.

Bake at 400° for 45 minutes.
Makes 4 servings.

    1 broiler-fryer, cut-up (about 3
         pounds)
    ½ cup buttermilk
    ½ cup packaged corn flake crumbs
    ½ cup all-purpose flour
    1 teaspoon salt
    1 teaspoon poultry seasoning
    ¼ cup (½ stick) melted butter or
         margarine.

1. Dip chicken pieces in buttermilk in shallow pan; coat with mixture of corn flake crumbs, flour, salt and poultry seasoning combined in second shallow pan; arrange chicken pieces

in single layer in a shallow baking pan; pour melted butter or margarine over. (This much may be done ahead.)
2. Bake in hot oven (400°) 45 minutes, or until tender and golden.

WHEAT GERM COATED CHICKEN

Nutrition-minded cooks will especially appreciate the coating on chicken breasts.

Bake at 375° for 45 minutes.
Makes 6 servings.

    3 whole chicken breasts, split (about
         12 ounces each)
    1 teaspoon salt
    ¼ cup (½ stick) melted butter or
         margarine
    1 can (6 ounces) frozen concentrate
         for orange juice, thawed
    ¼ cup honey
    ¾ cup toasted wheat germ
    ½ cup all-purpose flour
    1 teaspoon paprika
    ¼ teaspoon leaf thyme, crumbled

1. Sprinkle chicken breasts with ½ teaspoon of the salt. Brush with melted butter or margarine. Mix orange juice and honey in dish.
2. Combine toasted wheat germ, flour, paprika, thyme and remaining ½ teaspoon salt on wax paper. Roll chicken in orange-honey mixture, then in toasted wheat germ mixture. Place in single layer in shallow baking pan. Drizzle remaining butter and orange-honey mixture over chicken.
3. Bake in moderate oven (375°) 45 minutes, basting often with pan juices, until chicken is tender.

BREADED CHICKEN WINGS

A batch of tasty tidbits for nibblers.

Bake at 350° for 1 hour.
Makes 8 servings.

    24 chicken wings (about 3 pounds)
     ½ cup vegetable oil
     1 teaspoon seasoned salt
    1½ cups corn flake crumbs or bread
          crumbs

1. Trim tips from chicken wings. (Save for soup kettle.) Divide wings in half by cutting through remaining joints with a knife.
2. Mix vegetable oil and seasoned salt in a pie plate; place corn flake or bread crumbs in a second pie plate. Roll chicken pieces in oil mixture, then in crumbs to coat evenly. Place, not touching, in a large shallow pan.
3. Bake in moderate oven (350°) 1 hour, or until golden. Serve hot with prepared frozen French fries.

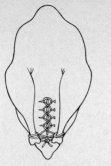

Pack bird lightly with stuffing. Close cavity by pressing poultry nails or wooden picks into skin and lace with string.

For cut up chicken, make a cut, at one side of wishbone, from neck to cavity, with a pair of kitchen or poultry shears.

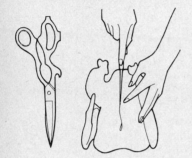

Turn bird over and flatten along backbone with palm of hand, then cut to one side of backbone with shears. (halves)

Cut across split bird, following the natural separation of breast and thigh, first with a knife, then shears. (quarters)

The whole bird—from broiler-fryer to holiday turkey, is always a treat when stuffed with a savory mixture and tied into shape.

STUFF OR BONE A BIRD

Have just the parts of the bird you want for a special recipe (even costly cutlets) by following our step-by-step pictures to cut up the whole bird.

Bend leg and thigh quarter and feel with fingers for joint. Cut through at this point with sharp knife and separate.

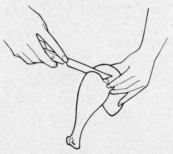

Bend wing and breast quarter and feel with fingers for joint. Cut through at this point with sharp knife and separate.

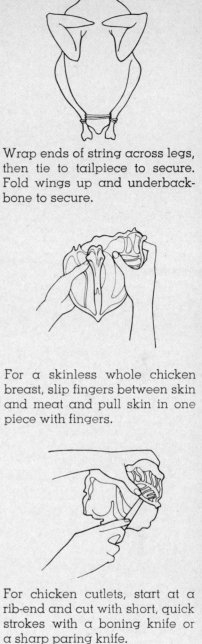

Wrap ends of string across legs, then tie to tailpiece to secure. Fold wings up and underbackbone to secure.

For a skinless whole chicken breast, slip fingers between skin and meat and pull skin in one piece with fingers.

For chicken cutlets, start at a rib-end and cut with short, quick strokes with a boning knife or a sharp paring knife.

Continue cutting towards wishbone, using finger to guide the knife away from meat, then cut into two oval pieces. (cutlets)

There is certainly nothing mysterious, or complicated, about learning how to carve meat. You don't have to be a chef, a butcher or a strong man. But you do have to be a little patient. Practice helps, too, and this is probably the key to learning this rather basic but artistic skill— along with directions like the ones here. And these guidelines are designed to help you not only learn how to carve, but learn to do it masterfully—just like a chef!

HOW TO CARVE LIKE A CHEF

Begin by learning a little about the anatomy of the bird by following the directions for cutting up raw poultry to discover where the joints are located. Next choose a carving set of good quality with a good feel in your hands. Then carve simply roasted chickens in the privacy of the kitchen, until you gain confidence, then recapture the past when carvers were the stars of the dining room.

Bend closest leg of bird toward serving platter while cutting through joint to separate leg and thigh from body with a long carving knife. Cut into thin slices on second serving platter.

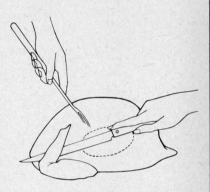

Insert a long-tined carving fork into breast near breastbone and cut off wing by slanting knife inward slightly, to hit joint. Place on platter.

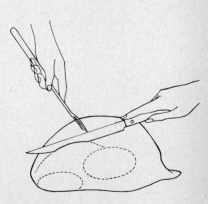

Slice breast meat into smooth even slices by starting to carve halfway up the side of the breast and slicing down, toward wing joint. Start each new slice higher on the breast. Slice only as much as needed.

QUARTERED DUCKLING

Roast duckling can be carved, as shown on this page, but it is often easier on both carver and guest, when a halved (split) or quartered bird is served. A poultry or kitchen shears will do a neat and quick job. Rock Cornish hens too can be split this way if the 1½ pound-size.

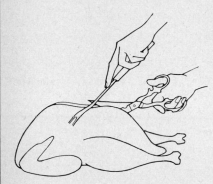

Place duckling, breast-side up, on a heated serving platter large enough to handle bird with ease. Present platter to guests with garnishes, then remove to side plate to add as garnish on individual plates. Cut through duckling breastbone, a little to one side of center, from neck to cavity, then follow along to one side of backbone to cut in half.

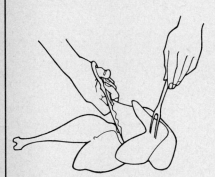

Halves of duckling may be too much for each guest, especially when served with a rich stuffing and sauce or gravy. To quarter duckling, continue using poultry shears or kitchen shears and cut across duckling, between breast and thigh, following the natural division, just below rib cage and breastbone. Serve with hot sauce or gravy.

GOOSE OR DUCKLING

Remove legs from bird by holding each leg, in turn, firmly with carving fork while severing skin at inside hip joint in easy strokes with a sharp, thin-bladed poultry carving knife at an angle.

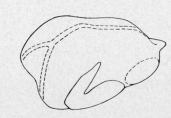

Twist drumstick and thigh away from body with knife until it loosens at the joint. Cut between drumstick and breast to pull drumstick quarter away from body. (It should separate easily, but if it does not, sever connecting joint with tip of carving knife.) Place quarter on second heated platter and separate thigh from leg. Hold thigh firmly on platter and cut into even slices, parallel to bones.

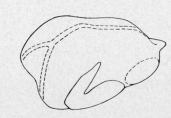

To carve the breast meat into more even slices, begin by cutting around area indicated by dotted lines in the picture above. (If carving a duckling, you can pull out breastbone with knife.)

Make a cut the length of the ridge of the breastbone, then slide knife down along ribs and loosen with blade as you go.

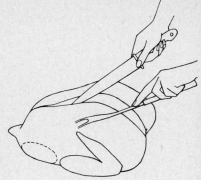

Continue to loosen breast meat from carcass until it can be removed in a single piece. Cut wings from breast at shoulder joint. (Carve goose breast on second platter into smooth even slices and arrange with thigh slices and legs to serve.) Serve half a duckling breast.

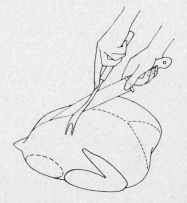

Note: Be sure to remove all pins, wooden picks or cord from poultry before placing onto a carving platter large enough to allow bird to be moved for ease in carving.

CARVING HINT

All poultry will carve more easily and the meat, especially the breast meat, will be more moist, if the bird is allowed to "rest" for at least 20 minutes after roasting. Put bird on a heated platter and place to the back of the range. "Tent" with foil to keep hot while making gravy.

A POULTRY COOK'S CHECK LIST

Most of the recipes in this book can be made with a minimum number of cooking utensils, but the creative cook usually enjoys adding a few specialty items to the kitchen cupboard that can make cooking a bit easier—and more fun. Here is a selection of knives, pans and thermometers that can often save time or work.

A copper hen-shaped salad mold also makes a decorative wall hanging when not in use.

Your fried chicken will be perfectly golden and crisp if you use a deep fat frying thermometer.

A turkey, duckling, goose, capon or roasting chicken will brown more evenly and be easier to remove from the roasting pan if you place it on a roast rack. The rack is designed to adjust to varying sizes of poultry, and holds the bird well above the pan drippings.

Any efficient cook knows the time-saving advantages of using this cook's knife with its heavy wide blade to slice, dice, crush, mince, or pound.

A pair of stainless steel poultry shears will make the job of cutting raw or cooked poultry much easier. You can find them in most gourmet stores.

Moroccan Couscous, (recipe is on page 20), is an exotic stew from North Africa that cooks to

perfection in this three sectioned cousisiere.

Chickens and other birds are always done to a turn, when a meat thermometer is pushed into the thickest part of the thigh, before roasting. Cooking is foolproof.

A heavy iron omelet pan can do double duty, both in making omelets with chicken fillings and as a perfect pan for crêpes.

An iron French fry kettle with its wire basket to lower poultry into the hot fat.

The classic French or chef's knife.

The sturdy boning knife with a sharp blade.

Carving is easier with a bayonet

fork that has extra long tines.

CHEESE AND TURKEY SALAD

Here's a main-dish salad planned especially for cold weather, for it's served hot.

Bake at 450° for 10 minutes.
Makes 4 servings.

  2 cups finely crushed potato chips (about a 4-ounce package)
  ½ cup grated sharp Cheddar cheese
  ½ cup chopped walnuts
  1 tablespoon butter or margarine
  2 cups cubed cooked turkey
  2 cups thinly sliced celery
  2 teaspoons grated onion
  ¼ teaspoon salt
  2 tablespoons lemon juice
  ½ cup mayonnaise or salad dressing

1. Mix potato chips and cheese in small bowl; pat half into bottom of a 6-cup shallow baking dish.
2. Sauté walnuts in butter or margarine in small skillet, stirring often, 5 minutes, or until lightly toasted; drain on paper towels. Toss with turkey, celery, onion, salt, lemon juice and mayonnaise or salad dressing in a medium-size bowl.
3. Spoon into prepared baking dish; sprinkle saved potato-chip mixture over top of casserole.
4. Bake in very hot oven (450°) 10 minutes, or until hot and golden.

QUICK TURKEY STROGONOFF

Heat cooked turkey in a no-fuss creamy sauce for this quickie with a Continental flavor.

Makes 4 to 6 servings.

  1 large onion, chopped (1 cup)
  2 tablespoons butter or margarine
  2 to 3 cups julienne strips cooked turkey
  1½ cups turkey gravy
     OR: 1 can (about 11 ounces) chicken gravy
  2 tablespoons catsup
  1 container (8 ounces) dairy sour cream
     Parsley noodles

1. Sauté onion in butter or margarine just until soft in a large skillet. Stir in turkey, turkey or chicken gravy, and catsup; simmer 5 minutes.
2. Stir part of hot mixture into sour cream in a small bowl; stir cream mixture into pan; bring just to boiling. Serve over hot noodles tossed with chopped parsley. Complete menu with a platter of marinated vegetables and fruit and cheese for dessert.

POULTRY POINTERS

• To braise poultry is to brown it first in a little fat in a heavy skillet or kettle, then to cook, covered, in a small amount of wine, broth, tomato juice or water in the oven or on a surface burner.
• For smoke-free sautéeing or frying of poultry, use equal parts butter or margarine and vegetable oil or olive oil. The addition of the oil increases the smoking temperature of the butter, giving you a more golden skin plus flavor of the butter.
• Add touch of leaf rosemary to broth when cooking chicken stew. Be sure to strain the broth for gravy.
• For extra crips crusts on chicken pot pies, cut the pastry into the shape of the casserole or individual casseroles; prick the top in several places and place on a cooky sheet. Bake in hot oven (400°) 10 to 15 minutes, or until golden. Slide baked pastry onto bubbly-hot chicken mixture and serve immediately.

GOOSE AND PASTA

Leftover goose goes international in this hearty pasta dish.

Makes 4 servings.

  1 medium-size onion, chopped (½ cup)
  2 tablespoons goose drippings or butter or margarine
  1 can (1 pound) red kidney beans, drained and mashed
  1 cup tomato juice
  1 can (6 ounces) tomato paste
  1 cup Goose Broth (recipe follows)
  1 cup chopped cooked goose
  1 teaspoon mixed Italian herbs, crumbled
  ⅛ teaspoon garlic powder
     Salt and pepper
  1 package (1 pound) thin spaghetti
     Grated Romano or Parmesan cheese

1. Sauté onion in fat in a large saucepan. Add kidney beans, tomato juice, tomato paste, GOOSE BROTH, cooked goose, Italian herbs, garlic powder and salt and pepper to taste.
2. Bring to boiling, then simmer, stirring several times, 15 minutes, or until sauce has thickened slightly.
3. Serve over hot cooked spaghetti and sprinkle generously with cheese. *GOOSE BROTH:* Place the carcass, neck and giblets and leftover skin in a large kettle. Add 1 large onion, chopped (1 cup), a few sprigs of parsley and 1 cup celery leaves. Cover with water, and bring to boiling; lower heat. Cover and simmer about 2½ hours. Strain, cool, then chill.

CASSOULET

A popular French casserole.

Bake at 350° for 1 hour, 30 minutes.
Makes 6 servings.

  1 package (1 pound) large dried lima beans
  4 cups water
  1 can (1 pound) tomatoes
  6 slices bacon
  1 cup grated raw carrots
  1 large onion, chopped (1 cup)
  2 teaspoons salt
  1 teaspoon leaf thyme, crumbled
  1 teaspoon leaf basil, crumbled
  1 bay leaf
  ¼ teaspoon pepper
  2 cups diced cooked turkey
  1 cup chopped celery
  ¼ cup whole-berry cranberry sauce

1. Combine lima beans and water in large kettle. Bring to boiling; cover; cook 2 minutes; let stand 1 hour.
2. Stir in tomatoes, bacon slices, carrots, onion, and seasonings; cover. Bring to boiling; simmer 1 hour.
3. Lift bacon slices from beans and save; remove bay leaf. Stir turkey, celery, and cranberry sauce into beans; pour into 10-cup bean pot or casserole; cover.
4. Bake in moderate oven (350°) 1 hour. Uncover; crisscross saved bacon slices on top. Bake 30 minutes longer, or until liquid is absorbed.

ROAST CAPON

This elegant fowl should be simply prepared so as not to detract from its own fine flavor.

Roast at 325° for 2 hours, 30 minutes.
Makes 6 servings.

  1 ready-to-cook capon (about 7 pounds)
     Salt
     Pepper
     Bread and Butter Stuffing (recipe, page 90)
  ¼ cup (½ stick) butter or margarine, melted

1. Sprinkle the capon inside with salt and pepper.
2. Pack stuffing lightly into neck cavity. Smooth neck skin over stuffing and fasten with wooden picks or skewers to back of bird; twist wing tips until they rest flat against fastened neck skin.
3. Stuff body cavity lightly; fasten opening, and tie legs together and fasten to tailpiece.

4. Place capon, breast-side up, on rack in a large roasting pan; brush well with melted butter or margarine.
5. Roast in slow oven (325°) 2½ hours, or until meaty part of drumstick is tender when pierced with a 2-tined fork; baste frequently.

SOUFFLÉ SUPREME

A puffy soufflé top adds a touch of elegance.

Bake at 375° for 40 minutes.
Makes 6 servings.

1 can condensed cream of shrimp soup
1 cup milk
2 cups diced cooked capon, turkey or chicken
3 tablespoons butter or margarine
¼ cup all-purpose flour
¾ cup milk
4 eggs, separated
¼ teaspoon cream of tartar (optional)
1 teaspoon salt
Few drops bottled red-pepper seasoning

1. Blend soup with the one cup milk. Combine with capon, turkey or chicken in 8-cup shallow baking dish.
2. Melt butter or margarine in small saucepan. Blend in flour; cook, stirring constantly, until bubbly. Stir in the ¾ cup milk; cook and stir until mixture thickens and bubbles 1 minute.
3. Beat whites with cream of tartar just until stiff peaks form. Beat yolks with salt and pepper seasoning in a large bowl. Beat in hot mixture. Fold whites, ½ at a time, into yolk mixture, just until well blended. Spoon soufflé mixture over poultry in dish.
4. Bake in moderate oven (375°) 40 minutes, or until puffed and browned.

BLUE-RIBBON TURKEY CASSEROLE

A make-ahead casserole with a light touch of sherry.

Bake at 350° for 25 to 30 minutes.
Makes 8 servings.

¼ cup (½ stick) butter or margarine
¼ cup all-purpose flour
1 teaspoon salt
2 cups chicken broth
2 cups milk
1 can (6 ounces) sliced mushrooms
¼ cup dry sherry
½ teaspoon leaf marjoram, crumbled
2 tablespoons chopped chives
1 package (1 pound) medium noodles, cooked and drained
4 cups diced cooked turkey
¼ cup grated Parmesan cheese

1. Melt butter or margarine in a large saucepan. Blend in flour and salt. Gradually stir in chicken broth, milk and liquid from mushrooms. Cook, stirring constantly, until mixture thickens and bubbles 3 minutes. Add sherry, marjoram and chives.
2. Combine with cooked noodles, diced cooked turkey and mushrooms. Turn mixture into a 12-cup shallow casserole. Sprinkle with grated cheese.
3. Bake in moderate oven (350°) 25 to 30 minutes, or until bubbly-hot.
COOK'S TIP: To make ahead, spoon mixture into a 12-cup shallow glass-ceramic freezer-to-oven casserole; cover and refrigerate. One hour before serving, place in moderate oven (350°). Bake 1 hour, or until bubbly-hot.

SANTA CLARA CHICKEN

Springtime vegetables are especially flavorful when you bake them with chicken in a clay pot. You must use an unglazed terra cotta pot that has been manufactured as a cooking utensil.

Bake at 450° for 1 hour.
Makes 8 servings.

2 broiler-fryers, cut up (about 3 pounds each)
12 small new potatoes, pared
1 Bermuda onion, sliced thin
4 cups shredded lettuce
1 tablespoon salt
¼ teaspoon pepper
1 teaspoon leaf rosemary, crumbled
3 envelopes instant chicken broth
3 cups hot water
3 cups frozen peas, cooked (from a 1 ½-pound bag)
4 medium-size yellow squash, tipped, sliced and cooked
⅓ cup cornstarch
¾ cup water

1. Do not preheat oven.
2. Soak a large-size unglazed clay pot, top and bottom, in water for 15 minutes before using.
3. Combine chicken with potatoes, onion, lettuce, salt, pepper and rosemary in clay pot.
4. Dissolve instant chicken broth in hot water in 4-cup measure; pour over chicken and vegetables; cover with drained top.
5. Place covered clay pot in the center of the rack in a cold oven.
6. Turn oven control to very hot (450°). Bake 1 hour, or until chicken and vegetables are tender; remove chicken and vegetables with a slotted spoon to the center of a heated serving platter; arrange cooked peas and squash in piles; keep warm while making sauce.
7. Strain juices in clay pot into a large saucepan; bring to boiling. Combine cornstarch and ¾ cup water in a cup; stir into hot liquid; cook, stirring constantly, until mixture thickens and bubbles 1 minute; spoon over platter.

PINE TOP PARTY CASSEROLE

Madeleine McNeil of this Arizona community developed this dish as the perfect way to use leftover turkey and entertain during the holidays.

Bake at 375° for 45 minutes.
Makes 16 servings.

8 cups cooked diced turkey
4 cans cream of chicken soup
2 cups light cream or milk
1 can (4 ounces) green chili peppers, seeded and chopped (optional)
1 bag (about 8 ounces) corn chips, crushed
2 Bermuda onions, chopped
2 cups shredded Monterey Jack Cheese (8 ounces)
2 cups shredded Cheddar cheese (8 ounces)

1. Combine turkey, chicken soup, cream or milk and chili peppers in a large kettle; heat slowly, stirring often, just until bubbly.
2. Divide ⅓ of the corn chips between two 12-cup casseroles; top with half the turkey mixture, chopped onion and shredded cheeses; layer ⅓ of corn chips, remaining turkey mixture, onion and cheeses; top with remaining corn chips.
3. Bake in moderate oven (375°) 45 minutes, or until bubbly-hot.
HOSTESS TIP: This is an especially good dish when guests arrive at various times. Bake one casserole and keep the other on hand for the second flow of company. A heaping platter of chilled marinated vegetables, sour dough bread and a bowl of sliced fruits in wine make a festive, yet easy open house menu.

POULTRY POINTER

Goose—These birds are less frequently seen in markets than chickens, turkeys or ducklings, but quick-frozen geese are beginning to appear in the big-city areas with some regularity. And, of course, they can also be ordered. Geese are tender and rich; they can weigh anywhere from 5 to 15 pounds. Those weighing 10 to 12 pounds are most appropriate for stuffing and roasting.

ROAST GOOSE

This method of roasting a goose at two temperatures was developed by the National Goose Council for a crisper skin and moist, tender meat.

Roast at 400° for 1 hour,
then at 325° for 1½ hours.
Makes 8 servings with leftovers.

- 1 frozen goose (8 to 10 pounds) thawed
  Salt and pepper
- 1 small onion, chopped (¼ cup)
- ¼ cup chopped carrot
- ¼ cup chopped celery

1. Remove neck and giblets from goose and cook immediately for goose broth. Remove excess fat from body cavity and neck skin. Season with salt and pepper; truss goose.
2. Place goose, breast-side up, on a rack in a large roasting pan. Insert a meat thermometer into the inside thigh muscle.
3. Roast in hot oven (400°) 1 hour, removing accumulated fat from roasting pan with a bulb baster every 30 minutes; reduce oven temperature to slow (325°); roast 1 hour longer; add onion, carrot and celery; roast ½ hour longer, or until temperature on meat thermometer reaches 180° and drumstick moves easily. Serve with POULTRY GIBLET GRAVY (recipe, page 91).
COOK'S TIP: Don't waste the goose fat, but keep to use in making leftover goose dishes or for a flavorful cooking fat. Melt down solid pieces of goose fat and add to the fat accumulated during roasting; strai through cheesecloth into a glass jar with a screw top; refrigerate and use within 1 month.

POULTRY POINTERS

Here are the most common members of the onion family. From top left:
• Garlic: This is actually an herb, but most cooks consider it part of the onion family. It is pungent and characteristic of Mediterranean and French cuisines like Chicken Cacciatori and Coq au Vin. The little piece is called a clove, and the whole is called a bud of garlic.
• Yellow Onion: The most familiar of the family. Chopped, it is added to stews and soups, and in slices it becomes a necessary part of most Chinese chicken dishes. It is also delicious over oven-baked chicken pieces.
• Green Onions: These are also called scallions. They are mild in flavor and lend color as well as texture and flavor when added to a chicken salad.
• Leeks: A new member of the family to many Americans, the leek has been part of European cooking for generations. Mild in flavor, yet especially delicious, they can be halved and braised in chicken broth or chopped and added to chicken soup.

BROILED CHICKEN BING

Elegant sweet-sour cherry sauce dresses up crisply broiled chicken.

Makes 6 servings.

- 3 broiler-fryers, split (about 2 pounds each)
- ¼ cup bottled oil-and-vinegar salad dressing
  Dark Cherry Sauce (recipe follows)

1. Place split chickens, skin-side down, on rack in broiler pan. Baste with salad dressing.
2. Broil, turning every 10 minutes, and basting with salad dressing, 40 minutes or until tender and brown. Remove to heated serving platter.
3. Pour DARK CHERRY SAUCE over.

DARK CHERRY SAUCE

Makes about 2 cups.
- 1 can (1 pound) pitted dark sweet cherries
- 2 tablespoons cornstarch
- 1 tablespoon prepared mustard
- 1 tablespoon molasses
  Few drops bottled red-pepper seasoning
  Dash salt
- 3 tablespoons lemon juice

1. Drain syrup from cherries into a 2-cup measure; add water to make 1½ cups liquid.
2. Blend a few tablespoons syrup into cornstarch in a small saucepan until smooth; stir in remaining syrup, mustard, molasses, red-pepper seasoning and salt. Cook over low heat, stirring constantly, until mixture thickens and bubbles 1 minute.
3. Stir in cherries and lemon juice; heat slowly just until bubbly.

KASHMIR TURKEY CURRY

Freeze this leftover turkey dish, then serve when the family least expects it.

Bake at 350° for 1 hour, 45 minutes.
Makes two 4-serving casseroles.

- 1 large onion, chopped (1 cup)
- 2 cups thinly sliced celery
- ¼ cup (½ stick) butter or margarine
- 2 to 4 teaspoons curry powder
- ¼ cup all-purpose flour
- 4 cups turkey broth
  OR: 2 cans (13¾ ounces each) chicken broth
- 1½ teaspoons salt
- 5 cups diced cooked turkey
- 8 cups hot cooked rice (2 cups uncooked rice)

1. Sauté onion and celery in butter or margarine until soft in a large saucepan; stir in curry powder and cook 2 minutes; stir in flour. Cook, stirring constantly, until bubbly. Add broth and salt; continue cooking and stirring until mixture thickens and bubbles 3 minutes; remove from heat: add diced cooked turkey.
2. Place hot cooked rice in a large bowl; stir in curry mixture.
3. Line two 6-cup shallow freezer-to-oven casseroles with heavy-duty aluminum foil, allowing enough overlap to cover food from casserole; return food to freezer.
4. Spoon rice and curry mixture into prepared casseroles; cool; cover with foil overlap; seal tightly. Label, date and freezer. When frozen solid, remove foil-wrapped food and return to freezer.
5. To bake: Remove foil from frozen food; return to same casserole; cover.
6. Bake in moderate oven (350°) 1 hour, 45 minutes, or until bubbly-hot.

CRANBERRY GLAZED ROAST TURKEY

Not every turkey has to be stuffed. You can serve the boxed kind, if you like.

Roast at 325° 2 hours, 30 minutes.
Makes 8 servings, plus leftovers.

- 1 frozen turkey, (about 10 pounds), thawed
- ¼ cup (½ stick) butter or margarine, softened
- 1 can (7 ounces) jellied cranberry sauce
- 1 teaspoon Worcestershire sauce
- ½ teaspoon leaf marjoram, crumbled

1. Place turkey, breast up, on a rack in a roasting pan; coat with soft butter or margarine.
2. Roast in slow oven (325°) 2 hours,

basting with pan drippings several times.

3. Pour off all drippings into a small bowl; measure 2 tablespoonfuls into a small saucepan; set remaining aside for making gravy. (Recipe is on page 91.)

4. Stir cranberry and Worcestershire sauces and marjoram into drippings in saucepan; heat, stirring constantly, just to boiling. Brush part of mixture over turkey.

5. Continue roasting, basting several times with remaining cranberry mixture, 30 minutes longer, or until drumstick feels very soft and a meat thermometer inserted into thigh registers 185°.

6. Remove turkey to a heated platter; carve and serve.

COOK'S TIP: If you wish to make gravy, fix it in another pan, as the cranberry drippings in the roasting pan tend to make the gravy too sweet.

TURKEY CROQUETTES

When you go to a little trouble with leftover poultry, it becomes a whole new dish.

Makes 8 croquettes.

    2 cups coarsely ground cooked
          turkey or chicken
    1 cup (2 slices) soft bread crumbs
    2 eggs, well beaten
    2 tablespoons plus ½ cup milk
    1 tablespoon minced green pepper
    1 tablespoon minced onion
    ½ teaspoon salt
    ¼ teaspoon leaf savory, crumbled
          Dash pepper
    ¼ cup finely chopped blanched
          toasted almonds
    ½ cup fine dry bread crumbs
          Vegetable oil or shortening
          Velouté Sauce (recipe, page 92)

1. Combine turkey or chicken, soft bread crumbs, eggs, 2 tablespoons milk, green pepper, onion, salt, savory, pepper and almonds in medium-size bowl; chill about 2 hours.

2. Shape into 8 cylindrical croquettes, each 1 inch in diameter; roll in fine dry bread crumbs; dip in ½ cup milk; roll again in crumbs; brush off any loose crumbs.

3. Pour oil or melt shortening to make a 2-inch depth in a small heavy saucepan; heat to 365° or 375° (a 1-inch cube of bread will brown in about 1 minute).

4. Fry croquettes, 2 or 3 at a time, 2 minutes, or until golden-brown; drain on paper towels.

5. Serve with VELOUTÉ SAUCE.

Chapter 4 (from page 36)

CAPE COD CHICKEN

Cranberry and spices are the special flavor secrets of this festive chicken dish. This recipe was developed to cook in an electric slow cooker.

Cook on 190° to 200° for 8 hours,
or   on 290° to 300° for 4 hours.
Makes 8 servings.

    2 broiler-fryers, quartered (about
          2½ pounds each)
    2 teaspoons salt
    ¼ cup vegetable oil
    1 large onion, chopped (1 cup)
    1 tablespoon grated orange rind
    ½ cup orange juice
    3 tablespoons lemon juice
    1 can (1 pound) whole-berry
          cranberry sauce
    1½ teaspoons ground cinnamon
    1½ teaspoons ground ginger

1. Rub chickens with salt to coat well. Brown, a few quarters at a time, in oil in a large skillet or an electric slow cooker with a browning unit; remove.

2. Sauté onion in pan drippings until soft; stir in orange rind and juice, lemon juice, cranberry sauce, cinnamon and ginger; bring to boiling; stir constantly.

3. Combine chicken quarters and sauce in slow cooker; cover.

4. Cook on low (190° to 200°) 8 hours, or on high (290° to 300°) 4 hours, or until chicken is tender. Serve with fluffy rice and buttered peas.

CORIANDER CHICKEN

Coriander is an herb that is used extensively in North African cooking for a spicy yet fresh flavor. This recipe was developed to cook in an electric slow cooker.

Cook on 190° to 200° for 8 hours,
or   on 290° to 300° for 4 hours.
Makes 6 servings.

    3 whole chicken breasts, split
          (about 12 ounces each)
    ¼ cup (½ stick) butter or margarine,
          melted
    1 small onion, grated
    1 tablespoon ground coriander
    1½ teaspoons salt
    ½ cup chicken broth
    1 tablespoon lemon juice
    1 container (8 ounces) plain yogurt
    2 tablespoons all-purpose flour

1. Roll chicken breasts in a mixture of melted butter or margarine, grated onion, coriander and salt in a pie plate to coat well.

2. Place in a 2½-quart electric slow cooker; pour chicken broth and lemon juice over; cover.

3. Cook on low (190° to 200°) 8 hours, or on high (290° to 300°) 4 hours, or until chicken is tender. Stir yogurt and flour together until well-blended in a small bowl. Stir into chicken, just before serving. Serve with rice pilaf and top with sliced green onions, if you wish.

CREOLE TURKEY ROYALE

Serving turkey the second time around can be delicious, when you follow this recipe.

Microwave for 10 minutes.
Makes 6 servings.

    1 tablespoon butter or margarine
    1 cup sliced mushrooms
    1 green pepper, halved, seeded and
          slivered
    3 cups cubed cooked turkey
          Velouté Sauce (recipe, page 92)
    ¼ cup dry sherry
    ¼ cup minced parsley
    1 can (4 ounces) pimiento, sliced
    1 teaspoon salt
    ¼ teaspoon pepper
    ¼ teaspoon paprika
    ¼ cup slivered toasted almonds

1. Heat butter or margarine in a 10-cup microwave-safe casserole in a microwave oven for 30 seconds.

2. Stir in mushrooms and green pepper; cook in oven 2 minutes.

3. Add cubed turkey, VELOUTÉ SAUCE, sherry, parsley, pimiento, salt, pepper and paprika. Cover casserole loosely with wax paper.

4. Microwave 8 to 10 minutes, turning dish several times. Stir; let stand 5 minutes. Sprinkle top with almonds.

POULTRY POINTER

Reheating and refreshing pasta or rice is simple. Place in a colander or strainer and set over boiling water in a pan; cover loosely with aluminum foil. Steam for 15 minutes. Toss with a bit of butter or oil, if not adding to a casserole immediately, to keep from sticking.

CHAFING DISH CHICKEN

Perfect for a company buffet. Shrimp and tiny meat balls add the final touch.

Makes 6 servings.

- 3 **whole chicken breasts, split (about 12 ounces each)**
- 4 **cups water**
  Few celery leaves
- 2½ **teaspoons salt**
- ½ **pound meat-loaf mixture (ground beef and pork)**
- 6 **tablespoons all-purpose flour**
  Dash pepper
- 1 **egg**
- 2 **teaspoons grated onion**
- ¼ **cup milk**
- 3 **medium-size carrots, pared and sliced**
- 1 **cup frozen peas (from a 1¼-pound bag)**
- ¼ **cup (½ stick) butter or margarine**
- ¼ **cup dry white wine**
  Few drops bottled red-pepper seasoning
- 1 **can (5 ounces) deveined shrimp, drained and rinsed**
- 2 **tablespoons chopped parsley**

1. Combine chicken breasts, water, celery leaves and 2 teaspoons of the salt in a large saucepan; cover. Simmer 30 minutes.
2. Remove from broth and cool until easy to handle. Pull off skin and take meat from bones in one piece; reserve.
3. Combine meat-loaf mixture, 2 tablespoons of the flour, remaining ½ teaspoon salt, pepper, egg, onion and milk in a medium-size bowl; mix with a fork until well-blended. Shape into 18 small balls.
4. Reheat chicken broth to boiling; add meat balls; cover. Poach 10 minutes or until cooked through; lift out with slotted spoon; place in bowl.
5. Cook carrots, covered, in part of the same chicken broth 20 minutes, or until tender; cook peas in remaining broth, following label directions. Drain liquid from each and strain into a 4-cup measure; add more water if needed, to make 4 cups. Keep carrots and peas hot.
6. Melt butter or margarine in a large saucepan; blend in remaining 4 tablespoons flour; cook, stirring constantly, just until bubbly. Stir in chicken broth; continue cooking and stirring until sauce thickens and bubbles 3 minutes. Stir in wine and red-pepper seasoning.
7. Cut each half chicken breast into three pieces; add to sauce with meat balls, carrots and peas. Heat slowly just to boiling; spoon into a chafing dish or heated serving dish. Arrange shrimp on top; sprinkle with parsley.

OKTOBERFEST GRILLED CHICKEN

Each September, 70,000 people gather in tents in the Munich fair grounds to celebrate the first tasting of the previous spring's beer. Called the Oktoberfest because it ends in that month, one of its culinary specialities is its chicken. It is customary to serve one whole chicken to each diner so the lovely parsley aroma may be savored. However, you may substitute 4 Cornish hens.

Makes 4 servings.

- 2 **broiler-fryers, (about 2 pounds each)**
- 2 **teaspoons salt**
- ¾ **teaspoon freshly ground pepper**
  Large bunch parsley, washed and dried
- ¼ **cup (½ stick) butter or margarine, melted**
- ¼ **cup vegetable oil**

1. Rub chicken cavities with 1 teaspoon of the salt and ¼ teaspoon of the pepper and stuff fairly full with parsley, stems and all. Truss; tie. Combine melted butter and oil and remaining 1 teaspoon salt and ½ teaspoon pepper in a bowl. Brush all over chickens.
2. Fasten to the spit of an electric rotisserie, following manufacturer's directions.
3. Roast slowly, brushing chicken frequently with the seasoned butter and oil. Chickens should be done, with skin a crisp golden-brown, in about 1 hour and 15 minutes. To serve, cut each chicken in half with poultry shears.

AU PORTO CHICKEN

Chicken in wine with a Portuguese touch —white Port is the cooking liquid. If you prefer a less sweet flavor, choose a dry white wine, such as Chablis. This recipe was developed to cook in an electric slow cooker.

Cook on 190° to 200° for 10 hours, or on 290° to 300° for 6 hours. Makes 4 servings.

- 1 **broiler-fryer (about 3 pounds)**
- 1½ **teaspoons salt**
- ½ **teaspoon pepper**
- 1 **large onion, chopped (1 cup)**
- 1 **clove garlic, minced**
- 2 **large carrots, pared and chopped**
- 2 **tablespoons olive oil or vegetable oil**
- 1 **teaspoon leaf rosemary, crumbled**
- 1 **cup white Port or dry white wine or chicken broth**
- ½ **pound mushrooms, quartered OR: 1 can (6 ounces) whole mushrooms**
- 2 **tablespoons all-purpose flour**

1. Season chicken with ½ teaspoon of the salt and ¼ teaspoon of the pepper. Skewer neck skin to back and tie legs.
2. Sauté onion, garlic and carrots until soft in oil in a large skillet or 3½-quart electric slow cooker with a browning unit. Stir in remaining 1 teaspoon salt, ¼ teaspoon pepper and rosemary. Spoon into the bottom of electric slow cooker.
3. Place chicken on top of vegetables; pour in wine or chicken broth; cover.
4. Cook on low (190° to 200°) 10 hours, or on high (290° to 300°) 6 hours, or until chicken is tender when pierced with a two-tined fork. Remove chicken to a heated platter and keep warm.
5. Turn heat control to high (290° to 300°). Add mushrooms and cook 15 minutes. Combine flour with ¼ cup cold water in a cup; stir into cooker until well-blended. Cover; simmer 15 minutes. Stir in a few drops bottled gravy coloring, if you wish. Slice chicken and pass sauce in heated gravy boat. Serve with a bottle of chilled dry white wine and a crisp salad of tossed greens with marinated artichokes, if you wish.

CHICKEN EGG ROLLS

Fill the rolls and chill overnight—this makes them extra crisp.

Makes 12 rolls.

Filling
- 1 **large onion, chopped (1 cup)**
- 1 **cup thinly sliced celery**
- 1 **teaspoon peanut oil**
- 1 **tablespoon soy sauce**
- 2 **cups diced cooked chicken**

Wrappers
- 4 **eggs**
- 1½ **cups water**
- 1½ **cups sifted all-purpose flour**
- 1 **teaspoon salt**
  Peanut oil
  Sweet Sour Sauce (recipe, page 92)

1. Make filling: Combine onion, celery, and oil in a small saucepan; cover. Cook over low heat 10 minutes, or until soft. Stir in soy sauce; pour over chicken in a medium-size bowl; toss to mix well. Let stand while making wrappers.
2. Make wrappers: Beat eggs with water until foamy in a medium-size bowl; beat in flour and salt just until smooth. (Batter will be thin.)
3. Heat an 8-inch crêpe pan or skillet slowly; test temperature by sprinkling in a few drops of water. When drops bounce about, temperature is right.

Add about 1 teaspoon oil, tilting pan to cover bottom completely.
4. Pour batter, ¼ cup for each wrapper, into pan. Bake 1 to 2 minutes, or until top appears dry and underside is golden. Lift out onto paper towels to cool. (Only one side is baked.) Repeat with remaining batter, adding a little oil before each baking, to make 12 wrappers; cool on paper towels.
5. When ready to fill, spoon ¼ cup chicken mixture slightly off center on baked side of each wrapper. Fold short end up over filling, then fold both sides toward center and roll up, jellyroll fashion, to cover filling completely; fasten with one or two wooden picks. Place in a shallow dish; cover. Chill overnight.
6. When ready to cook, heat a 1½-inch depth of oil to 400° in an electric skillet or an electric deep fat frying pan. Drop in chilled rolls, 2 or 3 at a time; fry, turning once, 5 to 8 minutes, or until golden. Drain on paper towels. Keep rolls hot in warm oven until all are cooked. Remove picks; serve rolls plain or with SWEET SOUR SAUCE.

POT-ROASTED CHICKEN

Beef broth and thyme are the flavor secrets to this French-style chicken dish developed to cook in an electric slow cooker.

Cook on 190° to 200° for 10 hours, or on 290° to 300° for 5 hours.
Makes 6 servings.

- 1 stewing chicken (about 5 pounds)
- 3 tablespoons butter or margarine
- 2 teaspoons leaf thyme, crumbled
- 1 can condensed beef broth
- 3 tablespoons all-purpose flour
- 1 small can evaporated milk

1. Brown chicken on all sides in butter or margarine and thyme until golden in a large skillet or an electric slow cooker with a browning unit.
2. Combine browned chicken and beef broth in slow cooker; cover.
3. Cook on low (190° to 200°) 10 hours, or on high (290° to 300°) 5 hours, or until chicken is tender when pierced with a two-tined fork. Remove chicken to a heated platter and keep warm.
4. Turn heat control to high (290° to 300°). Combine flour and evaporated milk in a cup; stir into liquid in slow cooker until well-blended. Cover; cook 15 minutes. Taste and season with salt and pepper, if you wish. Serve sauce separately. Serve with cooked elbow macaroni and buttered Italian green beans.

CHÂTEAU-STYLE DUCKLING

French cooks, too, are learning the advantage of using their microwave ovens with classic dishes.

Microwave for 25 minutes.
Makes 4 servings.

- 1 frozen duckling, thawed and quartered (about 4 pounds)
- ½ cup orange marmalade
- ½ cup orange juice
- 1 tablespoon soy sauce
- ½ teaspoon salt
- 1 tablespoon butter or margarine
- 1 tablespoon all-purpose flour
- ¾ cup dry white wine
- ¼ teaspoon black pepper

1. Place duckling pieces, skin-side down, in an 8-cup microwave-safe casserole.
2. Cook in microwave oven 10 minutes, turning duckling after 5 minutes. Drain off fat.
3. Combine marmalade, juice, soy sauce and salt in a 2-cup measure. Set ½ cup of the mixture aside. Brush duckling with remaining sauce; cook in oven, basting and turning pieces in dish at 5 minute intervals 15 minutes. (Test for doneness. Age of duck affects cooking time.) Cover dish; let stand while preparing sauce.
4. Melt butter or margarine in a glass bowl or 2-cup measure in oven for 30 seconds. Stir in flour. Add wine and pepper, stirring constantly. Cook in oven 1 minute. Mix well; stir in reserved marmalade mixture. Cook in oven 1½ minutes, stirring well. Spoon over duckling and garnish with orange slices and watercress, if you wish. Excellent with wild rice.

CHICKEN CROQUETTES

Croquettes have a noble origin, and this recipe proves it.

Makes 8 croquettes.

- 2 cups coarsely ground cooked chicken
- 1 cup (2 slices) soft bread crumbs
- 2 eggs, well beaten
- 2 tablespoons milk
- 1 tablespoon minced onion
- 1 tablespoon minced green pepper
- ½ teaspoon salt
- ¼ teaspoon leaf savory, crumbled Dash pepper
- ¼ cup finely chopped toasted almonds
- ½ cup fine dry bread crumbs
- ½ cup milk
  Shortening, lard, or vegetable oil
  Velouté Sauce (recipe, page 92)

1. Combine chicken, soft bread crumbs, eggs, the 2 tablespoons milk, onion, green pepper, salt, savory, pepper, and almonds in medium-size bowl; chill about 2 hours.
2. Shape chilled mixture into 8 cylindrical croquettes, each 1 inch in diameter; roll in fine dry bread crumbs; dip in the ½ cup milk; roll again in crumbs; brush off any loose crumbs.
3. Melt fat or add oil to a 1-inch depth in an electric frypan; turn heat control to 375°.
4. Fry croquettes, 2 or 3 at a time, 2 minutes, or until golden brown; drain on paper towels.
5. Serve on heated platter with VELOUTÉ SAUCE.

HONAN CHICKEN

Sweet and sour sauce originated in central China, but it's become very popular in the southern regions. With this same sauce one can make Sweet and Sour Pork, and Sweet and Sour Shrimp.

Makes 6 servings.

- 3 whole chicken breasts (about 10 ounces each)
- 1 tablespoon dry sherry
- 1 teaspoon salt
- 4 teaspoons cornstarch
- 1 can (8¼ ounces) pineapple chunks
- ½ cup sweet mixed pickles, cut into ½-inch pieces
- 2 medium-size tomatoes
- 1 small green pepper
- 2 cloves garlic, crushed
- ¼ cup vegetable oil
- 2 tablespoons soy sauce
- 1 tablespoon vinegar

1. Skin and bone chicken breasts. Cut into 1-inch cubes. Mix with sherry, salt and 2 teaspoons of the cornstarch in a medium-size bowl.
2. Drain the pineapple and sweet pickles; save the juice. Wash and cut each tomato into 6 to 8 wedges. Wash, seed, and cut pepper into wedges.
3. Heat garlic and oil in an electric wok or electric fry pan set at 375°; remove garlic. Add chicken pieces; stir-fry quickly for about 3 minutes, until all the meat turns opaque. Remove from wok; keep warm.
4. Add and heat soy sauce, vinegar and juices from pineapple and pickles to boiling. Combine remaining 2 teaspoons cornstarch with 1 tablespoon water. Stir into juices in wok.
5. Cook, stirring constantly, until thickened. Add pineapple, pickles, pepper wedges and tomato. Cook for about 10 seconds. Return chicken to wok and toss to coat with sauce.

DRUMSTICKS DIABLE

Sweet and spicy best describes this chicken treat. A cut-up chicken can be used in place of the drumsticks. This recipe was developed to cook in an electric slow cooker.

Cook on 190° to 200° for 8 hours, or on 290° to 300° for 4 hours. Makes 4 servings.

       8 **drumsticks (about 2 pounds)**
     ¼ **cup all-purpose flour**
   1½ **teaspoon salt**
         Dash pepper
       3 **tablespoons butter or margarine**
       1 **can (1 pound) tomatoes**
       2 **tablespoons brown sugar**
       2 **tablespoons cider vinegar**
       2 **tablespoons Worcestershire sauce**
       1 **teaspoon chili powder**
       1 **teaspoon dry mustard**
     ½ **teaspoon celery seeds**
       1 **clove garlic, minced**
         Few drops bottled red-pepper seasoning

1. Shake drumsticks in a plastic bag with flour, ½ teaspoon of the salt and pepper.
2. Brown in butter or margarine in a large skillet or an electric slow cooker with a browning unit; remove.
3. Stir tomatoes, brown sugar, vinegar, Worcestershire sauce, chili powder, dry mustard, celery seeds, garlic and red-pepper seasoning into pan with salt; bring to boiling.
4. Combine drumsticks and sauce in slow cooker; cover.
5. Cook on low (190° to 200°) 8 hours, or on high (290° to 300°) 4 hours, or until chicken is tender.

IMPERIAL CHICKEN

A bit of a production to make, but a splendid dish to serve. And if guests are late, this dinner will wait.

Bake at 350° for 1 hour, 15 minutes. Makes 8 servings.

       2 **cups soft bread crumbs (4 slices)**
     ¾ **cup finely diced cooked ham**
     ½ **cup chopped parsley**
     ½ **cup (1 stick) hard butter or margarine, sliced thin**
       4 **whole chicken breasts (about 12 ounces each)**
       4 **drumsticks with thighs (about 2 pounds)**
       1 **cup milk**
       1 **cup fine dry bread crumbs**
       1 **envelope (2 to a package) cream of mushroom soup mix**
       2 **cups cold water**
     ¼ **cup chili sauce**

1. Mix soft bread crumbs, ham and parsley in a large bowl; cut in butter or margarine quickly with a pastry blender; chill.
2. Halve chicken breasts, then cut out rib bones with scissors. Separate thighs and drumsticks at joints with a sharp knife. To make pockets for stuffing, pull each breast piece open on its thick side, and cut an opening along bone in each leg and thigh.
3. Stuff about ¼ cup chilled stuffing into each half breast and 2 table-spoonfuls into each leg and thigh.
4. Place ½ cup of the milk in a pie plate and dry bread crumbs on a sheet of wax paper. Roll stuffed chicken pieces in milk, then in bread crumbs to coat; chill while making sauce.
5. Combine mushroom soup mix and water in a small saucepan; cook, following label directions. Stir in remaining ½ cup milk and chili sauce; pour 1 cup of the sauce into a 12-cup shallow baking dish.
6. Place chicken pieces in sauce in dish; drizzle remaining sauce over.
7. Bake in moderate oven (350°) 1 hour and 15 minutes, or until tender and richly golden. Garnish with parsley, if you wish.
HOSTESS TIP: If dinner is delayed, simply lower oven heat to very slow (250°) and fit a sheet of foil, tent fashion, over casserole.

CHILI CHICKEN

Serve this chili in deep soup bowls, but add forks as well as spoons. A salad of shredded lettuce and toasted corn chips are the perfect accompaniment. This recipe was developed to cook in an electric slow cooker.

Cook on 290° to 300° for 2 hours, then on 190° to 200° for 6 hours. Makes 4 servings.

       1 **broiler-fryer, cut up (about 3 pounds)**
     ¼ **cup all-purpose flour**
   2½ **teaspoons salt**
     ¼ **teaspoon pepper**
     ¼ **cup vegetable shortening**
       1 **large onion, chopped (1 cup)**
       1 **clove garlic, minced**
       1 **green pepper, halved, seeded and chopped**
       1 **can (1 pound) tomatoes**
       1 **can condensed chicken broth**
       1 **cup chopped ripe olives**
     ½ **cup yellow cornmeal**
     ¼ **cup tomato paste**
       1 **to 3 tablespoons chili powder**
       1 **teaspoon sugar**

1. Shake chicken pieces in a mixture of flour, 1½ teaspoons of the salt and pepper in a plastic bag to coat evenly.
2. Brown chicken pieces in shortening in a large skillet or an electric slow cooker with a browning unit; remove and reserve. Pour off all but 2 tablespoons of the pan drippings. Sauté onion, garlic and green pepper in drippings until soft.
3. Place chicken pieces and onion mixture in slow cooker. Combine tomatoes, chicken broth, olives, cornmeal, tomato paste, chili powder, remaining 1 teaspoon salt and sugar in a medium-size bowl, pour over chicken; cover.
4. Cook on high (290° to 300°) for 2 hours. Stir at this point. Turn heat control to low (190° to 200°) and cook 6 hours longer, or until chicken is tender when pierced with a fork.

ROMAN TURKEY ALFREDO

Fettucini noodles are topped with browned slices of cooked turkey and a Supreme Sauce in this continental treat.

Makes 4 servings.

       1 **package (8 ounces) regular noodles**
       1 **cup freshly grated Parmesan cheese**
       8 **tablespoons (1 stick) butter or margarine**
         Supreme Sauce (recipe, page 91)
       1 **egg**
       1 **teaspoon leaf oregano, crumbled**
     ½ **teaspoon salt**
         Dash pepper
       2 **tablespoons water**
     ¾ **cup fine dry bread crumbs**
     12 **slices cooked turkey breast**
       3 **tablespoons olive oil or vegetable oil**

1. Cook noodles in a kettle, following label directions; drain; return to kettle. Add Parmesan cheese and 5 table-spoons of the butter or margarine; toss lightly with two forks until butter or margarine melts and noodles are evenly coated. Keep hot.
2. While noodles cook, make SUPREME SAUCE.
3. Beat egg with oregano, salt, pepper, and water in a pie plate; place bread crumbs on wax paper.
4. Dip turkey slices into egg mixture, then into bread crumbs to coat well. Brown slices, a few at a time, in the remaining 3 tablespoons butter or margarine mixed with oil in a large skillet.
5. Spoon hot noodles into an 8-cup shallow flame-proof dish; arrange turkey slices, overlapping, on top; spoon SUPREME SAUCE over middle of turkey slices.
6. Broil, 4 inches from heat, 5 minutes, or until sauce puffs and turns golden. Serve at once.

HAM'N CHICKEN MOUSSE

This refreshing gelatin salad is packed with fruits and vegetables to compliment the chicken.

Makes 8 servings.

2 whole chicken breasts (about 14 ounces each)
2 cups water
1 small onion, peeled and sliced
   Few celery leaves
1 teaspoon salt
1 bay leaf
4 peppercorns
1 can (8¼ ounces) crushed pineapple
2 envelopes unflavored gelatin
1 cup mayonnaise or salad dressing
1 tablespoon lemon juice
1 teaspoon prepared mustard
½ pound cooked ham
1 can (5 ounces) water chestnuts, drained

1. Combine chicken breasts, water, onion, celery, salt, bay leaf and peppercorns in a large saucepan; bring to boiling; cover. Simmer 30 minutes, or until chicken is tender.
2. While chicken cooks, drain syrup from pineapple into a 1-cup measure; add water, if needed, to make ½ cup. Stir in gelatin to soften; reserve pineapple.
3. Remove chicken from broth; strain broth into a 4-cup measure; add water, if needed, to make 3 cups. Return to same saucepan; stir softened gelatin into broth.
4. Heat slowly, stirring constantly, until gelatin dissolves; remove from heat. Blend in mayonnaise or salad dressing, lemon juice and mustard.
5. Pour into a shallow metal pan. Freeze 20 minutes, or just until firm about 1 inch from edges but still soft in middle.
6. While gelatin mixture chills, pull skin from chicken and take meat from bones; dice meat. (There should be about 1½ cups.) Dice ham and water chestnuts; combine with diced chicken and pineapple in a medium-size bowl.
7. Spoon partly frozen gelatin mixture into a chilled large bowl; beat until thick and fluffy. Fold in chicken-ham mixture; spoon into an 8-cup ring mold. Chill several hours until firm.
8. When ready to serve, loosen salad around edge and center ring with a knife; dip mold very quickly in and out of hot water. Cover with a large serving plate; turn upside down; gently lift off mold.

PARTY CHICKEN BURGERS

Open-faced sandwiches the crowd will love.

Makes 6 servings.

2 cups cubed cooked chicken
1 can condensed cream of celery soup
1 small onion, finely chopped (¼ cup)
¼ cup finely chopped green pepper
3 tablespoons chopped pimiento
1 can (3 or 4 ounces) sliced mushrooms, drained
1 tablespoon prepared mustard
½ teaspoon salt
½ teaspoon monosodium glutamate
6 hamburger buns, split

1. Combine chicken, cream of celery soup, onion, green pepper, pimiento, mushrooms, prepared mustard, salt and monosodium glutamate in a large bowl; stir to blend.
2. Spread an equal amount of mixture, about ¼ cup, on each bun half.
3. Broil 6 to 8 inches from heat for 7 to 10 minutes, until golden brown and bubbly. Serve immediately.

HEARTY SALAD SANDWICH

Delicious chicken salad makes summer suppers for two.

Makes 2 servings.

1 whole chicken breast (about 12 ounces)
1 cup water
1 small onion, sliced
   Handful celery leaves
¾ teaspoon salt
   Pepper
½ cup diced celery
¼ cup slivered almonds
¼ cup mayonnaise or salad dressing
1 tablespoon milk
⅛ teaspoon dry mustard
2 large Vienna rolls
   Butter or margarine
   Lettuce
   Cherry tomatoes

1. Place chicken breast in a medium-size saucepan with the water, onion, celery leaves, ½ teaspoon of the salt and a dash of pepper. Simmer, covered, 20 to 30 minutes, or until chicken is tender. Let stand until cool enough to handle, then skin chicken and remove meat from bones; dice.
2. Combine chicken, celery and almonds in medium-size bowl. Mix mayonnaise or salad dressing, milk, remaining ¼ teaspoon salt, mustard and a dash of pepper into chicken mixture, tossing lightly to mix.
3. Split Vienna rolls and butter. Line buttered rolls with lettuce; fill with salad. Garnish with cherry tomatoes.

PASTA CHICKEN SALAD

This one is a whole meal in itself. Almonds and apple add texture.

Makes 2 servings.

1 cup elbow macaroni
½ cup chopped red apple
1 cup diced cooked chicken
   OR; 1 can (5 ounces) boned chicken, diced
¼ cup toasted slivered almonds
1½ teaspoons grated onion
⅓ cup mayonnaise or salad dressing
2 tablespoons light cream
1 tablespoon lemon juice
½ teaspoon curry powder
¼ teaspoon salt
¼ teaspoon sugar

1. Cook macaroni in a saucepan, following label directions; cool to room temperature. Combine with apple, chicken, almonds and onion in a medium-size bowl.
2. Combine mayonnaise or salad dressing, cream, lemon juice, curry powder, salt and sugar in a small bowl; stir into macaroni mixture; chill. Garnish with red apple slices, if you wish.

SUPERMARKET SUPPER

A ready-barbecued chicken and prepared macaroni salad from the deli section of your supermarket can make dinner for two.

Makes 2 servings.

1 container (1 pound) prepared macaroni salad
½ package (4 ounces) shredded Cheddar cheese
1 small can (8 ounces) lima beans, drained
¼ cup chopped celery
¼ teaspoon mixed Italian herbs, crumbled
½ small head romaine, washed, dried and separated into leaves
1 medium-size tomato, cut in wedges
1 ready-to-eat barbecued chicken (about 2 pounds)
   Sweet mixed pickles
   Stuffed green olives

1. Combine macaroni salad, cheese, lima beans, celery and herbs in a large bowl; toss lightly to mix well. Chill at least an hour to season.
2. Line a platter with romaine leaves; break remaining into bite-size pieces in center, spoon macaroni salad on top. Tuck tomato wedges around edges of salad.
3. Cut chicken in half with kitchen scissors; place, skin-side up, on platter beside salad.
4. Garnish with pickles and olives.

SATAYS WITH PEANUT SAUCE

One finds delicious satays, really miniature kabobs, throughout Southeast Asia. Marinades vary from very mild and slightly sweet to scaldingly hot. The best sauce is this Malaysian version with a base of ground peanuts. Satays make excellent appetizers while guests wait for the rest of the meal to grill outdoors.

Makes 6 servings.

- 3 **whole chicken breasts, (about 12 ounces each) skinned, boned and cut into 1-inch cubes**
- 1 **teaspoon grated lemon rind**
- 3 **slices preserved ginger, finely minced**
  OR: ½ teaspoon ground ginger
- 1 **tablespoon crushed red chili peppers**
- 2 **teaspoons ground coriander**
- 1 **medium-size onion, minced (½ cup)**
- 2 **cloves garlic, minced**
  Pinch ground cumin
- ¼ **cup vegetable oil**
- 1 **teaspoon salt**
- 2 **teaspoons soy sauce**
- 1 **cup Coconut Milk (recipe follows)**
  Peanut Sauce (recipe, page 92)

1. Put chicken in a shallow glass or ceramic dish.
2. Whirl lemon rind, ginger, chili peppers, coriander, onion, garlic, cumin, oil, salt and soy sauce in the container of an electric blender 2 minutes to a smooth paste. Gradually pour in COCONUT MILK and whirl until smooth; pour over poultry.
3. Marinate for 2 hours. Thread meat onto four-inch wooden or bamboo cocktail skewers.
4. Grill, 3 inches above white-hot charcoal, 3 to 5 minutes, brushing with leftover marinade from time to time. Serve with PEANUT SAUCE.
SUGGESTED VARIATION: Although not authentic, you can prepare the above recipe with small chicken parts, such as drumsticks, wings and thighs, skinned but left on the bone, instead of cutting the meat and threading on skewers. Remove skin, cut a few gashes in meat and marinate twice as long as stated above. Grill, 4 inches above white-hot charcoal, for 15 to 20 minutes, basting with sauce and turning frequently. Be careful not to overcook. The pieces will be easy-to-handle finger-food.

COCONUT MILK: Makes 1 cup. To make this you will need a fresh coconut, or 1 can (3½ ounces) flaked coconut. If using a fresh coconut, crack open and remove white meat. Grate or chop until you have 1 cup.

Combine with 1 cup boiling water and let soak for 30 minutes. Or combine flaked coconut and 1 cup boiling water in a small bowl and let stand 1 hour. Pour through a cheesecloth-lined strainer, squeezing all juice out of coconut.

PÂTÉ SALAD

Crisp western lettuce and hearty pâté make the perfect supper salad on a hot day.

Makes 4 servings.

- 1 **large head iceberg lettuce**
  Pâté Maison (recipe, page 82)
  Wine Vinegar Dressing (recipe follows)
- 2 **hard-cooked eggs, shelled and sliced**
  Sliced green onion

1. Core, rinse and thoroughly drain lettuce. Chill in plastic crisper or disposable plastic bag. Prepare PÂTÉ MAISON and chill. Prepare WINE VINEGAR DRESSING.
2. Shortly before serving, line 6 shallow chilled individual salad bowls or plates with small lettuce leaves. Finely shred 4 cups lettuce and toss with dressing. Spoon into salad bowls and top with a scoop of PÂTÉ MAISON. Garnish with egg and green onion.

WINE VINEGAR DRESSING: Makes ½ cup. Combine ⅓ cup vegetable oil, 2 tablespoons wine vinegar, ¼ teaspoon garlic salt, ¼ teaspoon salt, ¼ teaspoon leaf basil, crumbled, ¼ teaspoon lemon-pepper and ¼ teaspoon curry powder in a jar with a screw top. Cover and shake well.

POULTRY POINTER

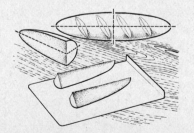

Barbecues are better when you have some crusty bread sticks to add to the menu. Simply cut a loaf of Italian or French bread, lengthwise, then crosswise to make 4 sticks. Then cut each stick in half lengthwise. Brush each with a mixture of 3 tablespoons softened butter or margarine and 1 clove garlic, crushed. Bake in hot oven (400°) 5 minutes.

SKEWERED CHICKEN CANTONESE

Flavors borrowed from mild Cantonese cooking give this chicken a special difference. It's delicious.

Makes 8 servings.

- 4 **whole chicken breasts, split (about 12 ounces each)**
- 1 **cup dry sherry**
- 2 **tablespoons vegetable oil**
- 1 **tablespoon soy sauce**
- ½ **teaspoon salt**
- ⅛ **teaspoon pepper**
- ¼ **teaspoon sugar**
- 4 **slices fresh ginger root (optional)**

1. Bone chicken breasts and cut each split breast into 4 pieces.
2. Combine sherry, oil, soy sauce, salt, pepper, sugar and ginger root in a large glass bowl; add chicken pieces. Marinate 4 hours in refrigerator.
3. Drain chicken; reserve marinade. Thread pieces loosely on 8 short skewers with pieces just touching.
4. Grill, turning and basting once, 10 minutes, or until chicken is golden.
5. Bring remaining marinade to boiling in a small saucepan; pour into shallow dish. Turn cooked chicken skewers in sauce immediately as they are removed from the grill. Serve on prepared packaged noodles with almonds mix, if you wish.

BONANZA BOBS

Thread chicken breasts on skewers with green pepper and onions and you're all set for the outdoor grill.

Makes 8 servings.

- 4 **whole chicken breasts (about 12 ounces each)**
- 4 **green peppers, halved, seeded and cut into 1-inch pieces**
- 2 **cans (1 pound each) onions, well drained**
- 2 **teaspoons monosodium glutamate**
- 2 **teaspoons salt**
- ½ **cup (1 stick) butter or margarine, melted**
- 1 **tablespoon dried leaf tarragon, crumbled**
- 1 **tablespoon lemon juice**

1. Bone chicken breasts; remove skin. Cut each breast half into 6 to 8 chunks, about 1½ inches square.
2. Alternate chunks on 8 skewers with green pepper and onions. Sprinkle with monosodium glutamate and salt.
3. Combine melted butter or margarine, tarragon and lemon juice. Brush over kabobs. Grill 3 inches from heat for 5 minutes. Turn and grill 5 minutes longer, brushing occasionally.

CHICKEN ON A SPIT

Currant jelly glazes this chicken as it twirls on the rôtisserie.

Makes 4 to 6 servings.

  2 cups ready-mix bread stuffing
      (from an 8-ounce package)
 ½ cup (1 stick) butter or margarine,
      melted
 ⅔ cup water
  1 roasting chicken (about 4 pounds)
 ½ cup currant jelly, melted

1. Prepare stuffing mix with ⅓ cup of the melted butter or margarine and water, following label directions.
2. Wash chicken, then dry. Stuff neck and body cavities lightly; skewer neck skin to body; secure body cavity closed and tie legs tightly to tail.
3. Place chicken on spit; brush with remaining butter or margarine. Set spit in position over hot coals; start spit turning.
4. Roast 1 hour; brush with melted jelly. Continue roasting, brushing often with more jelly, 30 minutes longer, or until chicken is tender.

CRUSTY CHICKEN WINGS

Crusty wing drumsticks, hot and savory from the oven, are great with frosty drinks.

Bake at 375° for 45 minutes.
Makes 8 servings.

 24 chicken wings (about 3 pounds)
  1 small can evaporated milk
  1 tablespoon prepared mustard
  1 clove garlic, minced
  1 cup fine dry bread crumbs
  1 teaspoon instant minced onion
  1 teaspoon seasoned salt
 ¼ teaspoon seasoned pepper
  1 envelope or teaspoon instant
      chicken broth

1. Trim tips from chicken wings. (Save for soup kettle.) Divide each wing in half by cutting through joint.
2. Blend milk, mustard and garlic in a shallow dish. Combine bread crumbs, onion, salt, pepper and broth in another dish.
3. Dip chicken pieces into milk mixture , then into crumbs to coat well.
4. Bake in moderate oven (375°) 45 minutes, turning once, until chicken is tender. Serve with potato salad and marinated vegetables for a simple, yet festive patio supper.
COOK'S TIP: To freeze: Place chicken wings in a single layer in buttered foil pans. Cover with foil or plastic wrap; freeze. Bake in moderate oven (375°) 1 hour, turning once, or until chicken is golden.

Chapter 6 (from page 59)

BACON AND CHICKEN LIVERS

These luscious morsels are oven baked and served on toast.

Bake at 400° for 30 minutes.
Makes 6 servings.

 ½ pound bacon
  1 pound chicken livers
 ¼ cup all-purpose flour
  1 teaspoon salt
 ½ teaspoon paprika
  6 slices hot toast
      Pepper

1. Lay bacon slices in a single layer on rack of broiler pan. (If slices don't separate easily, heat in oven for a few minutes.)
2. Bake in hot oven (400°) 10 minutes, or until crisp. (No need to turn.) Remove rack with bacon on it; keep warm. (Leave oven heat on.)
3. Shake chicken livers in mixture of flour, salt and paprika in a plastic bag to coat well; lay livers in hot drippings in broiler pan.
4. Bake in hot oven (400°) 10 minutes, or until browned on underside; turn; bake 10 minutes longer, or until browned on other side. Drain on paper towels.
5. Arrange toast slices in single layer on heated large serving platter; brush very lightly with bacon drippings from broiler pan. Arrange livers on top; sprinkle with pepper; top with criss-crossed bacon slices. Serve with chilled marinated vegetable.

POULTRY POINTERS

• Tip green beans in seconds, not minutes, by lining up a handful on the cutting board and cutting off all the tips of one end in a single motion. Turn and tip the other ends.
• For cut-up beans, keep them in line and make cuts at 1-inch intervals along beans.
• For French-style, draw the knife, lengthwise, down whole bean, then half, crosswise, if you wish.

RUBY PEAR AND CHICKEN SALAD

Canned pears and gelatin make a cool, yet special summer salad.

Makes 4 servings.

  1 can (1 pound) pear halves
  2 packages (3 ounces each)
      raspberry-flavored gelatin
  2 cups boiling water
 ¼ cup sherry or lemon juice
  2 cups diced cooked chicken
 ⅓ cup diced green pepper
 ⅓ cup chopped celery
 ½ cup mayonnaise or salad dressing
 ¼ cup toasted slivered almonds
 ¼ teaspoon ground ginger
      Salt and pepper

1. Drain pear halves into a 2-cup measure; add enough water to make 1¼ cups, reserving pears.
2. Dissolve gelatin in boiling water in a large bowl. Stir pear liquid into dissolved gelatin along with sherry or lemon juice. Chill until syrupy.
3. Arrange pear halves, cut side up, in a 5-cup ring mold. Pour gelatin carefully over pears. Chill 4 hours.
4. Combine cooked chicken, green pepper, celery, mayonnaise or salad dressing, almonds and ginger in a medium-size bowl; taste and season with salt and pepper. Chill until serving time.
5. Unmold gelatin ring by running a thin-bladed knife around edge and dip in and out of a pan of hot water; invert onto a lettuce-lined plate. Fill center with chicken salad.

CATALAN CHICKEN

Simmer and serve this rich Spanish dish in your most colorful kettle.

Makes 4 servings.

  1 roasting chicken, cut up (3½ to 4
      pounds)
  3 tablespoons olive oil
  1 teaspoon salt
  3 medium-size onions, sliced
  1 can (4 ounces) pimiento, sliced
  2 medium-size tomatoes, peeled and
      chopped
  2 tablespoons tomato paste
 ¼ cup water
 ¼ cup dry sherry
 ½ teaspoon sugar

1. Brown chicken pieces in oil with salt in a large kettle. Remove.
2. Add sliced onions to pan and cook until soft.
3. Add pimiento, tomatoes, tomato paste, water, sherry and sugar to kettle and bring to boiling; return chicken to kettle and simmer, covered, 40 minutes, or until fork-tender.

NECTARINE AND CHICKEN CURRY

California's special summer fruit adds flavor with little work to this tender chicken dish.

Makes 4 servings.

- 1 broiler-fryer, quartered (about 3 pounds)
  Salt
  Pepper
- 2 tablespoons butter or margarine
- 1 teaspoon curry powder (or more to taste)
- 3 large fresh nectarines
- ½ cup flaked coconut
- 2 green onions, sliced

1. Sprinkle chicken with salt and pepper. Heat butter or margarine and curry powder in a large skillet; cook 2 minutes.
2. Add chicken and brown slowly. Cover and cook about 45 minutes, or until fork-tender. Remove chicken to warm platter and keep warm.
3. Slice nectarines; add to drippings in skillet. Sprinkle with coconut and onion. Cook until lightly browned and heated through, turning as needed. Spoon over chicken. Serve at once with prepared frozen rice verdi.

PARMESAN BAKED CHICKEN

An easy and pleasing variation of the beloved Italian veal dish. This time it's chicken that's flavored with piquant Parmesan cheese.

Bake at 425° for 50 minutes.
Makes 8 servings.

- ⅓ cup vegetable oil
- 2 broiler-fryers, cut up (about 3 pounds each)
- 1 teaspoon leaf oregano, crumbled
- 1 teaspoon salt
  Paprika
- 1 can (3 or 4 ounces) sliced mushrooms
- 3 tablespoons grated Parmesan cheese

1. Line a shallow baking pan with aluminum foil. Pour oil into pan. Place in hot oven (425°) to heat, about 10 minutes. Remove pan from oven.
2. Place chicken pieces, skin-side down, in hot oil. Sprinkle with half the oregano and salt. Sprinkle lightly with paprika.
3. Bake in hot oven (425°) 30 minutes. Turn chicken pieces; sprinkle with remaining oregano and salt and paprika. Bake 15 minutes longer; remove from oven.
4. Spoon fat and drippings in pan over chicken. Pour mushrooms over chicken; sprinkle with Parmesan cheese; bake 5 minutes longer.

NECTARINE CHICKEN FRANCAIS

Star this recipe for summertime for a quick, yet delicious dish when nectarines are in season.

Makes 4 servings.

- 4 chicken cutlets
- 2 tablespoons cornstarch
- 1½ teaspoons paprika
- 1 teaspoon garlic salt
- ¼ teaspoon pepper
- 1 tablespoon vegetable oil
- 1 tablespoon butter or margarine
- 3 tablespoons brandy
- 4 fresh nectarines
- 1 cup heavy cream
  Fresh tarragon (optional)

1. Add chicken cutlets to a mixture of cornstarch, paprika, garlic salt and pepper in a plastic bag; shake until well coated.
2. Brown chicken slowly in heated oil and butter or margarine in a large skillet. Add brandy; cover and cook until almost tender, about 15 minutes. Halve nectarines remove pits. Cut fruit into thick slices. Add to chicken, pour cream over all and continue cooking uncovered, over moderate heat, about 10 minutes longer, until chicken is tender and nectarines are heated and lightly glazed. Serve from skillet or arrange in serving dish and garnish with fresh tarragon.

SKILLET CHICKEN AND TOMATO

The chicken pieces are browned and cooked with fresh rosy tomatoes and dill.

Makes 4 servings.

- 1 broiler-fryer, cut up (about 3 pounds)
- 1½ teaspoons salt
- ¼ teaspoon pepper
- 2 tablespoons butter or margarine
- 1 small onion, chopped (¼ cup)
- ½ cup chopped celery with leaves
- 4 medium-size tomatoes, peeled and chopped
- ¼ cup fresh dill
  OR:1 tablespoon dried dillweed
  Grated Parmesan cheese

1. Sprinkle chicken with 1 teaspoon of the salt and pepper. Heat butter in a large skillet. Add chicken and brown on all sides. Remove from skillet.
2. Add onion and celery; cook until tender. Add tomatoes and dill; sprinkle with remaining ½ teaspoon salt. Add chicken; spoon some of the tomato mixture over chicken.
3. Cover; simmer 30 minutes, until chicken is tender. Serve sprinkled lightly with grated Parmesan cheese.

CREOLE CHICKEN

This recipe will have dinner on the table in a little over half an hour.

Makes 4 servings.

- 1 broiler-fryer, cut up (about 3 pounds)
- 2 teaspoons salt
- ½ teaspoon paprika
- 2 tablespoons butter or margarine
- 1 medium-size onion, sliced
- 1 medium-size green pepper, halved, seeded and cut into strips
- ½ cup chopped celery
- 1 can (1 pound) tomatoes
- ½ teaspoon leaf thyme, crumbled
- 1 can (3 or 4 ounces) sliced mushrooms

1. Sprinkle chicken pieces with 1 teaspoon of the salt and paprika. Melt butter or margarine in a large skillet; add chicken and brown on all sides.
2. Add onion, green pepper, celery, tomatoes, remaining salt and thyme.
3. Bring to a boil, reduce heat, cover and simmer 20 minutes. Add mushrooms and liquid. Simmer 5 to 10 minutes longer.

FLORENTINE CHICKEN

Spinach takes on new elegance in this Italian chicken-cheese recipe.

Makes 4 servings.

- 1 package (10 ounces) frozen chopped spinach
- 3 tablespoons butter or margarine
- 3 tablespoons all-purpose flour
- 1 teaspoon monosodium glutamate
- 1 teaspoon salt
  Dash cayenne pepper
- 1½ cups milk
- ¼ cup grated Parmesan cheese
- ½ cup light cream
- 2 cups diced cooked chicken
- ⅓ cup dry bread crumbs

1. Cook spinach, drain well, and transfer to a 6-cup flame-proof casserole.
2. Melt 2 tablespoons of the butter or margarine in saucepan. Stir in flour, monosodium glutamate, salt and cayenne. Gradually add milk and cook, stirring constantly, until mixture thickens and bubbles 3 minutes.
3. Add cheese and cream; cook over low heat until cheese is melted. Add chicken; pour cream mixture over spinach. Sprinkle with bread crumbs, dot with remaining 1 tablespoon butter or margarine.
4. Place under broiler and heat until lightly browned. Serve with an antipasto salad and crisp bread sticks.

POTATO AND CHICKEN BOMBAY

Skillet dishes are always an easy-on-the-cook answer to what's for dinner.

Makes 4 servings.

    1 **broiler-fryer, cut up (about 2½ pounds)**
    ¼ **cup peanut oil**
    ¼ **cup frozen chopped onion**
    1 **clove garlic, crushed**
    ¼ **cup all-purpose flour**
    1 **tablespoon curry powder**
    2 **envelopes or teaspoons instant chicken broth**
  1½ **teaspoons salt**
    ¼ **teaspoon crushed red pepper**
  2½ **cups water**
    ¼ **cup dry sherry**
    1 **package (12 ounces) frozen French fried potatoes**

1. Brown chicken in oil in a large skillet; remove and reserve. Sauté onion and garlic in skillet.
2. Stir in flour, curry powder, instant chicken broth, salt and red pepper until smooth. Stir in water and sherry; cook, stirring constantly, until sauce thickens and bubbles; return chicken to skillet.
3. Cover skillet and simmer chicken 35 minutes. Arrange frozen French fried potatoes around chicken pieces and cover. Simmer 10 minutes, or until potatoes are heated through. Serve with tossed greens.

CHICKEN À LA KING

The chef at Delmonico's Restaurant in Victorian New York developed this recipe for Foxhall Keene and it was called Chicken à la Keene, later shortened to à la king.

Makes 4 servings.

    ¼ **cup (½ stick) butter or margarine**
    ¼ **cup all-purpose flour**
    2 **tablespoons finely chopped onion**
    1 **teaspoon salt**
    ½ **teaspoon Worcestershire sauce**
    2 **cups milk**
    2 **cups diced cooked chicken or turkey**
    ¼ **cup diced pimiento**
    1 **can (3 or 4 ounces) sliced mushrooms**

1. Melt butter or margarine in medium size saucepan; remove from heat.
2. Blend in flour, onion, salt, and Worcestershire sauce; stir in milk.
3. Cook over low heat, stirring constantly, until sauce thickens and bubbles 3 minutes.
4. Stir in chicken, pimiento, and mushrooms; heat through.
5. Serve over hot buttered rice or toast, if desired.

GOLDEN CHICKEN NUGGETS

These make-aheads will disappear fast at your next get-together.

Bake at 400° for 10 minutes.
Makes 4 to 5 dozen nuggets.

    4 **whole chicken breasts (about 12 ounces each)**
    ½ **cup unseasoned fine dry bread crumbs**
    ¼ **cup grated Parmesan cheese**
    2 **teaspoons monosodium glutamate**
    1 **teaspoon salt**
    1 **teaspoon leaf thyme, crumbled**
    1 **teaspoon leaf basil, crumbled**
    ½ **cup (1 stick) butter or margarine, melted**

1. Bone chicken breasts; remove skin. Cut each breast half into 6 to 8 nuggets, about 1½ inches square.
2. Combine bread crumbs, cheese, monosodium glutamate, salt, thyme and basil in a pie plate.
3. Dip chicken nuggets in melted butter, then in crumb mixture. Place in single layer on foil-lined baking sheets; do not crowd.
4. Bake in hot oven (400°) 10 minutes, or until golden. Chill until ready to use.

EAST-WEST RISOTTO

Cooked chicken or turkey on hand? Dice the meat and combine with rice in a soy-based sauce.

Bake at 375° for 30 minutes.
Makes 4 servings.

    2 **tablespoons thinly sliced green onion**
    1 **tablespoon butter or margarine**
    1 **cup chopped celery**
  1¼ **cups packaged precooked rice**
    1 **can condensed cream of chicken soup**
  1½ **cups milk**
    2 **tablespoons soy sauce**
  1½ **cups diced cooked chicken or turkey**
    1 **can (3 or 4 ounces) chopped mushrooms, drained**
    1 **can (4 ounces) pimiento, drained and sliced**
    1 **can (3 ounces) chow-mein noodles**

1. Sauté onion in butter or margarine until soft in a large skillet; stir in celery and rice; cook 1 minute longer.
2. Stir in the soup, milk, soy sauce, chicken, mushrooms and pimiento; bring to boiling. Spoon into an 8-cup shallow casserole; cover.
3. Bake in moderate oven (375°) 20 minutes; uncover. Sprinkle noodles over top. Bake 10 minutes longer, or until noodles are hot.

Chapter 7 (from page 71)

COQ AU VIN

Long slow cooking gives this French aristocrat its mellow flavor.

Bake at 325° for 2 hours.
Makes 6 servings.

    1 **stewing chicken, cut up (about 4 pounds)**
    ⅓ **cup all-purpose flour**
  1½ **teaspoons salt**
    3 **tablespoons butter or margarine**
    ½ **cup diced cooked ham**
  12 **small white onions, peeled**
    3 **cups dry red wine**
    1 **can (3 or 4 ounces) whole mushrooms**
    1 **clove garlic, minced**
    6 **peppercorns**
    6 **whole cloves**
    1 **bay leaf**

1. Shake chicken pieces with flour and salt in a plastic bag to coat thoroughly.
2. Brown pieces, a few at a time, in butter or margarine in a large skillet; place in a 12-cup casserole; sprinkle with ham and onions.
3. Stir wine, mushrooms and their liquid into drippings in pan; bring to boiling, scraping brown bits from bottom of pan. Pour over chicken.
4. Tie garlic, peppercorns, cloves and bay leaf in cheesecloth; add to casserole; cover.
5. Bake in moderate oven (325°) 2 hours, or until chicken is very tender.
6. Uncover; remove spice bag and let chicken stand for 5 to 10 minutes, or until fat rises to top, then skim off. Garnish chicken with parsley, if you wish. Serve with French bread and the same dry red wine.

POULTRY POINTER

Place small white onions in a large bowl; pour boiling water over; wait for 1 minute. Drain and cover with cold water for 3 minutes. Make a cut at the root-end with a paring knife, and the skins will slip off.

PARISIAN CHICKEN BOWL

Halved chicken breasts are glazed, French style, and served cold with seasoned vegetables for this fancy bowl.

Makes 6 servings.

    3 whole chicken breasts (12 ounces
         each)
    1 small onion, sliced
    1 teaspoon salt
  ⅛ teaspoon pepper
    1 bay leaf
    2 cups water
    1 envelope unflavored gelatin
  ½ cup mayonnaise or salad dressing
    6 pitted ripe olives
    1 package (10 ounces) frozen
         Fordhook lima beans
  ½ cup bottled Italian salad dressing
    4 cups broken mixed salad greens
    3 medium-size tomatoes, peeled and
         sliced
    3 hard-cooked eggs, shelled and
         quartered

1. Combine chicken breasts with onion, salt, pepper, bay leaf and water in a large saucepan; cover. Simmer 30 minutes, or just until tender.
2. Remove from broth cool until easy to handle, then pull off skin. Remove meat from each half of breast in one piece; place in one layer in a shallow dish. Chill.
3. Strain broth into a 2-cup measure; chill just until fat rises to top, then skim off surface.
4. Soften gelatin in 1 cup of the broth in a small saucepan. (Save any remaining to add to soup.) Heat gelatin mixture, stirring constantly, just until gelatin dissolves; pour into a small bowl. Blend in mayonnaise or salad dressing; chill, stirring several times, 20 minutes, or until as thick as unbeaten egg white.
5. Spoon part over chilled chicken breasts to make a thick layer, then repeat with remaining until chicken is evenly glazed. Cut each olive into 6 slivers; arrange, petal fashion, on top of each glazed chicken breast; chill until gelatin is firm.
6. Cook lima beans, following label directions; drain. Toss with ¼ cup Italian dressing in a small bowl; cover. (This much can be done early in the day, or even a day ahead.) If making ahead, store in the refrigerator until ready to use.
7. When ready to serve, place salad greens in a large shallow bowl; drizzle remaining ¼ cup Italian dressing over; toss lightly to mix, Top with tomato slices; mound lima beans in center, then arrange chicken breasts, spoke fashion, around beans; place quartered eggs around edge of bowl.

MELBOURNE CHICKEN

This delectable chicken has a light curry-and-fruit-flavored sauce.

Bake at 350° for 1 hour.
Makes 8 servings.

    4 whole chicken breasts (about 12
         ounces each)
    3 tablespoons all-purpose flour
    1 tablespoon curry powder
    2 teaspoons salt
  ¼ cup vegetable oil
    1 tablespoon sugar
    2 envelopes instant beef broth or 2
         beef bouillon cubes
    1 large onion, chopped (1 cup)
    1 cup water
    1 jar (about 5 ounces) baby-pack
         apricots
    2 tablespoons lemon juice
    2 teaspoons soy sauce

1. Pull skin from chicken breasts; halve each.
2. Shake with mixture of flour, curry powder and salt in a plastic bag to coat lightly and evenly.
3. Brown pieces in vegetable oil in a large skillet; place in a 10-cup baking dish.
4. Stir sugar, beef broth or bouillon cubes, onion, water, apricots, lemon juice and soy sauce into drippings in skillet; heat to boiling, crushing bouillon cubes, if used, with a spoon. Pour over chicken.
5. Bake, covered, in moderate oven (350°) 1 hour, or until chicken is tender and sauce is bubbly hot. Serve over hot fluffy rice or noodles.

CARROZZA TURKEY

Look for packages of turkey cutlets in the meat counter. If frozen, thaw before making this Italian version of Veal Cordon Bleu.

Makes 4 servings.

    8 small turkey cutlets (about 1
         pound)
    1 teaspoon salt
  ½ teaspoon black pepper
    2 ounces thinly sliced prosciutto
  ½ pound sliced mozzarella cheese
         Flour
    2 eggs, lightly beaten
    2 tablespoons cold water
         Packaged bread crumbs
  ½ cup vegetable oil
    2 tablespoons butter or margarine
         Lemon wedges

1. Pound cutlets with a wooden mallet or rolling pin between pieces of wax paper until very thin.
2. Sprinkle one side of each square with salt and pepper. Trim prosciutto to squares slightly smaller in size than the cutlet. Lay a piece of prosciutto on half of the cutlets. Top with slice of mozzarella and cover with remaining turkey squares. Gently press flat with the palm of your hand.
3. Dredge each "sandwich" with flour. Dip into beaten egg and water in a pie plate, letting excess drip off. Dredge with bread crumbs. Fry slowly in a large skillet in oil combined with butter or margarine 5 minutes or until first side is golden brown; turn and brown second side until outsides are crisp, golden brown and the cheese has melted. Drain on paper towels and serve with lemon wedges and a platter of marinated artichoke hearts and olives, if you wish.

KNISHES

A traditional Jewish snack, these delicious liver-filled appetizers should please all palates.

Makes about 3 dozen.

  1½ pounds chicken livers
    ¼ cup vegetable oil
      3 large onions, sliced thin
      3 teaspoons salt
    10 large potatoes, pared and
           sliced thin
      1 egg
  1¼ cups matzo meal or finely crushed
           unsalted cracker crumbs
           Shortening or vegetable oil for
           frying

1. Sauté chicken livers, turning once, in the ¼ cup vegetable oil in a large skillet 5 minutes, or just until they lose their pink color; lift out with a slotted spoon and place in a large bowl.
2. Stir onions into drippings in pan; sauté until soft; combine with livers. Put livers and onions through a food grinder, using a coarse blade; return to bowl. Stir in 1 teaspoon of the salt; chill mixture.
3. Cook potatoes, covered, in boiling salted water in a large saucepan 15 minutes, or until tender; drain well. Mash, then beat in egg, remaining 2 teaspoons salt, and ¼ cup of the matzo meal; chill.
4. When ready to finish cakes, measure remaining 1 cup matzo meal into a pie plate. Place potato mixture, a heaping tablespoonful at a time, into matzo meal and flatten into a 4-inch round; place a heaping teaspoonful liver mixture in center. Shape potato round up and over filling to cover completely. Roll in matzo meal to coat lightly.
5. Melt enough shortening or pour vegetable oil into an electric frypan

to make a depth of ⅛ inch. Set heat control to 375°. Add potato cakes, a few at a time, to hot fat and fry, turning once, 3 to 5 minutes, or until golden. (Add more shortening or oil between batches as needed.)

INDONESIAN CHICKEN AND PEARS

The special flavor of canned pears blends with chicken and lime for a memorable supper dish.

Makes 6 servings.

- 1 can (1 pound, 13 ounces) pear halves
- 6 chicken cutlets
- ½ cup frozen chopped onion
- 2 cloves garlic, crushed
- 1½ teaspoons salt
- ¼ teaspoon cayenne pepper
- 3 tablespoons vegetable oil
- 2 teaspoons grated lime peel
- 2 tablespoons lime juice
- 1½ cups light cream
- ½ cup flaked coconut
- 1 tablespoon soy sauce
- 2½ cups cooked rice
  Sliced green onions

1. Drain and slice pears, reserving syrup for another use.
2. Cut chicken cutlets into cubes; combine with onion, garlic, salt and cayenne in a large bowl; let stand 10 minutes to season.
3. Heat oil in a large skillet and sauté chicken until lightly browned. Add lime peel and lime juice, cream, coconut and soy sauce. Cook over low heat 20 minutes.
4. Mix in sliced pears and rice. Cook 5 minutes longer. Sprinkle top with sliced green onions.

CHICKEN KIEV

These great Russian-style chicken breasts take fussing, so fix them ahead for a special company dinner.

Makes 12 servings.

- ¾ cup (1½ sticks) butter or margarine
- 6 whole chicken breasts (about 12 ounces each)
- ¼ cup finely chopped parsley
- ½ teaspoon sugar
- 2 eggs
- 1 cup fine dry bread crumbs
- 1 teaspoon salt
- ⅛ teaspoon pepper
  Shortening or vegetable oil for frying

1. Cut the butter or margarine into 12 even-length sticks; chill in freezer while fixing chicken. (Butter should be very cold.)
2. Pull skin from the chicken breasts; halve breasts and cut meat in one piece from bones. Place each half, boned side up, between wax paper and pound very thin with a mallet or rolling pin to form a "cutlet." (Do not pound holes in meat.)
3. Place 1 piece very cold butter or margarine, 1 teaspoon parsley and a dash of the sugar on end of each cutlet; fold sides over to seal in butter, then roll up. Hold in place with wooden picks.
4. Beat eggs slightly in a pie plate; mix bread crumbs, salt and pepper in a second pie plate. Dip stuffed rolls in egg, then in crumb mixture to coat well. Chill at least an hour.
5. When ready to fry, melt enough shortening or pour in enough oil to make a 2-inch depth in an electric deep-fat fryer or large saucepan; heat to 350° or until a cube of bread turns golden in 65 seconds.
6. Fry rolls, 3 or 4 at a time and turning often, 7 minutes, or until tender and crisply golden. Lift out with a slotted spoon; drain well. Keep hot until all rolls are cooked.

FIESTA CHICKEN CACCIATORE

Men especially like this zesty Italian dish. It's also a good choice for guests, because it waits well.

Makes 8 servings.

- 2 broiler-fryers, quartered (about 3 pounds each)
- ¾ cup all-purpose flour
- 1 tablespoon salt
- ¼ teaspoon pepper
- ⅓ cup olive oil or vegetable oil
- 1 large onion, chopped (1 cup)
- 1 clove garlic, minced
- 1 can (about 2 pounds) Italian tomatoes
- 1 tablespoon sugar
- 1 teaspoon leaf basil, crumbled
- ½ teaspoon leaf thyme, crumbled
- 2 medium-size green peppers, halved, seeded and sliced

1. Shake chicken with flour, salt and pepper in a plastic bag to coat well.
2. Brown pieces, a few at a time, in oil in an electric frypan set at 375°; remove and reserve.
3. Stir onion and garlic into drippings in pan and sauté until soft; stir in tomatoes, sugar, basil and thyme; bring to boiling.
4. Return chicken to pan; spoon some of the tomato sauce over; lay sliced green peppers on top; cover;

lower temperature to 200°.
5. Simmer, basting several times with sauce in pan, 1 hour, or until chicken is tender. Serve with linguini and a hearts of lettuce salad.

ORANGE LEEK DUCK

Duck is considered very special and is served mainly as a banquet dish in the northern province of Soochow, China. Prepared correctly, the duck is so tender that no carving is necessary. Only forks or chop sticks are needed to separate the meat from the bones.

Roast at 350° for 1 hour.
Simmer 2 hours longer.
Makes 4 servings.

- 1 frozen duckling (about 4 pounds), thawed
- 1 teaspoon salt
- 2 California oranges
- 4½ cups water
- 2 leeks, cut into 2-inch pieces
- ¼ cup soy sauce
- ½ cup dry sherry
- 2 tablespoons dark corn syrup

1. Remove giblets from duck and use making broth. Sprinkle with salt.
2. Remove peel from oranges with a sharp knife in one continuous spiral, cutting through and removing white part and membrane around orange meat; reserve. Cut oranges in half; slice into ¼-inch slices.
3. Place duck on rack in roasting pan. (Add 2 cups of water to pan to catch drippings and prevent oven from smoking.)
4. Roast duck in moderate oven (350°) for 1 hour. Before removing from oven, pierce skin with tines of fork to let fat run out.
5. Combine leek, soy sauce and sherry in a Dutch oven or large kettle. Place duck on top, breast-side up. Bring to boiling. Add remaining 2½ cups water; bring to boiling again. Lower heat; cover; simmer 30 minutes, basting occasionally, then simmer 30 minutes longer.
6. Roll up orange spiral; stuff into cavity. Pour corn syrup over duck. Continue cooking for 1 hour more, basting once with pan juices.
7. Remove cover; simmer 10 minutes.
8. Place duck on platter. Arrange orange slices around and over it. Keep warm. Simmer juices remaining in Dutch oven until thickened. Pour over duck before serving.
HOSTESS TIPS: To fill out a festive dinner, serve FRIED SWEET POTATO SHREDS and HERBED PILAF (halve recipe) and GOLDEN SPICED PEACHES (All recipes are on page 94) with duckling.

Chapter 8 (from page 80)

JARDINIÈRE CHICKEN LIVERS

Jardinière means gardener-style, or served with an assortment of vegetables.

Makes 8 servings at 198 calories each.

- 2 tablespoons diet margarine
- 1 medium-size onion, chopped (½ cup)
- 2 pounds chicken livers
- 1 can (3 or 4 ounces) mushroom stems and pieces
- 1 can (5 ounces) water chestnuts, drained and sliced
- 3 stalks celery, cut into ½-inch pieces
- 1 package (9 ounces) frozen cut green beans
- 2 teaspoons salt
- ¼ teaspoon pepper

1. Melt margarine in a large skillet over medium heat. Add onion; sauté until soft. Add the chicken livers; cook, turning often, 5 minutes.
2. Add mushrooms and liquid, water chestnuts, celery and green beans. Cook over moderate heat until beans are completely defrosted. Add salt and pepper. Cover; simmer 10 minutes, stirring occasionally, or until vegetables are crisply-tender.

SMOTHERED CHICKEN

Old-fashioned eating with new-fashioned calorie-paring preparation.

Bake at 350° for 45 minutes.
Makes 6 servings at 267 calories each.

- 1 broiler-fryer, cut up (about 3 pounds)
- 1 teaspoon salt
- ½ teaspoon paprika
- 1 envelope (2 to a package) chicken-vegetable-soup mix
- 1½ cups boiling water
- ½ teaspoon poultry seasoning
- 1 cup evaporated skimmed milk
- 2 tablespoons cornstarch

1. Arrange chicken pieces on rack in broiler pan. Sprinkle with salt and paprika. Broil 10 minutes, until brown. Turn; brown other side.
2. Place browned chicken in an 8-cup casserole. Stir in soup mix, water and poultry seasoning; cover.
3. Bake in moderate oven (350°) 45 minutes, or until tender.
4. Remove chicken to heated serving platter; keep warm. Combine milk and cornstarch; stir into ingredients in casserole dish. Cook over low heat, stirring constantly, until sauce thickens and bubbles 1 minute. Pour over.

CHICKEN LIVER RAGOÛT

Your diet seems like something in the past when you try this dish.

Makes 4 servings at 323 calories each.

- 3 slices bacon, cut in 2-inch pieces
- 1 pound chicken livers, halved
- 2 medium-size onions, peeled and quartered
- 2 medium-sized green peppers, quartered and seeded
- 1 tablespoon all-purpose flour
- ½ teaspoon paprika
- 1 cup water
- 2 envelopes or teaspoons chicken broth
- OR: 2 chicken bouillon cubes
- ¼ teaspoon leaf thyme, crumbled
- 1 small bay leaf
- 2 cups hot cooked noodles

1. Sauté bacon until crisp in a medium-size skillet; remove and drain on paper towels. Pour off all drippings from skillet.
2. Sauté livers slowly in same pan 3 to 5 minutes, or just until they lose their pink color; remove and reserve.
3. Stir onions and green peppers into pan. Sprinkle with flour and paprika, then stir in water, chicken broth, thyme and bay leaf; cover. Simmer 15 minutes, or until onions are tender; remove bay leaf.
4. Add chicken livers to sauce; heat 5 minutes, or until bubbly.
5. Spoon noodles onto serving plates; top with liver mixture; sprinkle with bacon pieces.

POULTRY POINTER

Dieters can enjoy artichokes with a free conscience. To cook them, trim all leaves with kitchen shears; scoop out the choke with a sharp spoon (a grapefruit spoon is perfect). Place in a kettle with a bit of lemon juice and a few whole allspice; add a 1-inch depth of water. Cover and bring to boiling; lower heat and simmer 30 minutes, or until tender. Cool in cooking liquid. Serve with thin slices of poached chicken breast and a little low-calorie salad dressing.

SKINNY PAELLA

A low-calorie version of the favorite from sunny Valencia.

Bake at 350° for 1 hour.
Makes 8 servings at 303 calories each.

- 1 broiler-fryer, cut up (about 2 pounds)
- 1 large onion, chopped (1 cup)
- 1 clove garlic, minced
- 1 cup uncooked rice
- 6 small slices salami, diced
- 2 teaspoons salt
- ¼ teaspoon pepper
- ⅛ teaspoon crushed saffron
- 1 can (1 pound) tomatoes
- 1½ cups water
- 1 envelope or teaspoon instant chicken broth
- 1 pound fresh shrimps, shelled and deveined,
- OR: 1 package (12 ounces) frozen deveined shelled raw shrimp
- 1 can (4 ounces) pimiento, drained and cut in large pieces

1. Place chicken, meaty side down, in a single layer on rack of broiler pan.
2. Broil, 4 inches from heat, 10 minutes; turn; broil 10 minutes longer, or until lightly browned.
3. Pour drippings from broiler pan into a medium-size skillet. Stir in onion and garlic; sauté until soft; spoon into a 12-cup baking dish with rice, salami, salt, pepper and saffron.
4. Combine tomatoes with water and instant chicken broth in same pan; bring to boiling. Stir into rice mixture with shrimp. Arrange chicken and pimiento on top; cover.
5. Bake in moderate oven (350°) 1 hour, or until liquid is absorbed and chicken is tender. Garnish with parsley and serve with chopped green onions to sprinkle on top, if you wish.

POT AU FEU

A low-calorie version of a French classic.

Makes 4 servings at 380 calories each.

- 1 pound boneless round steak
- 3 cups water
- 1 can condensed beef broth
- 1 large onion, chopped (1 cup)
- 1 clove garlic, minced
- 2 teaspoons salt
- 4 sprigs parsley
- 1 bay leaf
- 6 peppercorns
- ½ teaspoon leaf thyme
- 1 whole chicken breast (about 12 ounces)
- 4 large carrots
- 2 medium-size zucchini
- 3 cups celery sticks

1. Trim all fat from beef. Place steak in a heavy kettle or Dutch oven. Add water, broth, onion, garlic and salt. Tie parsley, bay leaf, peppercorns and thyme in a small piece of cheesecloth; add to kettle.
2. Bring to boiling; lower heat; cover. Simmer 1 hour. Add chicken breast; simmer 30 minutes, or until meats are tender. Remove meats; keep warm.
3. While meats cook, pare carrots and cut in sticks; trim zucchini, cut in sticks about 4 inches long.
4. Reheat broth in kettle to boiling; add carrots; cover. Cook 15 minutes. Add zucchini and celery sticks; cook 5 minutes longer, or until tender. Remove.
5. Strain broth into a large bowl, pressing onion and garlic through sieve into liquid; let stand about a minute, or until fat rises to top, then skim off.
6. Carve meats; combine with broth and vegetables in a heated tureen.

CHICKEN CHOW MEIN

Chinese dishes are often lower in calories. This is so good even nondieters will want to make it.

Makes 6 servings at 247 calories each.

    1 tablespoon diet margarine
    2 medium-size onions, sliced
    ¼ cup dry sherry
    2 cups sliced celery
    ¾ pound mushrooms, sliced
    1 can (13 ¾ ounces) chicken broth
    1 cup drained bean sprouts
    1 cup water chestnuts, drained and
        sliced
    1 can (5 ounces) bamboo shoots,
        drained and sliced
    3 cups diced cooked chicken or
        turkey
    ¼ cup soy sauce
    2 tablespoons cornstarch

1. Melt margarine in a large skillet. Add onion; sauté 10 minutes. Add sherry; simmer until it is almost evaporated.
2. Add the celery, mushrooms and broth. Simmer over low heat for 5 minutes.
3. Stir in bean sprouts, water chestnuts, the bamboo shoots and diced cooked chicken or turkey.
4. Combine soy sauce and cornstarch in a small cup; mix until paste is smooth. Stir into skillet. Continue cooking over low heat, stirring frequently, until mixture thickens and bubbles 1 minute.
5. Garnish with 4 tablespoons fried chow mein noodles (55 calories), if you wish.

LOW-CALORIE CHICKEN ORIENTALE

A sweet and sour chicken dish that's off the "forbidden list."

Bake at 325° for 55 minutes.
Makes 6 servings at 248 calories each.

    2 broiler-fryers, cut up (1½ pounds
        each)
    1 can (1 pound) unsweetened
        pineapple chunks in pineapple
        juice
    3 tablespoons wine vinegar
    1 tablespoon soy sauce
    ½ teaspoon dry mustard
    1 teaspoon salt
    ¼ teaspoon pepper
    2 green peppers, seeded and cut in
        strips
    1 tablespoon cornstarch
    2 tablespoons water

1. Place chicken pieces, skin-side up, in a shallow baking dish and surround with pineapple chunks.
2. Mix juice with vinegar, soy sauce, mustard, salt and pepper and pour over chicken.
3. Bake in moderate oven (325°) for 40 minutes, basting occasionally. Add pepper strips.
4. Combine cornstarch and water in a cup. Stir into liquid in baking dish and bake an additional 15 minutes, or until bubbly.

POULTRY POINTERS

Guides for cooking with herbs:
• Keep herbs and spices in alphabetical order on the spice shelf and you will always be able to find them quickly.
• Use a new herb by itself the first few times you cook with it. Then you will learn how pungent it is, and how it blends with other foods.
• Give herbs time to season foods. If the cooking time is short, let the herb soak in part of the cooking liquid while preparing other ingredients.

• To determine the strength of an herb, crush a bit of it in the palm of your hand and sniff its aroma.

KOREAN CHICKEN

Quarters of chicken are baked in a soy-green onion sauce and served with golden pineapple chunks.

Bake at 350° for 1 hour.
Makes 4 servings at 323 calories each.

    1 broiler-fryer, quartered (about 3
        pounds)
    1 can (8 ounces) pineapple chunks in
        pineapple juice
        Water
    ¼ cup sliced green onions
        OR: 1 small onion, chopped (¼ cup)
    ¼ cup soy sauce
        Water chestnuts (optional)

1. Arrange chicken quarters, skin-side down, in a 12-cup shallow casserole.
2. Drain juice from pinapple chunks into a 2-cup measure; add enough water to make 1 cup; reserve chunks.
3. Add green onions and soy sauce to pineapple liquid; spoon over chicken.
4. Bake in moderate oven (350°) 30 minutes; turn chicken, skin-side up; bake 15 minutes longer; add pineapple chunks and baste with sauce. Bake 15 minutes longer.

ASPIC CHICKEN

Serve this cool salad on the first hot day of summer.

Makes 4 servings at 196 calories each.

    1 envelope unflavored gelatin
    ½ cup cold water
    1 can condensed chicken broth
    ¼ teaspoon salt
    2 tablespoons lemon juice
    2 cups diced cooked chicken or
        turkey
    ½ cup chopped celery
    ½ cup chopped green pepper
    2 tablespoons diced pimiento

1. Sprinkle gelatin over cold water in saucepan to soften. Place over low heat, stirring constantly, until gelatin dissolves, 2 to 3 minutes.
2. Remove from heat; stir in broth, salt, and lemon juice. Chill until mixture is the consistency of egg white.
3. Fold in the chicken or turkey, celery, green pepper and pimiento.
4. Turn into a 4-cup mold or four individual salad molds. Chill until set, about 3 hours.
5. When ready to serve, loosen salad around edge with a sharp knife; dip mold in and out of hot water. Cover with serving plate.

SKINNY CHICKEN À LA KING

Even this rich Victorian dish can be yours with our calorie-cutting directions.

Makes 8 servings at 242 calories each.

- 1 tablespoon diet margarine
- 1 large onion, chopped (1 cup)
- 4 cups cubed cooked chicken or turkey
- 1 envelope or teaspoon instant chicken broth
- 1 cup boiling water
- 2 teaspoons salt
- ⅛ teaspoon pepper
- ⅛ teaspoon leaf thyme, crumbled
- 1 cup water
- ⅓ cup all-purpose flour
- ½ cup instant nonfat dry milk
- 8 slices diet white bread, toasted

1. Melt margarine in skillet. Add onions; sauté over very low heat 15 minutes. Add chicken, broth, boiling water, salt, pepper, and thyme.
2. Combine water, flour and milk in a bowl; beat until smooth; add to pan. Cook over low heat, stirring occasionally, until mixture thickens and bubbles. Cook 2 minutes longer. Serve over toast.

CALICO CHICKEN FRICASSEE

Simmered chicken with a creamy gravy.

Makes 4 servings at 306 calories each.

- 1 broiler-fryer, cut up (2 pounds)
- 1 pound carrots, pared and sliced
- 1 large onion, chopped (1 cup)
- 1 cup thinly sliced celery
- 1 cup hot water
- 1 envelope or teaspoon instant chicken broth
- 2 teaspoon salt
- 1 teaspoon leaf sage, crumbled
- 1 cup frozen peas (from a plastic bag)
- 2 tablespoons all-purpose flour
- ½ cup skim milk
- 2 tablespoons chopped parsley

1. Place chicken pieces, skin-side down, in a large skillet over *very low* heat. (Do not add fat.) Cook until chicken is a rich brown on skin-side, about 10 minutes; turn and brown on other side; remove and reserve.
2. Add carrots, onion and celery to skillet; toss to coat with drippings from chicken. Cook and stir 10 minutes.
3. Add hot water, instant chicken broth, salt and sage; mix well; return chicken; cover; simmer 10 minutes; add peas, simmer another 10 minutes, or until chicken and vegetables are tender. Remove chicken; keep warm.
4. Mix flour and skim milk to a smooth paste in a cup; stir into vegeta-bles; bring to bubbling, stirring constantly. Cook 3 minutes, or until thickened and bubbly. Stir in parsley; spoon onto heated serving dish; top with chicken.

POULTRY POINTERS

Shell a perfect hard-cooked egg? It's easy if you follow these tips: Cover eggs with 1 inch cold water in a large saucepan. Bring slowly to boiling; lower heat to a slow simmer; cover saucepan; cook 14 minutes; remove from heat. Pour cold water over eggs until they are cool to the touch. Roll eggs gently on a counter top until shells crack. Peel shells off with thumbs. Store peeled eggs in plastic containers with tight seals.

For a calorie-saving stuffing for roast poultry, use a mixture of vegetables and herbs, rather than a bread or rice mixture. Then baste with chicken broth, rather than fat while cooking.

OVEN-BAKED "SOUTHERN FRIED" CHICKEN

Crisp and crunchy-perfect chicken every time, thanks to an inexpensive easy-do "convenience mix" you make yourself and keep in the pantry to use as needed.

Bake at 375° for 45 minutes.
Makes 6 servings at 244 calories each.

- ½ cup "Skinny Shake" (recipe follows)
- 2 broiler-fryers, cut up (about 2½ pounds each)

1. Measure out ½ cup of "SKINNY SHAKE" mix and put it in a plastic bag. Moisten the pieces of chicken with water and shake them up in the bag, a few pieces at a time.
2. Arrange chicken, skin-side up, in a single layer on a non-stick pan.
3. Bake in a moderate oven (375°) about 45 minutes, adding absolutely no other fats or oils. (Don't be alarmed if the chicken seems dry for the first 20 minutes; then the "SKINNY SHAKE" starts to work, and at the end of the baking period, it will be crisp and perfect.)

"SKINNY SHAKE": Makes enough to coat 5 cut-up chickens. Empty one 16-ounce container (about 4 cups, dry measure) of bread crumbs into a deep bowl and stir in ½ cup of vegetable oil with a fork or pastry blender until evenly distributed. Add 1 tablespoon salt, 1 tablespoon paprika, 1 table-spoon celery salt and 1 teaspoon pepper. This is a good seasoning for chicken. Or season it to suit yourself: Onion or garlic powder, sesame or poppy seeds, dried herbs.

CHINESE CHICKEN

This meal-in-one teams white meat with pineapple and vegetables.

Makes 6 servings at 398 calories each.

- 3 whole chicken breasts (about 12 ounces each)
- 3 tablespoons soy sauce
- 1 tablespoon vegetable oil or peanut oil
- 2¼ cups unsweetened pineapple juice
- ¼ cup cornstarch
- 1 can (8 ounces) pineapple chunks in pineapple juice
- 2 cans (3 or 4 ounces each) sliced mushrooms
- ½ teaspoon salt
- 1 package (10 ounces) frozen peas
- 6 cups shredded Chinese cabbage
- 3 cups cooked hot rice

1. Remove skin and bones from chicken breasts; slice meat into long thin strips.
2. Place soy sauce in pie plate; marinate chicken strips in sauce; brown quickly in oil in a wok or large skillet.
3. Stir ½ cup unsweetened pineapple juice into cornstarch in cup to make a smooth paste; reserve.
4. Stir remaining pineapple juice, pineapple chunks and mushrooms with liquid into chicken in pan; bring to boiling.
5. Stir in cornstarch mixture and salt; cook, stirring constantly, until sauce bubbles 1 minute. Cover; simmer 15 minutes.
6. Stir in peas; arrange cabbage on top. Cover; cook 8 minutes, or until peas and cabbage are tender. Serve over hot cooked rice.

BUYER'S GUIDE

Page 1: "Wild Strawberry" dinner plate by Wedgwood, 41 Madison Ave., N.Y., N.Y. 10010.

Pages 4-5: Enamel on steel frying pan, Denby Boutique Line by Aubecq, Denby, Ltd., Inc., 41 Madison Ave., N.Y., N.Y. 10010.

Pages 12-13: "Tiger's Eye" Touchstone flatware serving set by Denby, Ltd., Inc., 41 Madison Ave., N.Y., N.Y. 10010.

Page 22: Silver platter by Mayer Silverware, 136 E. 57th St., N.Y., N.Y. 10022.

Page 26: Number 2: "Florentine Green" china by Wedgwood, 41 Madison Ave., N.Y., N.Y. 10010; "Gold Aegean" silver flatware by Wallace Silversmiths, Wallingford, Conn. 06492. Number 3: casserole from the Pottery Barn, Inc., 231 Tenth Ave., N.Y., N.Y. 10011.

Page 37: Top: "Rhapsody" flameproof oval casserole by Royal Worcester Porcelain Co., 11 E. 26th St., N.Y., N.Y. 10010. Middle: "Palmyra" individual baker also by Royal Worcester Porcelain Co. Bottim: "Palmyra" oval platter also by Royal Worcester Porcelain Co.; "Onyx" Touchstone flatware serving spoons by Denby, Ltd., Inc., 41

Madison Ave., N.Y., N.Y. 10010.

Pages 50-51: Clock from Clocks and Things, 972 Second Ave., N.Y., N.Y. 10022.

Page 52: "Tea Party" Fine China oval platter by Denby, Ltd., Inc., 41 Madison Ave., N.Y., N.Y. 10010.

Page 73: "Avignon" Fine Stoneware dinner plate, salad plate and soup tureen by Denby, Ltd., Inc., 41 Madison Ave., N.Y., N.Y. 100?0.

Page 76: "Clifden" crystal goblet and salad bowl by Galway Irish Crystal, 41 Madison Ave., N.Y., N.Y. 10010; "Fruit Sprays" oven to table platter by Wedgwood, 41 Madison Ave., N.Y., N.Y. 10010.

Pages 106-107: All items from Bazaar De La Cuisine Inc., 1003 Second Ave., N.Y., N.Y. 10022. Add $1.50 per item for postage and handling, except $1.75 for couscous and French fry outfit. Top page 106: Copper hen mold ($13.50); Taylor deep fat thermometer ($5.75); roast rack E2V ($2.45); 10" Sabatier cook's knife ($10.95); poultry shears ($5.95). Page 107: Couisiere ($14.95); Taylor meat thermometer SS ($4.00); iron French fry outfit ($9.95); 8" iron omelet pan ($5.95); 10" Sabatier slicer ($9.95); 5" Sabatier boning knife ($4.95); Sabatier bayonet fork ($8.95).

Editor's Note: All items not listed in the Buyer's Guide are part of a private collection and not for sale.

CREDITS

Photography Credits: Douglas Kirkland: page 11, page 61. **Mort Mace:** pages 18-19. **George Nordhausen:** page 17, pages 22-23, page 26, page 27, pages 62-63, page 64. **Bob Stoller:** pages 38-39. **Gordon Smith:** Cover, page 1, pages 4-5, pages 6-7, pages 12-13, pages 30-31, page 37, page 40, page 49, pages 50-51, page 52, page 73, page 76. **René Velez:** pages 106-107.

Herb Chart Illustration: Betty Frasier: pages 74-75.

Illustrations: Maggie Zander.

Poultry Illustrations: Adolph Brotman: pages 103, 104, 105.

ACKNOWLEDGMENTS

The editor gratefully acknowledges the help of: American Egg Board; American Spice Trade Association; California Bartlett Pears; California Fresh Nectarines; College Inn Chicken Broth; Frozen Potato Products Institute; Kretchmer Wheat Germ Products; National Broiler Council; National Peanut Council; National Turkey Federation; Pacific Kitchens: Pacific Coast Canned Pear Service Inc., Alaskan King Crab Association; Sunkist Growers Incorporated; The National Goose Council; Western Iceberg Lettuce.

A&B

A Poultry Cook's Check List, 106-107

Accompaniments, 93-95

Appetizers, 82-83

Apple and Chestnut Stuffing, 86

Apple and Cornbread Stuffing, 89

Apple-Wine Broiler Chicken, 54

Apricot Walnut Stuffing, 89

Arroz con Pollo, 96

Arroz con Pollo (Diet), 80

Arroz con Pollo Criollo, 71

Artichoke Hearts, 94

Aruba Chicken Sancocho, 21

Aspic Chicken, 123

Au Porto Chicken, 112

Avocado Chicken Salad, 42

Avocado Double-Deckers, 42

Bacon and Chicken Livers, 117

Barbecue Chicken, 78

Barbecue Chicken Drumsticks, 48

Barbecue Sauce, 58

Basic Barbecue Sauce, 90

Basic Broiled Chicken, 56

Basic Chicken Broth, 83

Basic Fried Chicken, 34

Basic Poultry Glazes, 90

Basil Fried Chicken, 54

Batter for Chicken, 100

Biscuits and Chicken Casserole, 55

Biscuit Wedge Topping, 55

Blue-Ribbon Turkey Casserole, 109

Bonanza Bobs, 116

Boneless Chicken Cacciatore, 80

Bowling Night Salad, 43

Bread and Butter Stuffing, 90

Breaded Chicken Wings, 102

Breasts

Bonanza Bobs, 116

California Chicken, 16

Chafing Dish Chicken, 112

Chicken Kiev, 121

Chicken Veronique, 41

Chinese Chicken, 124

Chinese Wok Chicken, 32

Classic Chicken Almond, 68

Cordon Bleu Chicken, 72

Coriander Chicken, 111

Deviled Chicken, 80

Diet Chicken Cacciatore, 78

Dieter's Chicken en Aspic, 77

French Chicken in Sherry

Sauce, 78

Golden Chicken Nuggets, 119

Grilled Chicken Breasts Supreme, 44

Honan Chicken, 113

Hong Kong Chicken Almond, 35

Imperial Chicken, 114

Japanese Chicken, 70

Low-Cal Chicken Teriyaki, 77

Mandarin Chicken Breasts, 16

Mandarin Supper, 34

Melbourne Chicken, 120

Monterey Chicken and Artichokes, 36

Parisian Chicken Bowl, 120

Pennsylvania Chicken, 101

Poulet en Croûte Lutèce, 65

Raisin and Almond Chicken, 53

Satays with Peanut Sauce, 116

Shredded Chicken and Vegetables, 59

Skewered Chicken Cantonese, 116

Sweet and Sour Chicken, 78

Tahitian Chicken, 47

Veracruz Chicken, 58

Weight Worrier's Fricassee, 79

Wheat Germ Coated Chicken, 102

Zesty Lemon Chicken Breasts, 55

Bridie's Really Great Chicken, 97

Broiled
Apple-Wine Broiler Chicken, 54
Basic Broiled Chicken, 56
Broiled Chicken Bing, 110
Capri Chicken Broil, 47
Chili-Broiled Chicken, 56
Curry-Broiled Chicken, 56
French Chicken Broil, 60
Garlic-Broiled Chicken, 56
Lemon-Broiled Chicken, 56
Lemon-Mint Broiled Chicken, 53
Massachusetts Grilled Chicken, 34
Orange-Broiled Chicken, 56

Broiled Chicken Bing, 110
Brown Chicken Fricassee, 14
Brown Rice Stuffing, 89
Brunswick Chicken, 97
Brunswick Chowder, 84
Budapest Chicken Livers, 101
Bulgar, 69
Butter Baked Wings and Drumsticks, 16
Buttermilk Fried Chicken, 99

C&D

Calico Chicken Fricassee, 124
California Chicken, 16
California Chicken Roasts, 9
Canadian Chicken with Cream Sauce, 58
Cape Cod Chicken, 111
Cape Cod Sauce, 92
Capri Chicken Broil, 47
Caribbean Roast Chicken, 8
Carrozza Turkey, 120
Cassoulet, 108
Catalan Chicken, 117
Chafing Dish Chicken, 112
Château-Style Duckling, 113
Cheese and Turkey Salad, 108
Chestnut Stuffed Turkey, 20
Chicken à la King, 119
Chicken Baked with Barbecue Sauce, 58
Chicken Broth, 41
Chicken Chowder, 84
Chicken Chow Mein, 123
Chicken Clubs, 46
Chicken-Corn Salad, 46
Chicken Croquettes, 113
Chicken Egg Rolls, 112
Chicken Gravy, 41, 45
Chicken, Hunter's Style, 10

Chicken in Orange Sauce, 59
Chicken Kiev, 121
Chicken-Lemon Soup, 83
Chicken Liver Bounties, 46

Chicken Liver Ragoût, 122
Chicken Marengo, Diet-Style, 78
Chicken on a Spit, 117
Chicken Sauce alla Romeo, 21
Chicken Scallopine, 59
Chicken Slices with Supreme Sauce, 56
Chicken Soup with Dumplings, 85
Chicken Veronique, 41
Chili-Broiled Chicken, 56
Chili Chicken, 114
Chilled Chicken Cream, 86
Chinese Chicken, 124
Chinese Chicken Salad, 44
Chinese Wok Chicken, 32
Chowder Diamond Head, 84
Chunky Chicken-Beef Soup, 84
Chutney Chicken, 95
Chutney Fruit Sauce, 91
Cinnamon-Sugar Toast Triangles, 93
Classic Chicken Almond, 68
Coach House Chicken Pie, 10
Coconut Milk, 116
Cold Cucumber Soup with Chicken, 86
Cold Curried Chicken Soup, 86
Company Soup, 86
Coq au Vin, 119
Cordon Bleu Chicken, 72
Coriander Chicken, 111
Corn Crisped Drumsticks, 57
Corn Crisped Fried Chicken, 78
Corn Flake Chicken, 102
Cornish Hens en Casserole, 32
Cornmeal Dumplings, 15
Corn 'n' Chicken Chowder, 84
Country Captain, 8
Country Chicken Fricassee, 96
Country Roast Chicken, 99
Cranberry Glazed Roast Turkey, 110
Creamy Boiled Dressing, 45
Creamy Gravy, 90
Crème d'Oie, 85
Creole Chicken, 118
Creole Jambalaya, 98
Creole Turkey Royale, 111
Crêpes, 98
Crisp Batter Chicken, 66
Crisscross Chicken Pie, 97
Crostini Salvatore, 94
Crusty Chicken Wings, 117
Cucumber-Chicken Cup, 85
Cucumber Dressing, 41
Cumberland Sauce, 92
Currant Jelly Glaze, 90
Curried Chicken Coronet, 47
Curry-Broiled Chicken, 56
Curry Cream Sauce, 97
Curry Glaze, 29
Curry Sauce, 90

Cutlets
Canadian Chicken with Cream Sauce, 58

Chicken Scallopine, 59
Indonesian Chicken and Pears, 121
Nectarine Chicken Français, 118
Parmigiana Chicken Cutlets, 36

Dappled Dumpling Fricassee, 96
Dappled Dumplings, 96
Dark Cherry Sauce, 110
Deep Dish Chicken Pie, 55
Deviled Chicken, 80
Deviled Dunking Sauce, 57

Diet, Chicken on a
Arroz con Pollo, 80
Aspic Chicken, 123
Barbecue Chicken, 78
Boneless Chicken Cacciatore, 80
Calico Chicken Fricassee, 124
Chicken Chow Mein, 123
Chicken-Liver Ragoût, 122
Chicken Marengo, Diet-Style, 78
Chinese Chicken, 124
Cordon Bleu Chicken, 72
Corn Crisped Fried Chicken, 78
Diet Coq au Vin, 80
Diet Chicken Cacciatore, 78
Dieter's Chicken en Aspic, 77
Dieter's Hawaiian Chicken, 79
Deviled Chicken, 80
French Chicken in Sherry Sauce, 78
Jardinière Chicken Livers, 122
Korean Chicken, 123
Low-Cal Chicken Teriyaki, 77
Low-Calorie Chicken Orientale, 123
Maytime Chicken Breast Soup, 72
No-Fat Fried Chicken, 79
Orange Chicken, 79
Oven-Baked "Southern Fried" Chicken, 124
Peachy Low-Calorie Chicken, 80
Pot au Feu, 122
Roast Chicken with Wild Rice, 77
Skinny Chicken à la King, 124
Skinny Paella, 122
"Skinny Shake," 124
Slick Chick, 79
Smothered Chicken, 122
Sweet and Sour Chicken, 78
Tandoori Chicken, 77
Weight-Worrier's Fricassee, 79

Dindonneau au Vin, 14
Dipping Sauce, 67

Drumsticks and thighs
Barbecue Chicken Drumsticks, 48
Butter Baked Wings and Drumsticks, 16
Corn Crisped Drumsticks, 57
Drumsticks Diable, 114
Imperial Chicken, 114
Orange Chicken, 79
Salami-Chicken Duo, 32

Sautéed Chicken Legs Isabel, 101
Sesame Seed Glazed Kabobs, 48
Stuffed Drumsticks Napoli, 102
Western Chicken and Iceburg, 102
Drumsticks Diable, 114
Dunking Chicken, 82
Dutch Chicken Salad, 43

E&F

East-West Risotto, 119
Favorite Chicken Salad, 41
Fiesta Chicken Cacciatore, 121
Figaro Sauce, 92
Florentine Chicken, 118
Fluffy Hollandaise Sauce, 91
French Chicken Broil, 60
French Chicken in Sherry Sauce, 78
French Pâté Stuffing, 90
Fried
  Basic Fried Chicken, 34
  Basil Fried Chicken, 54
  Buttermilk Fried Chicken, 99
  Corn Crisped Drumsticks, 57
  Corn Crisped Fried Chicken, 78
  Crisp Batter Chicken, 66
  Ginger Crisp Chicken, 98
  Iowa Fried Chicken, 14
  Marie Walsh's Fried Chicken, 41
  Mrs. McCollum's Fried Chicken, 45
  No-Fat Fried Chicken, 79
  Oven-Baked "Southern Fried" Chicken, 124
  Southern Fried Chicken, 100
  Tempura, 66
  Tempura Fried Chicken, 69
Fried Rice, 36
Fried Sweet Potato Shreds, 94
Fruit Stuffing, 54
Fruited Giblet Dressing, 88
Fruited Rice Stuffing, 88

G&H

Garden Chicken Casserole, 43
Garden Patch Soup, 85
Garlic-Broiled Chicken, 56
Giblet Gravy, 20
Ginger Batter, 99
Ginger Crisp Chicken, 98
Ginger-Honey Glaze, 54
Ginger-Marmalade Glaze, 90
Ginger Sauce, 90
Golden Chicken Nuggets, 119
Golden Croutons, 68
Golden Rice, 48
Golden Spiced Peaches, 94
Goose Broth, 108
Goose and Pasta, 108
Goose Liver Pâté, 82
Gourmet Stuffing, 89
Grape and Chicken Omelet, 57

Gravies & Sauces, 90-92
Grilled Chicken Breasts Supreme, 44
Guacamole Sauce, 92
Halved Chicken Italiano, 57
Ham and Chicken Mousse, 115
Harissa Sauce, 21
Harvest Pumpkin Soup, 93
Hawaiian Chicken, 100
Hawaiian Stuffing, 88
Hearty Salad Sandwich, 115
Herb Vinaigrette Dressing, 41
Herbed Chicken Livers, 57
Herbed Pilaf, 94
Hilo Stuffing, 90
Holiday Turkey Platter Indienne, 35
Holstein Schnitzel, 24
Honan Chicken, 113
Hong Kong Chicken Almond, 35
Honolulu Jumbos, 46
Hot Senegalese Soup, 85
How to bone a bird, 103
How to Carve Like a Chef, 104-105
How to cut up a bird, 103
How to stuff a bird, 103

I&J

Ile d'Orléans Chicken, 34
Imperial Chicken, 114
Indonesian Chicken and Pears, 121
Indonesian Rijsttafel, 36
Iowa Fried Chicken, 14
Italian Herb Sauce, 90
Jamaica Chicken Feast, 70
Jamaica-Style Pimiento Rice, 70
Jambalaya, 8
Japanese Chicken, 70
Jardinière Chicken Livers, 122
Jardinière Dressing, 88
Jumbo Chicken Popover, 10

K&L

Kashmir Turkey Curry, 110
Kentucky Burgoo, 102
Knishes, 120
Korean Chicken, 123
Lemon-Broiled Chicken, 56
Lemon-Mint Broiled Chicken, 53
Lemon Swirl Cups, 8
Liberian Chicken, 33
Little Livers Specialty, 15
Londonderry Turkey Pie, 36
Long Island Duck Bigarade, 65
Low-Calorie Chicken Oriental, 123
Low-Cal Chicken Teriyaki, 77

M&N

Macaroni Chicken Chowder, 84
Madeira Turkey Pâté, 15
Mediterranean Chicken, 100
Make-Ahead Chicken Casserole, 59

Mandarin Chicken Breasts, 16
Mandarin Supper, 34
Maple-Butter Glazed Carrots, 93
Marie Walsh's Fried Chicken, 41
Mashed Butternut Squash and Yams, 93
Massachusetts Grilled Chicken, 34
Maytime Chicken Breast Soup, 72
Melbourne Chicken, 120
Mexicali Chicken, 66
Mexican Turkey Mole, 71
Molded Chicken Indienne, 48
Monterey Chicken and Artichokes, 36
Mornay Sauce, 91
Moroccan Couscous, 20
Mousseline Sauce, 92
Mrs. McCollum's Fried Chicken, 45
Mulligatawny Soup, 86
Mushroom-Liver Kabobs, 46
Napa Sonoma Chicken, 43
Napoli Chicken, 35
Nectarine and Chicken Curry, 118
Nectarine Chicken Français, 118
Neopolitan Chicken, 67
No-Fat Fried Chicken, 79
Normandy Chicken, 70

O&P

Oktoberfest Grilled Chicken, 112
Old-Fashioned Chicken Pie, 95
Old-Fashioned Goose Giblet Soup, 85
Onion Roast Chicken, 95
Orange-Broiled Chicken, 56
Orange Chicken, 79
Orange Chicken Hors d'Oeuvre, 83
Orange Curry Dunk, 83
Orange-Honey Glaze, 90
Orange Leek Duck, 121
Orange-Lemon Cranberry Relish, 93
Orange Pecan Stuffing, 87
Orange Sauce, 91
Oriental Chicken, 8
Oriental Omelet, 57
Outdoor Party Chicken, 45
Oven-Baked "Southern Fried" Chicken, 124
Oyster Stuffing, 87
Paprikash Chicken, 98
Parisienne Chicken, 32
Parisian Chicken Bowl, 120
Parmesan Baked Chicken, 118
Parmesan Sauce, 91
Parmigiana Chicken Cutlets, 36
Parsley-Buttered Spaghetti, 56
Party Chicken Amandine, 96
Party Chicken Burgers, 115
Pasta Chicken Salad, 115
Pasta Taormina, 56
Pâté-Cheese Mold, 82
Pâté Maison, 82
Pâté Salad, 116

Peachy Low-Calorie Chicken, 80
Peanut Coated Chicken, 58
Peanut Sauce, 92
Pecan-Fruit Stuffing, 87
Pennsylvania Dutch Potato Stuffing, 89
Perfection Chicken, 9
Perfection Chicken, 28
Pickup Chicken Sticks, 16
Pimiento Biscuits, 9
Pimiento Chicken Stew, 9
Pine Top Party Casserole, 109
Pineapple-Curry Glaze, 90
Piquant Fruit Sauce, 44
Polynesian Chicken Wings, 14
Pot au Feu, 122
Potato and Chicken Bombay, 119
Potato Flake Chicken, 16
Pot-Roasted Chicken, 113
Poulet aux Tomates, 69
Poulet Bretonne, 8
Poulet en Casserole, 71
Poulet en Croûte Lutèce, 65
Poulet Marengo, 68
Poultry Giblet Gravy, 91
Poultry Herb Chart, 74-75
Poultry Pointers
    Calorie-saving tips, 77
    How to barbecue poultry kabobs, 48
    How to broil chicken, 54
    How to defrost frozen birds, 29
    How to freeze fresh chickens, 55
    How to store cooked poultry, 29
    How to store frozen birds, 58
    Money-saving tips, 99
    Stuffing tips, 20

Quiche Americain, 9
Quick Brown Sauce, 65
Quick Cacciatore, 58
Quick Chicken Livers Stroganoff, 100
Quick Turkey Stroganoff, 108
Raisin and Almond Chicken, 53
Raisin-Nut Stuffing, 88
Refried Beans, 94
Rice Ring, 96
Rich Pie Crust, 10
Risotto alla Milanese, 66
Roast Capon, 108
Roast Chicken and Butternut Squash, 53
Roast Chicken with Wild Rice, 77
Roast Goose, 110
Roasts
    California Chicken Roasts, 9
    Caribbean Roast Chicken, 8
    Chestnut Stuffed Turkey, 20
    Country Roast Chicken, 99
    Cranberry Glazed Roast Turkey, 110
    Jamaica Chicken Feast, 70

Long Island Duck Bigarade, 65
Onion Roast Chicken, 95
Roast Capon, 108
Roast Chicken and Butternut Squash, 53
Roast Chicken with Wild Rice, 77
Roast Goose, 110
Tandoori Chicken, 77
Rock Cornish Hens Nöel, 29
Roman Forum Chicken, 56
Roman Turkey Alfredo, 114
Romeo Salta's Chicken Scarpariello, 60
Rosemary Chicken, 42
Ruby Pear and Chicken Salad, 117

Salami-Chicken Duo, 32
San Angel Pollo Ranchero, 97
San Fernando Pepper Chicken, 101
San Fernando Valley Salad, 45
Santa Clara Chicken, 109
Satays with Peanut Sauce, 116
Sauce Perigourdine, 65
Sausage and Apple Stuffing, 87
Sausage and Turkey Cacciatore, 67
Sautéed Chicken Legs Isabel, 101
Savory Mushroom Gravy, 101
Savory Stuffing, 87
Scaloppine Milanese, 24
Scrambled Eggs and Liver, 55
Sesame Seed Glazed Kabobs, 48
Shredded Chicken and Vegetables, 59
Simmered Chicken, 96
Simple Simon, 44
Skewered Chicken Cantonese, 116
Skewered Chicken Livers with Mushrooms, 42
Skillet Chicken and Tomato, 118
Skillet Hungarian Chicken, 56
Skillet Jambalaya, 54
Skillet Turkey Scramble, 32
Skinny Chicken à la King, 124
Skinny Paella, 122
"Skinny Shake," 124
Slick Chick, 79
Slow Cooker Coq au Vin, 33
Smothered Chicken, 122
Soufflé Supreme, 109
Soups, 83-86
Southampton Turkey, 34
Southern Fried Chicken, 100
Southern Turkey and Kale, 33
Soy Baked Chicken, 59
Soy Dressing, 44
Spanish Rice Chicken Bake, 67
Spicy Cornbread Stuffing, 87
Springtime Party Platter, 53
Springtime Sauce, 92
Stroganoff Rounds, 47
Stroganoff Sauce, 92
Stuff or Bone a Bird, 103

Stuffed Crèpes, 98
Stuffed Drumsticks Napoli, 102
Stuffed Onions, 93
Stuffed Salad Rolls, 45
Stuffed Whirlybird, 54
Stuffings, 86-90
Summer Chicken Divan, 42
Summer Salad Heroes, 47
Supermarket Supper, 115
Supreme Sauce, 91
Sweet and Sour Chicken, 78
Sweet Sour Sauce, 92
Tagine, 69
Tahitian Chicken, 47
Tandoori Chicken, 77
Tarragon Chicken Champignons, 54
Tempura, 66
Tempura Batter, 67
Tempura Fried Chicken, 69
Tennessee Club Chicken, 101
Tibetan Rice, 44
Tijuana Chicken, 66
Tobago Chicken-Avocado Soup, 83
Turkey Croquettes, 111
Turkey Cutlets Bolognese, 29
Turkey Cutlets Kiev, 35
Turkey Liver Pâté, 82
Turkey Time Pears, 94

Uganda Peanut Butter Chicken, 55
Vegetable and Sausage Stuffing, 87
Vegetable Bouquet, 94
Velouté Sauce, 92
Veracruz Chicken, 58
Weight Worrier's Fricassee, 79
Weiner Schnitzel, Turkey-Style, 15
Western Chicken and Iceberg, 102
Wheat Germ Coated Chicken, 102
White Wine Sauce, 42
Whole-Wheat Bread Stuffing, 89
Wild Rice Pilaf, 29
Wild Rice Stuffing, 89
Wine Vinegar Dressing, 116
Wings
    Breaded Chicken Wings, 102
    Butter Baked Wings and Drumsticks, 16
    Crusty Chicken Wings, 117
    Kentucky Burgoo, 102
    Pickup Chicken Sticks, 16
    Polynesian Chicken Wings, 14
Winter Garden Salad Tray, 95
Yorktown Walnut Stuffing, 88

Zesty Lemon Chicken Breasts, 55
Zing Sauce, 90
Zippy Tomato Dunk, 83
Zurich Baked Chicken, 71